Junior Ministers
in British Government

To Breda

Junior Ministers
in British Government

KEVIN THEAKSTON

Basil Blackwell

First published 1987

Basil Blackwell Ltd
108 Cowley Road, Oxford, OX4 1JF, UK

Basil Blackwell Inc.
432 Park Avenue South, Suite 1503
New York, NY 10016, USA

British Library Cataloguing in Publication Data

Theakston, Kevin
    Junior ministers in British government.
    1. Junior ministers (Political science)
    —Great Britain—History
    I. Title
    354.41'04   JN406
    ISBN 0–631–15156–7

Library of Congress Cataloging in Publication Data

Theakston, Kevin, 1958–
    Junior ministers in British government.
    Includes index.
    1. Government executives—Great Britain. I. Title.
    JN406.T48   1987   354.4107'4   86–26342
    ISBN 0–631–15156–7

Typeset by Cambrian Typesetters, Frimley, Surrey
Printed in Great Britain by T. J. Press Ltd, Padstow

Contents

Preface

'Few people in British politics exist in such deep obscurity as junior ministers.' So began a newspaper review of the personalities and promotion potential of Conservative junior ministers in 1979.[1] This book aims to dispel a little of that obscurity by exploring the role of junior ministers in British government since 1830. It is the first comprehensive study of the subject. Hitherto, junior ministers have been only briefly discussed in books on British government and have been the focus of a mere handful of articles in academic journals.

It is important to study junior ministers for a number of reasons. First, because they are the pool of talent from which between half and three-quarters of future Cabinet ministers will be drawn. Three-quarters of all junior ministers never rise above the bottom rungs of the ministerial ladder, but one in five eventually reaches the Cabinet. Any assessment of the skills and abilities of our chief political executives must take account of the nature and value of their junior ministerial apprenticeships. Secondly, the study of junior ministers can help us to understand better the problems involved in ensuring continuing political control of the Whitehall machine. Junior ministers are part of the team of democratically elected and accountable politicians to whom we look to translate political promises into government programmes. Are junior ministers of much use in ensuring that decisions reflect political rather than bureaucratic aims and values? How do they fit into the structures and processes of government? How do junior ministers actually spend their time? Are there too many junior ministers? There is a gap in our understanding of British public administration here which needs to be filled. And, thirdly, there is the intrinsic importance of the tasks junior ministers undertake: these are often unglamorous, and win very little public attention, but they are nevertheless essential. Indeed, without junior ministers to support them, Cabinet ministers would be hopelessly overloaded with work and their jobs would be quite simply impossible. Junior ministers are, of course, subject to a number of major constraints that limit their authority and ability to take decisions or make policy. Much of this book constitutes an analysis of the different constitutional and political factors that define the outer limits of junior ministers' power. Sometimes it is true that a junior minister has little or no scope for independent action. But Macaulay overstated the position when he wrote that, 'A man in office, and out of the Cabinet, is a mere slave.'[2]

It is necessary to explain that throughout this book the term 'junior minister' is taken to refer to both parliamentary under-secretaries of state (or parliamentary secretaries) *and* to ministers of state (some of whom have special titles, such as Economic Secretary to the Treasury, Minister for Trade, Minister for the Environment and so on). Official lists refer to ministers of the rank of minister of state as 'Ministers not in the Cabinet', and designate only parliamentary under-secretaries as 'Junior Ministers'. However, constitutionally, both ministers of state and parliamentary under-secretaries are in a similar position, as will be shown below, and politically there can sometimes be little difference in their role and weight in decision-taking. During many interviews with serving and former office-holders at all levels (MPs, parliamentary under-secretaries, ministers of state, Cabinet ministers, senior civil servants), no one demurred at my working assumption that ministers of state were also junior ministers: no minister of state objected to my questioning him or her on the grounds that my subject was nothing to do with them!

I have tried where possible to use the first-hand experience of office-holders to describe the role of junior ministers: the jobs they do, how they do them, how they work with other office-holders in government. The analysis of the activities of junior ministers in the nineteenth century in chapter 1 draws heavily on the evidence of ministers and civil servants to House of Commons Select Committees. These Victorian parliamentary papers offer the researcher a wealth of evidence which reflects the personal experience of 'insiders' at different levels. Interviews with nearly 60 serving and former political and civil service office-holders conducted in 1981, 1982 and 1986 provided information and insights not available from other sources. The '30 year rule' means that documentary evidence for ministerial activities in the 1960s, 1970s and 1980s is simply not available. Other sources – *Hansard*, the press, politicians' memoirs or biographies, official publications – do not allow a complete understanding of the role of junior ministers. Interviews were especially valuable for eliciting information on political and personal relations, an important area to investigate as the role and authority of junior ministers depend crucially on those factors rather than on the intrinsic powers of the office.

All interviews were conducted on the understanding that they were not for personal attribution, and are quoted on that basis. Ministerial appointment diaries give an invaluable picture of how ministers divide their time and what the detail of their jobs comprises. To my knowledge, this is the first book in the field of British public administration to print extracts from the diaries of serving ministers.

I am very grateful to the editors of *The Political Quarterly* for kindly permitting me to use material from my article 'The use and abuse of junior ministers', which appeared in vol. 57, no. 1 of the journal (January–March 1986). Quotations from government documents in the Public Record Office are made by permission of the Keeper of the Public Records. I am grateful to the Controller of Her Majesty's Stationery Office for permission to quote from its published material. I take this opportunity to thank the many politicians and civil servants who agreed to be interviewed, and to thank the junior ministers who sent me copies of their appointments diaries, particularly William Waldegrave and David Trippier, whose diaries are used in this book. The Trustees of the Kennedy Memorial Trust awarded me a Kennedy Scholarship to study at Harvard University in the academic year 1982–3, for which I am deeply grateful. Professor Hugh Heclo of Harvard University made many constructive suggestions and comments on my work and showed a kindly interest in my esoteric concerns. Professor George Jones of the London School of Economics has been extremely generous in his patience and encouragement. He gave invaluable help at every stage of this project, and his criticisms of earlier drafts improved this book beyond measure. Responsibility for errors of omission or commission, however, is strictly my own.

Kevin Theakston

1

Historical Background

Contemporary British government, in its organization and operation, is largely the constitutional and political inheritance of the nineteenth century. The basic institutions, personnel and methods of British government emerged in roughly their present form in the years from about 1830 to 1914. Subsequent change has been substantial but piecemeal and evolutionary. Consequently, an understanding of this process of historical development is an essential prelude to the study of modern government. It is particularly important to consider in detail the development of the office of junior minister over the past 150 years because so much of its present scope, potential and limitations has been shaped by the circumstances of its emergence and evolution.

The Emergence of Junior Ministers

'Junior ministers' cannot be properly identified before about 1830. In the eighteenth century, the class of under-secretaries (meaning the under-secretaries to the secretaries of state and the secretaries to the Treasury and the Admiralty) was formally undifferentiated, in the sense that there were no distinctions drawn between 'permanent' and 'parliamentary' positions. All were alike in their legal, administrative and political subordination to their ministerial chiefs. The ministers at the head of government departments formulated policy and monopolized decision-taking. Departments were very small: the staff of the Home Office in 1782, for instance, consisted of two under-secretaries, a chief clerk, four senior clerks and six junior clerks. While the clerks were chiefly engaged in copying letters, the functions of the under-secretaries were variable. The Commissioners on Fees reported in 1786 that their duties were 'to attend to the execution of such orders, to prepare drafts of such special letters and instructions as occasion may require; to transact themselves whatever is of the most confidential nature; and generally to superintend the business of the office in all its branches'.[1] It was common for one of the two under-secretaries in each department to serve a succession of ministers, and for the other to come and go with his patron. His personal relations with his minister were important in determining the political content of an under-secretary's work. There was no clear separation between parliamentary and bureaucratic functions or careers: either of the two under-secretaries in a department might have been an MP, handling much of the day-to-day work in the House of Commons, without thereby becoming a 'parliamentary under-secretary'.

Eighteenth-century under-secretaries' political subordination was matched by their social standing, for, on the whole, they lacked the aristocratic birth and landed property that were prerequisites for Cabinet careers. Ambitious men generally sought a junior lordship at the Admiralty or the Treasury before moving through a number of ministerial positions or sinecures outside the Cabinet and then securing Cabinet appointments. Under-secretaryships were not regarded as a desirable rung on the political ladder. Charles Jenkinson, later the First Earl of Liverpool, was the first under-secretary to reach the Cabinet, in 1791; George Canning was the first to serve as a secretary of state, in 1807, and the first to become prime minister, in 1827. Such eminence was at that time unique. For the most part, eighteenth-century under-secretaries had careers, like their duties, of secondary importance.

In the period 1780–1830, administrative and political pressures began to force some measure of differentiation between under-secretaries. The administrative pressures were the growing volume and complexity of business, and the changes demanded in the internal structures and styles of departments. On the political level were the intensified demands of political and parliamentary life: more legislation, debates, committees and deputations. Departments were doing more and in a changing political environment. These pressures continued throughout the nineteenth century and beyond; what concerns us here is the effects on the organization and duties of the ministerial cadre of government. Henry Parris wrote that under-secretaries 'bore the brunt' of these administrative and political pressures which led to a division in the office:

> As it became increasingly difficult for a man with a seat in the Commons to deal adequately with a heavy burden of office work also, some went one way, some the other. The position of one stream steadily approximated to that of the ministers, so that on a change of government they were the lowest office-holders to go. The position of the remainder, on the other

hand, drew gradually closer to that of the officials, so that on a change of government, they were the most senior to keep their places.[2]

The pressures were inexorable, but the actual adaptation of government was piecemeal. In 1786, the Commissioners on Fees considered that for the necessary official business of the Home and Foreign Offices one under-secretary was sufficient, who should be 'stationary' to prevent 'the confusion and serious consequences that may arise in business of such high importance, from frequent changes'. For his 'private and confidential business', each secretary of state should 'on his coming into office, have the nomination of an assistant under-secretary'. The emphasis was on personal rather than *parliamentary* assistance to a secretary of state, though the advantages of permanent help were conceded. At the Treasury, the Commissioners suggested, one secretary should be 'permanent' and excluded from parliament, while the other should be an MP, and leave office with the government. At the time, these recommendations were rejected by the government, but over the next 45 years their underlying principles came to be accepted.

If financial rewards are any guide, the benefits of permanent assistance were realized by ministers sooner than those of parliamentary assistance for, from 1799, under-secretaries were to receive a supplement of £500 to their salary of £2,000 after three years' service. The qualifying time was extended to seven years in 1817, and in 1822 the extra payment was abolished only to re-emerge in 1831.

The duties of under-secretaries were also more clearly distinguished, though the process was uneven over different departments. At the Treasury the spheres of the two secretaries were divided in 1804, one being assigned financial, the other non-financial (including patronage) business. They were both political appointments and MPs who by that time invariably lost office on a change of government. In 1805 an assistant secretary was added – as the senior permanent official he was declared ineligible for parliament. At the Colonial Office a second and permanent under-secretary was appointed in 1825 to free the political under-secretary to concentrate more on his parliamentary tasks, and also to serve as 'the depository of all knowledge of which the Secretary of State must daily avail himself'.[3] Until the 1840s the two under-secretaries were regarded as having a coordinate authority, subordinate to the secretary of state, and divided the work between them on a geographical basis.

The Home Office had a great deal of parliamentary business and, after 1806, it was rare for it not to have an under-secretary in the Commons. In 1822, planning the appointment of his brother-in-law as his under-secretary, the Home Secretary, Robert Peel, wrote that:

the mere official duties were light ... the parliamentary duties would be far
the heaviest, and also of the greatest importance to me ... these
parliamentary duties consisted in the attendance on committees ... The
Secretary of State could not attend all of these, and must devolve on his
Under Secretary the charge of attending such as he could not, and watching
the progress of business there. If at any time the Secretary of State were
unavoidably absent from the House, the Under Secretary would have to
conduct such business there as belonged to the office, for it would be a
mortification to him to see that business in the hands of another ... the
performance of those duties must be difficult at first ... nothing but
experience could render them less so, but ... experience would.[4]

At the Foreign Office, in contrast, although from 1807 one under-
secretary was 'permanent' and held office through a change of
government, the non-permanent under-secretaryship was not necessarily
a parliamentary position. Indeed, in 1807, Canning virtually insisted that
Charles Bagot give up his seat on appointment as under-secretary: 'The
labour is very hard, and it is daily and constant. It requires entire
devotion to it. I think Parliament is wholly incompatible with the due
discharge of the duty.'[5] Palmerston seems to have shared this view and
what he called the 'junior under-secretary of State' was not invariably a
parliamentarian – in either House – until after 1852. In the office, each
under-secretary supervised the correspondence of particular divisions
dealing with groups of countries, and they substituted for one another as
necessary, but it is clear that by 1840 the permanent under-secretary
dealt with the major powers, though that did not yet give him a great
influence over policy, which was still the preserve of the secretary of
state.

The career patterns of under-secretaries further distinguished political
from permanent office-holders. The rise of Jenkinson and Canning
marked a fundamental change in the conception of political careers. They
demonstrated that under-secretaryships could be used as stepping stones
to the front ranks of politics. Canning realized that potential in 1795:
'the business of the office was I thought such as would at once open to me
great opportunities of general information, and assign to me also, in
some measure, in the House of Commons, that sort of province which
[is] so desirable.'[6] Peel was appointed Under-secretary for War and
Colonies in 1810, his Secretary of State, the Second Earl of Liverpool,
explaining that he would receive a training in 'all the necessary habits of
official business', a view which Peel came to adopt himself when prime
minister.[7] By the beginning of the nineteenth century the junior lordships
at the Admiralty were being filled by naval officers and those at the
Treasury were associated with whipping duties in the Commons and seen

as of lower political status than under-secretaryships. Thus, when in 1835 Gladstone was moved by Peel from a junior lordship at the Treasury to the post of under-secretary at the Colonial Office, it was regarded by the Prime Minister as a promotion. And Gladstone's new Secretary of State, Lord Aberdeen, was clear that 'it is a fine opening for a young man of talent and ambition and places him in the way to the highest distinction.'[8]

In 1831 the distinction between 'permanent' and 'parliamentary' under-secretaries was first officially made, confirming and institution-alizing the *ad hoc* developments of the preceding decades. A Select Committee inquiring into official salaries observed that 'the Under Secretaries who habitually remain in office during different changes of administration, and who thus make a profession of official life, may be distinguished from those who merely appear there for short periods.' In response, the Treasury, setting the salaries of 'permanent Under Secretaries' at £2,000 and those of 'Parliamentary Under Secretaries' at £1500 (secretaries of state were to receive £5,000), stated that it was necessary to secure 'the services of men of high character, experience and acquirements for the discharge of duties of the most confidential and responsible description'. The permanent under-secretaryships were 'generally speaking, the commencement of a laborious course of profession of great trust and close application'. The appointments of parliamentary under-secretaries were 'more exclusively of a political character, and connected with parliamentary duties' and, moreover, 'frequently lead to advancement in the higher offices of the government'.[9]

That Treasury minute was the first official statement of the difference between parliamentary and permanent under-secretaries. The differences were fundamental: titles, salaries, methods of appointment, duties and career possibilities. The permanent secretary had been formally instituted, as had the junior minister.

Appointments and Careers, 1830–1914

The size of the junior ministerial cadre grew from only 11 to 15 during the years 1830–1914 (not counting the parliamentary secretary to the Treasury, the government chief whip). Earl Grey's government of 1830 included: the financial secretary to the Treasury, parliamentary under-secretaries of state at the Foreign Office, Home Office and for War and Colonies, the parliamentary secretary to the Board of Control for India, the civil lord and the first secretary at the Admiralty, the vice-president of the Board of Trade and the clerk, storekeeper and surveyor-general at the

Board of Ordnance. Asquith's government included in 1914: the financial secretary to the Treasury, parliamentary under-secretaries of state at the Foreign Office, Home Office, India Office and Colonial Office, the parliamentary under-secretary and the financial secretary at the War Office, the civil lord and the parliamentary and financial secretary at the Admiralty, parliamentary secretaries at the Board of Trade, Board of Education, Board of Agriculture and the Local Government Board, the assistant postmaster-general and the vice-president of the Department of Agriculture and Technical Instruction for Ireland. The small increase in the overall number of junior ministerial posts before 1914 reflected the creation of new departments (Education, Agriculture, Local Government) and the addition of junior ministers to existing departments (Post Office, Ireland). Reorganizations in the military and colonial departments reduced the complement of junior ministers from four to three by the end of the nineteenth century.

Formally, junior ministers were the personal appointees of their ministers or secretaries of state rather than Crown appointments and so, under an Act of 1707, were not required to resign their seats and seek re-election on appointment, unlike the junior lords of the Treasury, the civil lord of the Admiralty and all full ministers. Not removed until 1918, this provision did at times influence the ministerial dispositions of prime ministers and chief whips, and a safe seat was undoubtedly an asset for an ambitious politician.

As late as 1880, Gladstone could write to Queen Victoria that, 'The position of the Crown, and also of the Prime Minister, with regard to these appointments is peculiar. They are the appointments of the Secretary of State.' But this formula was to mollify the monarch; in reality, the premier was deeply involved in these appointments. In 1795, the Prime Minister, Pitt, appears to have insisted that Lord Grenville appoint Canning as his under-secretary at the Foreign Office. Gladstone received his junior appointments in 1834, 1835 and 1841 after being summoned to see the Prime Minister, Peel, in person. Peel explained to the Select Committee on Official Salaries in 1850 that the First Lord of the Treasury – the prime minister – could not officially and formally make an appointment in any department but his own, but he added that there would probably be communication between ministers before important appointments. The prime minister's powers of patronage were not strictly defined. Much would depend on the situation and on the character of the prime minister, but ministers 'would probably consider that the Prime Minister was responsible for the general conduct of the affairs of the government, and would be ready to acquiesce in the appointment of any capable man to . . . office; [they] might express a wish in favour of some person in whom [they] had particular confidence; but I do not recollect any practical difficulties in the adjustment of those things.' Peel summed up the power of appointment as one of 'joint action' between a minister and the prime minister.[10]

The real meaning of such 'joint action' depended on the political circumstances and personalities involved. Strong, determined and senior ministers could insist on choosing their own juniors, or at least installing protégés elsewhere in the lower ranks of the government. Ministers may have been consulted if their junior ministers were to be replaced. On the whole, most ministers would have some selection offered, or have a final veto power, or merely be informed as to who their junior was to be. Only rarely did rising young politicians attempt to bargain with the prime minister, make conditions or refuse a junior office. Most, at an early stage in their careers, were not indispensable, and only occasionally could exploit political or personal connections to negotiate successfully.

The chief constraints on the prime minister's power to appoint junior ministers were political in the widest sense. Prime ministers faced two problems when forming a government. The first was 'strategical', involving 'the task of conciliating all the elements in the party and therefore of attaching to his ministry men who represented different political views'. In addition to forming a government 'commanding the allegiance of a parliamentary majority', there was the 'tactical' problem of ensuring 'routine administrative competence and parliamentary skill'.[11]

'Strategical' considerations would be brought to bear on junior appointments through the medium of discussions among an inner circle of senior ministers: men with weight, representative character, allies and clients. The prime minister could not act unilaterally without securing at least the acquiescence of those ministers in his junior dispositions. The political instability of the 1850s disrupted party alignments and produced coalition governments to which appointments were made by bargaining among the leaders of the various political groupings. The chief whip was particularly influential in junior appointments. As one was to write, 'his counsel was essential. He knew the men, their hopes and expectations, what weight they carried and – always subject to qualifications for particular posts – what the views and wishes of the party were as regards appointments.'[12]

On the 'tactical' level – appointing competent individuals – prime ministers considered parliamentary skills essential in those selected for junior office. The executive was a parliamentary one: ministers were chosen from parliament and sat there; one of their most important duties was to represent and defend their departments in parliament. Parliament was the great forcing-ground of political talent. Salisbury observed in 1894 that 'when party leaders have to select, for a certain number of the offices of the government, members of the House of Commons *who have never held office before*, one of the qualifications which they consider with the greatest care, is that of being able to speak and act in a manner acceptable to the House of Commons' (my italics). Sir Francis Baring, who progressed smoothly from a junior lordship at the Treasury, through the financial secretaryship, to become Chancellor of the Exchequer, told a Select Committee in 1848 of the importance of a parliamentary reputation for junior lords seeking promotion to the ranks of junior ministers: 'I was at the Treasury almost every day in the week . . . and I used to take home papers to read at night.' Not all his colleagues were so diligent, 'But you generally get gentlemen who are anxious to do a great deal of business, as much as is put upon them, which makes them speak and brings them forward in Parliament; but the work unconnected with Parliamentary distinction is not so popular.'[13]

A substantial parliamentary apprenticeship was necessary to secure junior ministerial office, and it was an advantage to enter parliament young. Gladstone considered that 'as a rule, it would be as rational to begin training for the ballet at forty-five or fifty, as for the real testing work of the Cabinet.'[14] In the period 1830–1914, the average age on appointment to junior office was 40 years for those who rose no higher, and 37 years for those men who later served in the Cabinet. The former class was appointed to junior posts after an average of eight years in the Commons, the latter after an average of six years. The logic of career politics in a parliamentary system explains why the landed classes provided the majority of office-holders in the governments of the nineteenth century: young aristocrats and gentry were advantaged by their early debut in public life, their tenure of safe seats and the absence of financial distractions to full-time politics.[15]

Parliamentary distinction, acquired through debate on the floor of the House, rather than specialist subject qualifications, marked men out for office. Contemplating the appointment of a parliamentary secretary at the Board of Trade in 1908, Asquith thought 'Rea is an admirable economist but an unimpressive parliamentary figure, and much junior in H of C standing to Tennant.' (Tennant was appointed in January 1909.) Sir Edward Grey did not think that a prospective junior minister had to be an 'expert'. He wrote of his appointment to the Foreign Office in 1892, 'I had had no special training for Foreign Office work, nor had I till then paid special attention to foreign affairs. But special knowledge is not a necessary qualification in a young man appointed to a Parliamentary Under-Secretaryship.'[16]

Lawrence Lowell outlined two pathways to ministerial office. One course was for an individual to speak and vote loyally with the party leaders and come to be regarded as 'a promising young man of sound principles who can be relied upon'; the opposite course – not so slow or safe – was to become 'the candid friend', criticizing or attacking the leader and his policies, and gaining a position as 'a dangerous critic who must be conciliated' by office. Indeed, at times junior office was offered to muzzle able and energetic backbench critics. Disraeli wrote in 1874, 'I have contrived in the minor and working places to include every "representative" man, that is to say everyone who might be troublesome.' Gladstone made Courtney under-secretary at the Home Office in 1880 as 'he would certainly be safer in a secondary office, than he could be with his great industry, and tenacity of purpose, on the independent benches.'[17]

To parliamentary and political qualifications were sometimes added ties of kinship or personal affiliation. The endogamous nature of the British landed and political elite often worked to the advantage of young aristocrats. The 30-year-old Marquis of Hartington (heir of the Duke of Devonshire) was made under-secretary at the War Office in 1863. His biographer considered that the appointment 'shows the handicap then possessed . . . by . . . young men in high aristocratical positions . . . that things may be made too easy for them'.[18] Three prime ministers gave their sons junior posts: Grey (Viscount Howick) in 1830, Derby (E.H. Stanley) in 1852 and Gladstone (Herbert Gladstone) in 1892.

The emphasis on parliamentary generalists did not prevent the appointment of a small minority of specialist non-parliamentarians to junior office. Of the 294 junior ministers serving from 1830 to 1914, 22 were neither MPs nor peers at the time of their appointment; 15 of these in the military departments of the Ordnance, Admiralty and War Office, where experienced officers were sometimes selected, and four Foreign Office under-secretaries from 1830 to 1852 were outside parliament. As late as 1847–8, the political under-secretary at the Home Office was not in parliament: Sir Denis Le Marchant, who served as permanent secretary at the Board of Trade 1836–41 and 1848–50 and finished his career as Clerk of the House of Commons. Horace Plunkett, Vice-President of the Department of Agriculture and Technical Instruction for Ireland, was an MP on his appointment in 1899, but out of the House between 1900 and 1907 and served across a change of government. He owed his appointment and retention to his personal character and the peculiarities of Irish politics.

Junior ministerial posts were the bottom rung of the ministerial ladder, but increasingly after 1830 it was thought not only possible but also desirable to recruit Cabinet ministers from the ranks of those with junior ministerial experience, and to replenish continuously the government through recruitment at the base. Although lingering on until the 1880s, the view that former ministers and under-secretaries had a right to be given their old post on the return of their party to office was generally rejected in favour of keeping the hierarchy moving. In 1841, Peel complained of 'everybody fancying that to any office they had ever held they had a sort of vested right and title, and forgetting that *younger men must be brought forward*' (my italics).[19]

Sir James Graham stated the conventional view in 1861, that a junior post was a 'training in public life, and the means of . . . rising to high offices in the state'. The value of junior ministerial experience for future Cabinet service was widely appreciated. In 1869, George Ward Hunt said:

> I consider it an honourable ambition for a man to wish to serve the Crown in high offices of state, and it is seldom that a man can do so without first beginning in the lower ranks . . . Nothing gives a man so great an advantage towards his being selected for high official position as two or three years experience in Office, and no one will deny that he is a much more competent man for Office than if without that experience.

Similarly, Sir Edward Grey thought that a junior minister was 'trained in capacity for public affairs', receiving a 'steady training in industry and despatch'. And in 1908 Churchill was clear that there were 'disadvantages in bestowing under-secretaryships upon men at the end of their careers, who are not likely to be able to use that invaluable experience in more responsible positions later on'.[20]

Of the 294 junior ministers who served between 1830 and 1914, 93 eventually reached the Cabinet and 27 full ministerial positions outside the Cabinet: 40 per cent of all junior ministers received promotion, 60 per cent rose no higher. Figures on age of appointment and parliamentary service have been cited above: they show that junior ministers who reached the Cabinet started on the path early, but so did a large number of men who were tried and found wanting at this first hurdle. Of the 174 who never rose above the rank of junior minister, 77 were appointed at the age of 45 or over, which lends some support to Gladstone's dictum. However, 15 of the 93 who reached the Cabinet, and nine of the 27 who received posts outside the Cabinet, first became junior ministers at 45 years or older. Whereas 102 of the 174 men who stayed at junior minister level held only one post in their 'career' (58.6 per cent), and 45 held two posts; of the 93 reaching the Cabinet, 44 had held only one junior post (47.3 per cent), 31 had held two, and 18 had held three or more posts. It would appear that many of the latter group were given a rigorous ministerial apprenticeship, and that many of those who never rose off the bottom rung were 'day-labourers'. It is noteworthy that 23 of the 93 who reached the Cabinet had at one time been financial secretary to the Treasury; only 44 men held that post between 1830 and 1914, so that 52.3 per cent of them reached the Cabinet. A further six former financial secretaries reached non-Cabinet ministerial positions, confirming that experience in that office particularly qualified a man for higher posts.

Five junior ministers in this period moved outside the boundaries of the ministerial hierarchy, finishing their careers as civil servants, four of them at permanent secretary rank. Sir Denis Le Marchant, Home Office under-secretary 1847–8, was noted above. The financial secretary to the Treasury, Hamilton, became assistant (permanent) secretary of that department in 1859, serving until 1870; Hawes, junior minister for War and Colonies 1846–51 became permanent secretary at the War Office in 1857; Vivian moved from being financial secretary to become permanent secretary at the War Office in 1871. After this date, such fluid career patterns were not found, any movement in the twentieth century being from permanent secretaryship to ministerial office rather than the reverse.

By the end of the nineteenth century, while it was possible for men to enter the Cabinet without prior ministerial experience, it had become exceptional (see table 1.1). Willson calculated that each new Cabinet minister had, on average, 14–15 years' experience as an MP and had served for about three and a half years in subordinate office in the period from 1868 to 1916. (He defined this to include experience as a whip or in non-Cabinet ministerial posts, in addition to service as a junior minister.)[21] Individually, only exceptional political talent or 'representative' quality carried men from the backbenches straight into the Cabinet. The idea that junior office was an apprenticeship for the Cabinet was bi-partisan. Though Peel and Gladstone self-consciously espoused it, and the latter was in a position over a long period to mould the careers of a whole generation of Liberal ministers, Conservative prime ministers also embraced the idea. Long periods in Opposition naturally affected the background of ministers – it was then possible to move onto the frontbench without junior experience in government (Liberals 1895–1905) – but did not overturn the conventional notion of an appropriate ministerial apprenticeship.

Just as generalist parliamentary talents won initial junior ministerial appointments, so the generalist model prevailed in career movements up the hierarchy. Of the 93 junior ministers who finally reached the Cabinet (17 of whom did so only through non-Cabinet posts, while 76 moved

TABLE 1.1   Junior ministerial experience of Cabinet ministers, 1830–1914

Government		Total Cabinet ministers	Cabinet ministers appointed directly to the Cabinet	Cabinet ministers with service as junior ministers
1830–4	(Grey/Melbourne)	24	12	5
1841–6	(Peel)	21	8	9
1868–74	(Gladstone)	19	3	14
1874–80	(Disraeli)	17	7	9
1880–5	(Gladstone)	19	3	14
1886–92	(Salisbury)	21	2	11
1892–5	(Gladstone/ Rosebery)	18	3	10
1895–1905	(Salisbury/ Balfour)	35	7	17
1906–14	(Campbell-Bannerman/ Asquith)	36	10	16

directly into the Cabinet), 46 (49.5 per cent) rose to head departments they had not worked in as junior ministers or took non-departmental offices; 47 (50.5 per cent) were promoted to head departments they had served in as junior ministers. However, in this second group there were only 18 *straight promotions* within departments (for instance, financial secretary of the Treasury to Chancellor of the Exchequer or under-secretary for Colonies to Colonial Secretary), and of these six ministers served in only óne department in their careers. In contrast, 29 junior ministers later headed departments they had *once served in* as a junior minister, but in a career involving either several junior assignments or several Cabinet appointments, or both. Thus, only one minister in five experienced the direct promotion with a single department which would allow the accumulation of experience necessary to become expert in a subject. The number of ministers specializing in the affairs of one department was very small. Most ministers were generalists in that they specialized not in particular subjects but in whatever tasks they were responsible for at the moment. They won promotion by their competence as ministers and as political figures rather than by single-subject knowledge and experience.

As with initial appointments, so promotions up the ministerial hierarchy were subject to both 'strategic' influences such as party management and representative quality and to 'tactical' considerations such as competence in office, House of Commons reputation and senior colleagues' assessment of administrative ability. A significant development was the manner in which the operation of the ministerial hierarchy came to precondition the Cabinet choices of prime ministers. As they came, increasingly, to look to the ranks of junior ministers to replenish the Cabinet, they drew upon men who had started their careers under different leaders. One prime minister's junior appointments constrained subsequent prime ministers' Cabinet dispositions. Understandably, three-quarters of those who stayed at the level of junior minister served only one prime minister. However, only one in ten of those junior ministers later reaching Cabinet rank served their whole career under one prime minister; a third served two, another third three, and the remainder more than three premiers. A prime minister's Cabinet choice was, to an increasingly significant extent, restricted by the pool of available junior ministers, in whose initial appointments he may have had little or no say. As they moved up the hierarchy, successful junior ministers could accumulate the experience in office and political support to compel a (later) prime minister to appoint them to the Cabinet.

Junior Ministers in Parliament

Parliament came to be the main field of activity of junior ministers in the nineteenth century. As the demands of the House of Commons intensified, departmental ministers needed parliamentary assistants to help them deal with debates on legislation, Estimates and general matters affecting departments, the probing of Select Committees, and the increased use of questions to seek information and to harry the government. The impact on individual departments was uneven, but the overall and cumulative effects of these pressures were of general significance. Sir Charles Wood told the Select Committee on Official Salaries in 1850 that he did not think that anything had added more to the work of ministers than 'the searching nature of the inquiries which the ... House of Commons ... is perpetually making into public business, which requires very constant attention in all ... offices, in addition to the increased business which has been thrown upon them.'[22]

The constitutional convention of the individual responsibility of ministers for the work of their departments, which replaced earlier notions of Board administration, implied that junior ministers did not carry any responsibility to parliament. Constitutionally, they had only a derivative authority, as the agents of their ministers and, politically, the responsibility of the department's head encompassed their actions. Junior ministers were regarded as responsible not to parliament, but to their chiefs, who carried responsibility for every act that they permitted them to do. Sir Francis Baring stated the principle succinctly in 1848: 'the Parliamentary responsibility would be the same if there did not exist any Parliamentary Secretary.'[23]

As late as May 1870, there was an instance of a question being asked of the Chancellor of the Exchequer, and when the financial secretary rose to answer, the Member left the House in protest, returning to ask the same question the next day and to argue that the Chancellor had to answer in the name of access to responsible ministers. If that attitude had been common, the *raison d'etre* of junior ministers would have been destroyed, and Cabinet ministers overwhelmed by work. So, junior ministers had to be presented as acceptable departmental spokesmen, but subordinate to their ministers, to preserve the convention of ministerial responsibility. Disraeli's view was that 'in every branch of the administration there [should] be someone in either House of Parliament who can explain or indicate its policy if called upon to do so . . . The government is as much represented, in any public statement of its policy, by an Under Secretary of State, as by a Secretary of State.'[24]

The pressures to have leading party and government figures in the Commons were irresistible. In 1863, Cowper could say that 'Every department intrusted with the expenditure of public money must be represented either by its head *or by its Secretary* in the House' (my italics). In fact, the House of Commons was more insistent. Much depended on the political salience of a department or a policy at a particular time, whether its activities were controversial or of enduring importance, the expenditure involved and the weight of legislation carried. For instance, when, in 1863–5, the Admiralty and the War, Foreign and Colonial Offices were all headed by peers and represented by junior ministers in the lower House, Palmerston detected 'growing dissatisfaction . . . at finding so many important departments represented in the House of Commons by Under-Secretaries.'[25]

During the years 1830–1914, Treasury ministers were always in the Commons. For most of this period, all Board of Trade, Home Office and Poor Law Board (Local Government Board after 1871) ministers and junior ministers sat there too: these departments usually had heavy legislative loads, and being of domestic concern aroused continuous interest among MPs. In the case of the Admiralty, either all of its ministers were found in the Commons, or else the First Lord was a peer rather than a junior minister (except for 1870–4). The War Office reorganization of 1870 meant that a team of ministers could cover both Houses between them: the financial secretary was always in the Commons to move the Estimates, but the parliamentary under-secretary was to be the chief representative for 'military' questions in whichever House the secretary of state did not sit. Until the post was abolished in 1887, the surveyor-general of Ordnance could also relieve the Secretary of State for War of 'many hours of labour each week, which are . . . devoted to the learning up of answers to small questions'.[26] Most other departments had one minister in each House, or else the junior minister would assist his chief in the Commons, leaving non-departmental figures (Household or sinecure appointments, or other department's peers) to answer in the Lords. Between Canning and Grey, only three foreign secretaries were in the Commons, leaving the under-secretary to carry the burden of parliamentary duties, assisted for major debates by the prime minister or the leader of the house.

The absence of a junior minister for Ireland was anomalous. The chief secretary was the main representative in the Commons for the Irish administration. The assistance of the Irish law officers was never guaranteed; they were often unable to find seats. There was a heavy load of parliamentary work: there were always many Irish questions, and much minor legislation. In addition, the chief secretary had to travel to Dublin frequently, and was sometimes in the Cabinet. Attempts to replace the bicephalous Irish executive (lord lieutenant and chief secretary) with a more conventional secretary of state and under-secretary model failed. In 1887, the chief secretary was particularly hard-pressed and a temporary (and unpaid) parliamentary under-secretary for Ireland, Edward King Harman, was appointed. A Bill was introduced to make the post permanent: the chief secretary was to keep full responsibility, but the under-secretary would deputize for him, representing the Irish Local Government Board and answering a wide range of Irish questions. The Bill received a second reading, but when King Harman died in June 1888 the government abandoned the scheme. Intense opposition had been aroused among the Irish MPs, who had created scenes in the House and who wanted to pin responsibility for policy on the chief secretary in person. After 1899 the vice-president of the Department of Agriculture and Technical Instruction was in a position to offer parliamentary assistance to the chief secretary, but up until 1914 he was in the Commons for only half the period, which reduced his usefulness.[27]

The parliamentary duties of the financial secretary to the Treasury were particularly onerous. He was truly 'the maid of all work for the government'.[28] Specially involved in the parliamentary management of public financial business, he would move the Civil Estimates, in the presence of the Chancellor and the departmental ministers concerned, to help defend any special vote or item. Any unusual or controversial vote would be moved by the Chancellor, or even the First Lord, the prime minister. He would lead for the government during the protracted committee stages of the Finance and Appropriations Bills, often till after midnight, and sit on the Public Accounts Committee. In addition, the financial secretary usually answered for any department not represented in the Commons. The postmaster-general, for instance, was not eligible for membership of the Commons until 1866, and was often a peer thereafter; the office of assistant postmaster-general was not created until 1910.

The burdens which the Commons placed on senior ministers were intense. Lowe defended the representation of departments by junior ministers in the Commons, and the assignation of secretaries of state to the Lords:

> There is an inconvenience in that, but it is not all on one side; the work of those public departments is immensely laborious, the details are enormous, the responsibility is absolutely frightful, and I think that there is a good deal gained when you have a man at the head of a department who has his evenings disengaged, and who is not overpowered by that enormous labour of attendance in the House of Commons.

In the period 1830–1914, about half of all Cabinet ministers were peers, but only one-sixth of all junior ministers (45). In the 1868–74 government, 11 out of 19 Cabinet ministers were in the Commons, but 17 out of 20 junior ministers. Before this government, Cabinets always contained a majority of peers, after it a minority. As a larger proportion of Cabinet ministers came to sit in the House of Commons, the position of junior ministers as indispensable parliamentary assistants was confirmed, as was their subordinate status. The absence of such parliamentary assistance led Home Secretary Harcourt in 1881 to lament the fact that his junior minister, Rosebery, was a peer: 'Already I find the department in confusion and despair at the loss of a House of Commons Under-Secretary.'[29]

If a minister was in the Lords, his junior carried the burden of departmental representation in the Commons. Questions would then, in form, be addressed to him and not to his master; he would take the department's Estimates through. Having to answer for the department on all matters, he would be drawn more closely than other under-secretaries into the major decisions. Such assignments were coveted by ambitious young politicians who wanted to make a name for themselves in the Commons and to play a significant administrative role. Churchill may have realized this potential when he chose to go to the Colonial Office under Lord Elgin in 1906, rather than be financial secretary to the Treasury under Asquith. Edward Grey's wife, Dorothy, wrote on his securing such a posting, 'I am trying to remember which of Dizzy's novels contains a man who prided himself on possessing a gallery of the portraits of Under-Secretaries whose chiefs were in the Lords. They are splendid beings it seems.' It was natural that some ministers were wary of alloting glamorous parliamentary work to their junior ministers. Graham, in 1861, considered that since the Reform Act of 1832, nothing shook the power of the First Lord of the Admiralty as much as being represented in the Commons by a subordinate.[30]

The pressures of parliamentary business on junior ministers worked to limit their administrative capabilities. Particularly from the 1850s, the post was defined primarily in terms of a parliamentary rather than a departmental role. At the Foreign Office, for instance, the permanent under-secretary acquired control of more divisions as the parliamentary under-secretary's parliamentary role became more burdensome. In 1858 an assistant under-secretary was created for the junior minister's divisions as his work on parliamentary committees took him away from the office. The relentless demands of parliament, especially after 1868 when all foreign secretaries were peers until 1906, meant that the junior minister had to spend more time being briefed for, and appearing in, the Commons to defend the course of foreign policy without having had a chance to influence it. Parliamentary duties could not be delegated by the junior minister and came to acquire a priority over departmental tasks. The position was the same in other departments. In 1850, Earl Grey noted of the Colonial Office junior minister, 'It must necessarily interfere with his attentions to the details of the ordinary official business, very much indeed, to pass a great number of hours every day in the House of Commons.' And in 1886, the permanent secretary of the Home Office minuted that, 'Practically the bulk of the work falls upon the Permanent Under-Secretary and the Assistant Under-Secretary, for, except as to Estimates, the Parliamentary Under-Secretary cannot be counted upon to a great extent, so much of his time being occupied with Deputations, committees, attendance in Parliament etc.'[31] Attendance at committees of the House of Commons, generally meeting at midday, and then during sittings of the House, for about eight hours a day, and often until midnight or after, ate into the time and energy that could be devoted to administrative work. Official boxes often had to be dealt with at home, or in the Commons Library or in offices in the Commons.

While junior ministers were facing more definite parliamentary duties, they were not free agents in their dispatch. Palmerston, in 1861, may have overstated to overcome the Queen's opposition to the appointment of Layard, but still maintained that 'an Under-Secretary of State is only the instrument and mouthpiece of his principal to say what he is told, and to write what he is bid . . . [He is] useful to answer unimportant questions as to matters of fact . . . knowing the details of matters discussed, able to make a good speech . . . [and shaping] his course in strict conformity with the line which might be chalked out for him.' A junior minister's discretion would be limited. His answers to questions and speeches would be drafted by civil servants and cleared with the permanent secretary and the secretary of state. He may have been forbidden to depart from the exact wording of statements prepared in advance.[32]

Some junior ministers tried to argue that as they had to defend policy in the Commons they ought to have a say in the major decisions or at least more information. They were usually rebuffed, though when Curzon complained to Salisbury that he did not always know what was going on in the Foreign Office and asked to see the records of the foreign secretary's meetings with ambassadors, to have access to private telegrams and dispatches sent to his chief, and to be present when he received deputations, Salisbury agreed to all of these requests. What is striking is not the nature and volume of information that Curzon then acquired, but that so much had been earlier denied to him and, presumably, to other junior ministers. In fact, in the Foreign Office, Salisbury considered that a 'discreet man' was needed for the under-secretaryship. As Low put it:

> It is not deemed necessary to set a statesman of weight and influence to advise with the People's Chamber on foreign policy. It is enough to have there a fluent and accomplished young official, who can act as a telephone for the greater powers above, and convey with neatness and point such limited information as it is thought occasionally desirable for the nation's representatives to possess.[33]

The convention of ministerial responsibility and the expectations and behaviour of MPs and ministers themselves ensured that junior ministers could never usurp their masters' positions. They were answerable, but not responsible. They could appear in parliament to defend a department, but on their secretary of state's responsibility, not their own. In that sense, they were not deputies to ministers but assistants. On important occasions – which meant any occasion when the Commons had been aroused on an issue – attention focused on the ministerial heads of departments, not their subordinates. Northbrook considered in 1887 that:

now there is such an enormous mass of questions put, which occupy very much time in the House of Commons ... it would certainly be desirable that the Secretary of State should have one man who is able to answer questions for him, [so] that he should not be troubled by having to answer a mass of detailed questions ... [But] if anything important arises, the House of Commons will not be satisfied without an answer from a Secretary of State, and the other parliamentary officers are not of any considerable value for important parliamentary purposes.[34]

The secretary of state, not the junior minister, was also the important political figure for the deputations of interest groups and individuals lobbying departments. At the Treasury, explained Sir Francis Baring, 'Parties generally wish to see the Chancellor of the Exchequer, and his time is a great deal wasted in interviews ... [They] would not be satisfied with seeing the Secretary of the Treasury, who probably decided the case.' And at the Foreign Office, the secretary of state devoted a good deal of his time to receiving ambassadors; in his absence, the permanent under-secretary, not the junior minister, received them.[35]

Junior Ministers in Departments

In the eighteenth century the style of ministerial administration was largely personal: the press of business was not beyond the capacity of one man to deal with, and under-secretaries were something between office-managers and personal assistants. In the course of the nineteenth century departmental structures and the style of administration began to change profoundly, affecting the executive position of both types of under-secretary: as the permanent secretary's place in the administrative machine was confirmed and extended, the parliamentary under-secretary, for the most part, ceased to play a significant administrative role.

Palmerston insisted that the minister, in consequence of his responsibility to parliament, completely dominated his department:

In England the ministers who are at the head of the several departments of the state, are liable any day and every day to defend themselves in parliament; in order to do this, they must be minutely acquainted with all the details of the business of their offices, and the only way of being constantly armed with such information is to conduct and direct those details themselves.

By a prodigious effort of labour at the Foreign Office, he was able to read 'every report, every letter, every despatch received ... down to the least important letter of the lowest vice-consul'. Not only his junior ministers but also his senior officials were excluded from policy work and confined to routine chores, such as correcting drafts. But that degree of personal control involved him in at least eight hours a day of paperwork, in addition to a similar time spent at the Commons. Palmerston's style was probably unique by the time he came to formulate his principle, and it was not one that he was able to sustain in the late 1840s and 1850s. The Duke of Richmond, in 1830, described a procedure which was to become more typical: 'no Postmaster-General would think himself justified in signing a paper, unless it was accompanied by a minute and by proper explanations . . . The secretary places before the Postmaster-General all the papers relating to the case, *with his opinion*. The Postmaster-General then writes his decision, and signs it' (my italics).[36]

Ministerial responsibility to parliament fundamentally influenced the nature of departmental administration and decision-taking. Ministers at the head of departments were responsible, not their subordinates who acted at their behest. This principle shielded the bureaucracy, underwrote its developing permanence, neutrality and anonymity, and deprived it of alternative political leaders. But it also meant that the powers of a junior minister were inherently derivative: 'He has not and cannot have any independent executive and administrative powers and responsibilities.' Consequently, his role came to be largely dependent on his relationship with his ministerial superior. As Buxton, under-secretary to Ripon at the Colonial Office 1892–5, observed:

> the position of an Under-Secretary of State in a great department – even where specific and prescribed duties are alloted to him – is somewhat difficult and anomalous. He feels not unfrequently that he is neither fish nor flesh nor fowl nor good red herring. His use and wont, his authority and responsibilities, his enjoyment of and interest in his post, depend in a very large degree on his Chief.[37]

Any delegation of business to a junior minister was a political and personal arrangement but, of course, there were not always close political or personal ties, or trust and confidence, between ministers and their juniors. To some extent, the prime minister's patronage, and the career interests of competing politicians, played a part in creating such tension, but there were also the inevitable pressures generated by a parliamentary and Cabinet system of government, which compelled departmental heads to deal personally with all major administrative problems and policy decisions. They alone could represent the department in Cabinet, and parliament insisted on the top minister being personally accountable to it. All this meant that it was possible for junior ministers to find themselves on the sidelines. W.E. Baxter, Parliamentary Secretary to the Admiralty, described in 1871 how the First Lord, Childers, guided him in framing the Estimates, with 'many conversations' on the policy, and 'even a part of the detail'. Childers was an exceptionally energetic minister. Baxter complained, 'I find that I have now very little to do. I believe that I am the best paid, and the least hard-worked officer in the government.'[38]

The principle and practice of ministerial responsiblity meant that a junior minister could never be an official deputy minister. One instance where a junior minister could perhaps have been considered such proved to be difficult to work in practice – namely, the vice-presidency of the Board of Trade. His position was in fact ambiguous. He was not explicitly subordinated to the President, had the same salary of £2,000, and was generally – unlike other junior ministers – a Privy Councillor. Gibson, President of the Board of Trade, stated in 1864 that 'The Vice-President of the Board of Trade has a sort of co-ordinate authority with the President. I have no authority over the Vice-President whatever that I am aware of.' The vice-president deputized for the President when he was absent, and may have represented the Board in the House other than that in which the President sat. The Board had long been, according to Bagehot, a 'hypothesis', the President and vice-president conducting the work through two joint (permanent) secretaries. However, the vice-president was never properly fitted in to the organization of the department. He had, strictly, no function as vice-president, except what was arranged between himself and the President. Bagehot wrote, 'if the two are not intimate, and the President chooses to act himself, the Vice-President sees no papers and does nothing.' Gladstone delegated railway business to his Vice-President, Dalhousie, in the early 1840s, but when the latter became President he kept personal control. Both a Treasury committee of inquiry and a Commons Select Committee recommended the replacement of the vice-president by a parliamentary secretary, expressly subordinate to the President of the Board, as was done in 1868. The change of status to that of a parliamentary secretary only made de jure what had been the vice-president's de facto responsibility and position.[39]

A final handicap, apart from the heavy loads of parliamentary work they carried, was the limited time in office of junior ministers. The average length of time a junior minister held a particular office in the period 1830–1914 was only 23 months. Moreover, they changed more frequently than both their ministerial chiefs and permanent secretaries (see table 1.2). Short tenure limited the experience and knowledge brought to office. The permanent secretary's experience was greater than either the secretary of state's or the junior minister's, but, of course, the secretary of state had the formal and political authority over officials which the junior minister lacked.

The place of junior ministers in departmental administration, their relations with their chiefs on the one hand and with senior civil servants on the other, and the problematic role they played can be conveniently analysed through an examination of a handful of departments: the Treasury, the War Office, the Colonial Office and the Foreign Office. The administrative structures and practices of these departments, while differing in detail, illustrate more generally the position of junior ministers.

TABLE 1.2 Number of ministers and officials serving in selected departments in the mid-nineteeth century

Department	Period	Permanent secs	Secs of state (or equivalent)	Junior ministers	
Treasury	1840–70	2	8	17	
Admiralty	1840–70	5	12	19	Civil Lords
				13	Parliamentary secs
Foreign Office	1840–70	3	7	12	
Home Office	1840–70	2	9	19	
War Office	1854–70	3	9	11	
Colonial Office	1854–70	2	12	7	

At the Treasury, the financial secretary had substantial administrative responsibilities. He was formally in charge of the revenue departments, and Estimates and expenditure papers were routed through him. Until 1869 the formal chain of authority ran: Chancellor – financial secretary – assistant secretary (styled permanent secretary after 1867) – clerks. After 1869 the permanent secretary assumed a more important formal position by virtue of a right of appeal to the Chancellor against the financial secretary.

In 1848 Sir Francis Baring had asserted that 'everything of the slightest importance should go through a Parliamentary officer.' The assistant secretary sieved papers before submitting them to the financial secretary. According to the procedure established, he would decide some matters himself and refer others on, the criteria chiefly being whether an increase in expenditure was involved or if the matter was likely to arouse parliamentary attention. The financial secretary, in turn, would settle certain matters without reference to the Chancellor. Gladstone wrote to his financial secretary, Childers, on that point in 1865:

> The relation between our two offices is one of peculiar intimacy; greater, I think, in reality (in most cases at least) than between Secretary and Under Secretary of State, because the [Financial] Secretary to the Treasury dispatches great masses of business without referring it to . . . [the Chancellor], and it requires much tact and discernment on his part to know when he ought to refer.[40]

Sir Charles Wood, in 1848, said that the Chancellor decided questions 'of principle', relying on his subordinates to conduct the 'preliminary investigation which brings the matter into a small compass, and ripe for decision', and then carrying out all the other questions arising of the same description, and working out in detail the matter. 'A great deal is done by them without coming to me . . . If a matter of more than ordinary importance occurs, it is looked into by them, and brought to me for final decision.'[41] In practice, the financial secretary would take business to the Chancellor only when he had a novel or important case and was doubtful whether he had the political authority to settle it, or where pressure was brought to bear and he expected appeals by other ministers to the Chancellor or to the Cabinet. The initial meetings at a ministerial level between the Treasury and other departments would fall to the financial secretary; appeals to the Chancellor were not common.

All the papers brought before the financial secretary had been seen by the assistant/permanent secretary, and usually the financial secretary was content to initial and approve the minutes he was presented with; only rarely did he reject the chief official's advice. In 1867 the permanent secretary sought from Disraeli the power to appeal to the Chancellor against the financial secretary in cases where his advice had been rejected, and was turned down. However, in 1869 he appealed successfully to Lowe against a decision of Ayrton's, and was thought to have set a precedent that in certain cases it was the right of the permanent secretary to appeal.[42]

The circumstances surrounding the precedent of 1869 are interesting, for the arrangements inside the Treasury were unusual at that time. In December 1868, James Stansfeld was appointed a junior lord of the Treasury, but styled 'Third Lord' and given £2,000 a year and a Privy Councillorship to distinguish him from the others. The aim of this appointment was to relieve the pressure of work on the financial secretary, who was to concentrate on expenditure business while the Third Lord took revenue matters. The permanent secretary was to send the papers on those subjects directly to him; no longer would all the business go through the financial secretary. This system lasted only until October 1869, when Ayrton was promoted out of the department and Stansfeld succeeded him as financial secretary. In July 1869, Lowe had overruled Ayrton in favour of the permanent secretary – the financial secretary by that time being politically estranged from the Chancellor, and one of the most unpopular members of the government by reason of his inflexible approach to economies. The permanent secretary protested that he found coordination between three political heads too difficult, and Gladstone considered Lowe and Stansfeld strong enough to conduct the Treasury by themselves.[43]

After this incident it was clear that the position of the permanent secretary in relation to the financial secretary was strengthened. The latter always had a heavy load of parliamentary business; in most cases he accepted the permanent secretary's advice; and when they disagreed, the permanent secretary could appeal to the Chancellor. The Chancellor's delegation to the financial secretary would hold only if he supported him in the face of civil service appeals. Determined civil service argument, or political doubts about his junior minister's case or judgement, might make him give way.

After 1870 the Secretary of State for War had three ministerial subordinates. The financial secretary was responsible to him for the finance of the department and involved in Estimates work; the parliamentary secretary had a primarily parliamentary role in whichever House the secretary of state did not sit; the surveyor-general of Ordnance had charge of the manufacturing, supply and munitions departments. Allowing for differences of detail, the difficulties of the surveyor-general's position mirror general problems experienced by junior ministers in all departments.

It was thought desirable that the surveyor-general should have a military background, but also be a parliamentary representative for the War Office. The first surveyor-general when the office was revived in 1870, Storks, was an experienced military officer, who was found a seat to support the secretary of state in the House. Thereafter, appointees were generally young MPs; only Adye (1880–3) had a similar background to Storks and was outside parliament. A Royal Commission in 1887 recommended that the surveyor-general be replaced by a permanent official, the junior minister's position by then being impossible: 'He changes so often that he is rather at the mercy of the permanent heads of the branches . . . as a parliamentary official he has not got the requisite detail[ed] knowledge.' In the years 1880–5, there were five successive surveyors-general. The continuity necessary to build up sufficient experience to perform the intended functions was being sacrificed to 'the exigencies of the Prime Minister . . . it has become merely a vehicle for finding a place for a parliamentary supporter.'

The surveyor-general was supposed to relieve his chief from dealing with the finance and administration of the ordnance side of the War Office. In fact, his position was undermined by both the secretary of state and his own civil servants. 'He must go very much indeed by what the Secretary of State says, and he must refer to him upon every single little point', recalled a former surveyor-general. Storks was experienced enough to be able to do the job effectively. After him, 'the practice grew up of constantly appealing from the decision of the Surveyor-General . . . to the Secretary of State. So that, in point of fact, the Secretary of State had to consider the question all over again, and to give a decision.' Sometimes the surveyor-general was ruthlessly bypassed: 'the Inspector General of Fortifications . . . for instance, would go straight to the Secretary of State, and having, in the ordinary phrase of the day, interviewed him, would produce a decision from the Secretary of State before the Surveyor-General understood that any appeal was going to be made.'

One member of the 1887 Royal Commission, Lord Lingen (Permanent Secretary of the Treasury 1870–85), identified the crucial factor: 'if the Secretary of State invariably confirmed the opinion of the Surveyor-General, people would very soon cease to appeal.' The fact that an appeal route existed, because of the final responsibility of the secretary of state, and that secretaries of state allowed the military and officials to go behind the surveyor-general's back to press their cases, undermined his authority in the department. The hapless surveyor-general was often bypassed or appealed against from below and overruled from above. The secretary of state's constitutional responsibility, and his political inclination to support the military in their demands so as not to be blamed for deficiencies in equipment, combined to render the surveyor-general powerless and redundant inside the War Office.[44]

In the early part of the nineteenth century the parliamentary and permanent secretaries at the Colonial Office divided the Empire between them on a geographical basis and had equal status. However, the problems thrown up in a department dealing with many diverse colonies, and with many aspects of each colony's business, forced changes in structure and style, first made under the powerful permanent secretary, Sir James Stephen (1835–47).

From 1848 the system was that the senior clerks in charge of departments examined incoming letters, minuted them with the prominent points and suggested the form of answer or course of action. These

précis and drafts were then sent either to the assistant under-secretary or
to the permanent under-secretary (who saw all important papers), who
passed them on to the parliamentary under-secretary, with their
observations on them, and from the junior minister they reached the
secretary of state. In 1850 Colonial Secretary Earl Grey said that 'all
ordinary business is expected to be brought before me in such a form that
it can be disposed of simply by adding my initials.'[45]

In outline, the system of minuting at the Colonial Office would seem to
have placed the junior minister in a good position to contribute to
decisions on policy and administration. In fact, the procedure served to
enhance the influence of the permanent officials, for they could arrange,
comment on and propose solutions to problems confronting the
department. Their tenure and experience were strong advantages. As
minutes progressed up to ministers, junior ministers would find that in
most cases they could not disagree with the officials. Even if they did, the
whole file would reach the secretary of state, who would have to weigh
the comments and arguments of the civil servants and the junior minister.
Henry Taylor, a senior clerk, wrote, 'In ninety-nine cases out of a
hundred the consideration which has been given to a subject by the
Secretary of State has consisted in reading the draft submitted to him and
his decision has consisted in adopting it, and the more important the
question has been the more I have found my judgement to be leant upon.'
One study of the Colonial Office found that some junior ministers
'scarcely ever minuted a despatch, or confined their attention to certain
phases of the work such as finance.'[46]

The Colonial Office junior minister had an assured place in the flow of
business, but it served to inform him and brief him for his parliamentary
duties rather than facilitate his contribution to policy. The decisive
relationship was between the secretary of state and the top officials. Only
in exceptional cases, as in Churchill's contribution to South African
policy in 1906–8 for instance, did a junior minister have a real say in
major decisions, depending on the constellations of personalities and
circumstances involved. Even then, according to Elgin's private secretary,
Churchill found that:

> he couldn't do anything without the approval of the Secretary of State. The
> Secretary of State was completely dominant ... As under-secretary
> everything went through him and [Churchill] wrote long minutes ... and
> then these would go up to the Secretary of State. 'E.' That's all – 'E.' for
> Elgin, and then that was the end of that file. You couldn't do anything
> more. You could not appeal. There was nobody to appeal to. You couldn't
> go beyond that.

On one occasion, Churchill wrote a long memorandum finishing with the words, 'These are my views.' Elgin simply wrote, 'But not mine'.[47]

The under-secretaries in the Foreign Office shared the work on a geographical basis in the early nineteenth century. From 1828 the permanent secretary supervised the divisions dealing with the Americas, Russia, Prussia, Austria, France, Spain and Turkey – areas where Britain had enduring political, strategic and commercial interests. None of the major powers came under the supervision of the junior minister. Such an inequality in the distribution of business hardly mattered when Palmerston confined the under-secretaries to routine and quasi-clerical duties. The growth in the complexity and burden of the work; the appointment of the resolute and energetic Edmund Hammond as permanent secretary in 1854; the appointment of secretaries of state less forceful and experienced than Palmerston; and the weight of the parliamentary work of the junior minister all combined to shift the central axis of advice and decision inside the department. The 1850s and 1860s were crucial years in this process, in the Foreign Office as indeed in other departments around Whitehall.

Developments in both the distribution and conduct of business strengthened the permanent secretary at the expense of the junior minister. The bulk of the important political work fell to the permanent secretary, who supervised the major divisions. After 1864 the junior minister had charge of only two small divisions, and after 1874 only one, which he finally surrendered in 1898. His parliamentary duties were so pressing that an assistant under-secretary had been appointed in 1858 to support the junior minister in the department. The most decisive factor behind the pre-eminence of the permanent secretary was the manner in which business was conducted. From the 1850s new emphasis was placed on the advisory functions of the under-secretaries, and the permanent secretary advised on a greater range of more important problems and over a longer period of time than any junior minister.

The Foreign Office system of minuting meant that papers went to the secretary of state from the under-secretary supervising each division, with his opinion on them. The secretary of state then considered the matter, and the under-secretary's opinion, and made his decision. The other under-secretary saw the papers on their way *down* the hierarchy, after the secretary of state's decision had been taken, and while the boxes were on their way to the prime minister. This arrangement served to keep each under-secretary informed about the business of the other's divisions but, given the unequal distribution of business, made it rather difficult for the junior minister to intrude his voice into the decision-taking process. As one Foreign Office junior minister described his position:

> A man possessed of some deference towards his chief does not like, when
> he finds a paper that has been approved by the Secretary of State and a
> Permanent Under Secretary of immense experience, to set his opinion
> against theirs . . . When a paper came back, having received the approval
> of the Secretary of State and the Permanent Under Secretary of State, I was
> very loath to give a contrary opinion.[48]

The secretaries of state after Palmerston, with less experience in
foreign affairs, and more willing to solicit advice, looked to the
permanent secretary to maintain continuity in administration, and for
advice on decisions. Malmesbury said that the permanent secretary was
'the minister of the interior of the office', and Clarendon admitted that 'if
a case came before me, and I did not feel myself quite able to decide it, [I]
should ask the Under Secretary's opinion.' Hammond's forceful personality drove him to acquire more of the business and vigorously to press
his advice. One of his parliamentary colleagues, Layard, wrote in 1866:

> My position is not a comfortable or a satisfactory one . . Hammond is so
> determined to have his own way that it is impossible unsupported to fight
> against him . . . [He] monopolises the whole work of the Office and
> renders it impossible for the Parliamentary Under-Secretary to do anything
> or almost to have a voice in any matter . . . I have got on well with
> Hammond by giving way to him in everything – in most things I willingly
> yield to his great knowledge and experience – but when you have to defend
> a policy to which you may not agree and in the carrying out of which you
> have had no voice at all the position becomes a very painful one.[49]

There were compelling reasons to follow the permanent secretary's
advice: his experience and detailed knowledge of the business of the
Office gave his voice special weight. All ministers – secretaries of state
and junior ministers alike – relied on the permanent officials, and
especially on the permanent secretary, for information and guidance. The
dependence of the junior minister may have been even greater than that
of the secretary of state, who probably had considerable previous
ministerial experience; the junior minister may have been completely new
to office. One parliamentary under-secretary, Otway, explained that 'On
any important question I should never have thought of putting my
opinion against Mr Hammond's; indeed, we seldom differed.' James
Bryce spoke of his method of work in 1890: cases 'always come up with
the minute from the department which had dealt with them, and one
could, generally speaking, run through them pretty quickly, and unless
one saw any strong reason to dissent, one adopted the conclusion at
which the department had arrived.' And if the junior minister dissented
from the advice of the civil servants? Otway was clear that 'the Secretary
of State did that which I should have been very much inclined to do in his

place, namely, he took the experience of the Permanent Under Secretary.'[50]

The Foreign office system was usually defended on the grounds of permitting a rapid transaction of business and guaranteeing consistency in administration. It also allowed the junior minister to concentrate on his parliamentary duties: he could easily become acquainted with what passed in the department in order to defend the decisions in the House. Informal consultations between the two under-secretaries each morning on current business helped the junior minister to learn quickly about subjects likely to come up in the House of Commons, and gave the permanent secretary a more complete knowledge of everything going on in the department.

The junior minister's administrative and policy-making role in the Foreign Office, relative to that of the permanent secretary, was thus slight. The relationship between the secretary of state and the permanent secretary was crucial in decision-taking. Even until late in the nineteenth century everything passed across the desk of the secretary of state. Otway said, 'it used to make me melancholy to see the heap of trash sent up to the Secretary of State, every paper of which he had to read and put his initials to.' Bryce commented that 'the Secretary of State is far more overloaded with work than the Parliamentary Under Secretary . . . The old traditions of the office require an enormous number of things to be settled by him.'[51] But even then, the secretary of state relied extensively on his civil service staff. In the Foreign Office, as in other departments, ministerial style was no longer so much personalized as systematized – and in the system a special place was alloted to the permanent officials.

The Inter-war Years

The general nature and significance of the office of junior minister as it had developed over the course of the nineteenth century was confirmed during the inter-war years. The continuities from the earlier period are striking: a similar proportion of junior ministers promoted up the ministerial hierarchy; an emphasis on the parliamentary functions of under-secretaries; the importance of relations with the top minister in determining the weight of the junior minister in the department. This period was noteworthy for an experiment – placing junior ministers in charge of small, semi-independent departments (Overseas Trade and Mines) – the failure of which served to demonstrate the manner in which constitutional, political and administrative influences could interact to sustain a particular definition of the appropriate character of a political office – in this case, the office of junior minister.

Standing at 15 in 1914, the size of the junior ministerial layer of government had grown to 22 by August 1939. Chamberlain's government of that month included: the financial secretary to the Treasury, parliamentary under-secretaries of state at the Foreign, Home, Colonial, Dominions, India and Scottish Offices and at the Air Ministry, the under-secretary of state and the financial secretary at the War Office, the civil lord and the parliamentary and financial secretary at the Admiralty, the assistant postmaster-general, parliamentary secretaries at the Board of Agriculture and Fisheries, the Education Board, and the Ministries of Health, Labour, Transport and Supply, and three parliamentary secretaries at the Board of Trade (one called the Secretary for Mines, another the Secretary for Overseas Trade).

The increase since 1914 was due to the creation of a Scottish Office under-secretaryship and the two specially titled junior ministers at the Board of Trade, and to the appearance of new departments: Air, Transport, Labour, Dominions and Supply. For half of the inter-war period, the Ministry of Pensions did not have a parliamentary secretary (during the two short-lived Labour governments and after 1932), and the Office of Works had a junior minister only during 1922–3. On the other hand, the Foreign Office had two parliamentary under-secretaries from August 1935 to May 1939 (until February 1938 the second one was designated as under-secretary for League of Nations Affairs). This additional Foreign Office junior minister was appointed shortly after Eden was made Minister without Portfolio for League of Nations Affairs, and at his insistence; the special title was retained until Eden resigned as Foreign Secretary, taking his under-secretary, Cranborne, with him.

As in the nineteenth century, so in the inter-war period prime ministers constructed their governments through a process of bargaining with leading colleagues. As Ramsay MacDonald noted in his diary in 1924, 'Consultation with Thomas, Henderson, Clynes, Snowden, Spoor. Produced my proposals for Ministers and under Secys, etc. List generally approved after explanations of why & wherefore.' Senior and powerful figures could insist on choosing their own junior ministers, as Henderson did with Dalton at the Foreign Office in 1929. Others may not even have been consulted; according to Dalton, Herbert Morrison first knew Lord (Arthur) Ponsonby was to be his new parliamentary secretary at the Ministry of Transport when he read it in *The Times*.[52]

The most detailed study of parliamentary careers in the years 1918–1955 (extending beyond the period discussed here) shows that of the MPs serving as junior ministers in this period, 65.7 per cent served only as junior ministers, 20.4 per cent were promoted to ministerial office outside the Cabinet, and 13.9 per cent ultimately received Cabinet appointments. One-third of parliamentary private secretaries (PPSs) advanced into the ranks of ministers; 28.8 per cent of junior ministers had previously been PPSs. In all, 64.5 per cent of Labour Cabinet ministers and 75.8 per cent of Conservatives had had some experience in junior office. Only one cabinet minister in eight had no prior experience of ministerial office at the time of appointment to the Cabinet – more than half of these served in the first two Labour Cabinets.[53] These figures show that the notion of politicians making their careers on a moving hierarchy of ministerial offices, established in the nineteenth century, had become the orthodox pattern (though, of necessity, fully adopted by Labour only after 1945).

Some junior ministers, of course, could not expect promotion. As H. E. Dale, a senior civil servant between the wars, put it, 'A few may be veterans who have not the qualities for a seat in the Cabinet but have deserved a consolation prize by long service and hard work in the party head-quarters or on the platform.' But for the others, Dale believed that promotion depended mainly on parliamentary reputation:

> One characteristic of Cabinet Ministers is likely to be even more obvious in Parliamentary Secretaries: their concentration on parliamentary business. A Secretary of course desires to get into the Cabinet. He is competing against a score of fellow Secretaries. His success depends not entirely but mainly on his performance in the House of which he is a member and the degree of esteem that the House accords to him. Unless he is in the Commons and his Minister in the Lords, his opportunities of distinguishing himself at question-time or in debate are not frequent. He is even more emphatically 'on the make' than Cabinet Ministers. When, therefore a piece of Parliamentary business does fall to him, he takes great pains over it – sometimes excessive pains, it seems to the officials who have to cherish him. The question 'What will the House think of this?' is an even more frequent subject of anxious thought to him than to his chief.[55]

If anything, those successful junior ministers who attained Cabinet office were slightly less likely than their Victorian forebears to have had previous experience in the department they were to head on promotion. Of the 51 junior ministers who moved into the Cabinet in the inter-war period, 28 (54.9 per cent) assumed non-departmental Cabinet posts or headed departments they had not previously served in (the corresponding figure for 1830–1914 was 49.5 per cent). Twenty-three former junior ministers (45.1 per cent) later headed departments they had worked in (50.5 per cent in the earlier period). Eighteen of this latter group, though, had a career involving several junior appointments, several Cabinet appointments, or both – thus diluting their 'specialist' character. Only five made their careers within one department in this period. Ministers successful in scaling the career ladder largely continued to be generalists.

Despite his own career success, Duff Cooper was not sure that this model was a good way of training future Cabinet Ministers:

> The life of a junior minister . . . is not a disagreeable one, but it provides little in the way of training for the higher responsibilities to which it should lead. At the same time, it deprives the young politician of opportunities of distinguishing himself or of improving his technique in the House of Commons. He sees no Cabinet papers and remains therefore hardly better informed on matters of high policy than his contemporary backbenchers . . . Nor is it open to [him] to enlighten his ignorance by asking questions in the House of Commons . . . junior ministers are in fact put into cold storage, and if they remain there too long their faculties may suffer from lack of employment and even become atrophied. Too often it happens that a promising back-bencher, who has been a capable Under-Secretary, proves a great disappointment upon higher promotion.[55]

These doubts had not been entertained before 1914 when, as we noted above, Sir Edward Grey and Winston Churchill, among others, regarded junior office as a valuable apprenticeship for higher things. However, Duff Cooper's scepticism does not appear to have been widely shared in this period; not until the 1960s and 1970s was the appropriateness of this method of training British Cabinet ministers to become more widely questioned. If he felt underemployed as a junior minister, Duff Cooper at least put his free time to good use, producing a two-volume biography of Field Marshal Lord Haig in 1935, written during two and a half years when he was successively financial secretary to the War Office and financial secretary to the Treasury!

Again, as in the nineteenth century, relations with his departmental chief were crucial in determining whether or not a junior minister cut much of a figure in his department. A number of examples will illustrate this point. At the Foreign Office, 1929–31, Henderson trusted and liked his junior minister, Dalton, and delegated widely to him, giving him 'an unusually large share of responsibility over the detailed working of the Office and in the handling of papers'. In contrast, R. A. Butler at the India Office, 1935–7, found his chief, Lord Zetland, exceptionally wooden. He was 'too punctilious to be informal and too straightlaced to be communicative. Interviews with him were not to be held by "breaking in" to his room, but required to be arranged by correspondence or through the channels of his Private Office.' Zetland was equally aloof in his personal and political advice to Butler; asked about Indian problems, he told him, 'Read my books'. As parliamentary secretary at the Board of Agriculture and Fisheries from 1929 to 1930, Addison had 'far more influence upon Cabinet policy in his department than most Under

Secretaries could reasonably expect'. He actually had more experience as a Cabinet minister than his chief, Buxton, whose job he coveted. His biographers describe how Addison was effectively in charge of the department: 'Buxton and Addison formed an excellent partnership . . . largely, it must be said, on the basis that Buxton gave way on practically everything and increasingly let Addison take command of his own department.' As Addison wrote to his wife, 'Buxton is very decent and defers to me a lot.' Within a year Buxton left the Cabinet and was replaced by his junior minister.[56]

The memoirs of Sir Geoffrey Shakespeare, who was a junior minister for ten years after 1932, in four governments, serving in five departments and under seven ministers, show what junior ministerial life was like from the perspective of a man who, like the majority of his colleagues, was not a high-flier. His first assignment was as parliamentary secretary to the Ministry of Health, a department 'always in the parliamentary firing line', where, in four years, he helped put onto the Statute Book 30 Acts of Parliament. However, at first he did not have much of an administrative role:

> One of the drawbacks of the post of Parliamentary Secretary to the Ministry of Health was that, unlike the corresponding post in some other departments, he had no administrative responsibilities. His Minister, receiving information from any Division of the Department, might or might not pass it on to him. Hilton Young [the Minister] immediately remedied this defect and put me in charge of the actual administration of the slum crusade subject, of course, to his general direction and supervision. All information and memoranda on housing in future was to pass through me and I was part of the administrative machine.

In 1937 Shakespeare moved across to become parliamentary and financial secretary at the Admiralty, 'one of the plums among the junior appointments'. Except for parliamentary questions and the annual presentation of the Navy Estimates, his parliamentary duties were light. His job was instead a highly technical and laborious administrative one, presiding over the Admiralty's Finance Committee which, starting in the autumn, held daily meetings for several months to prepare the Estimates, and also approving contracts for the purchase of naval equipment and supplies. The day-to-day work on dossiers was burdensome, and Shakespeare was clear that as a junior minister it was not his job 'to initiate or decide questions of policy'. As a rule he minuted his opinion and passed the file onto the First Lord for his final decision. A variety of minor business came his way: the question of marriage allowances for naval officers, procedures for promoting ratings from the lower decks, steering the Anglo-German Naval Treaty through the House, and a great many visits to ships and naval dockyards. ('We civilians were caught up in the traditions of the Navy and inspired by its sense of mission.')[57]

Reviewing Shakespeare's autobiography for the *New Statesman*, Richard Crossman described him as 'the natural Under-Secretary', adding 'every Prime Minister requires for the majority of the posts in his Administration, honest, unassuming career politicians, who can read a Departmental brief almost as though they had composed it; put a questioner off the scent without actually saying what is untrue; and accept without frustration the unimportance of their own activities.'[58]

If senior ministers were not unhappy with the conventional role of the junior minister in this period, neither were top civil servants dissatisfied. The increase in work had led to a greater delegation from ministers to officials, and the generalist civil servant emerged in the inter-war period to dominate the Whitehall machine and to handle functions of a quasi-political character. Senior officials actually opposed the appointment of a greater number of junior ministers to support departmental heads. When, in early 1936, Conservative peers complained at the absence of direct Board of Agriculture representation in the Lords (the department's junior minister was always a peer in this period, except for 1924, 1929–30 and November 1935–July 1936 when Baldwin arranged a limited reshuffle to meet this criticism), and suggested the appointment of promising young peers as extra unpaid 'assistant under-secretaries', who could at least speak with more authority and knowledge than lords-in-waiting, Sir Warren Fisher (Head of the Civil Service) and Sir Horace Wilson (ostensibly the government's Chief Industrial Adviser, in reality a key No. 10 adviser) were quick to argue that extra ministers would not be welcome: it would be difficult to find any departmental work for them and there were problems of locating suitable accommodation. Fisher said that additional parliamentary secretaries would be 'a nuisance' to the departments.[59]

The expectations and practices of Cabinet ministers and senior civil servants together kept junior ministers on the fringes of decision-taking on the major policies. They were deliberately kept in the dark about matters other than the limited field of subjects they personally dealt with. For instance, the procedure of the Cabinet Office, from its establishment in 1916, was to circulate the decisions and conclusions (minutes) of the Cabinet to 'the Political and Civil Heads of the departments concerned'. Permanent secretaries and the ministers at the head of departments thus knew directly the decisions of the Cabinet; junior ministers were not officially informed. In his note on 'Cabinet Procedure' in 1937 Chamberlain allowed that there was a convention that ministers were permitted to show Cabinet conclusions and other documents to their junior ministers 'in their discretion'. Much depended on the attitude of the top minister and his relations with his junior. Duff Cooper was probably not the only junior minister to make a gaffe because of being in 'entire ignorance of what questions the Cabinet might be discussing'.[60]

Not surprisingly, some junior ministers chafed at this restricted access to official information. In 1938, Crookshank, the Secretary for Mines, wrote to Lord Halifax, the Foreign Secretary, asking if junior ministers could see the Foreign Office telegrams circulated to Cabinet ministers 'on the grounds that without such means of keeping themselves informed it was difficult for Junior Ministers . . . to understand and defend Government policy.' Halifax forwarded the request to Prime Minister Chamberlain, who in turn asked for the opinion of Sir Maurice Hankey, the Secretary to the Cabinet. Hankey thought that it would be best for junior ministers to see the Foreign Office 'prints' (paraphrased selections of the telegrams) rather than the copies of incoming and ingoing telegrams circulated to all Cabinet ministers and to the Secretary for Overseas Trade (a junior minister with a departmental interest). Alternatively, junior ministers might be shown copies of the telegrams after their superiors had dealt with them, but by then they would be 'obsolescent' and the issues referred to closed. Even in these modified forms Hankey opposed the proposal. He argued that it could be anticipated that once junior ministers had seen the telegrams or prints, they would soon ask – 'with some justification' – to see dispatches, including the 'more secret and important' circulated to the Cabinet 'concerned with the formulation and execution of policy'. If they saw Foreign Office material, it would be difficult to resist requests to see papers from other departments – the Dominions Secretary, Malcolm MacDonald, objected to circulating his papers to junior ministers. Last, there would be a great risk of leakage to newspapers. Overall, Hankey concluded, 'it is a most dangerous proposal.' His arguments were endorsed by the Prime Minister, who wrote to Halifax rejecting Crookshank's request.[61] Junior ministers were thus bound by the convention of collective ministerial responsibility to support in public decisions which they had not participated in taking on issues they had no official information about, a state of affairs which did not appear to trouble either Cabinet ministers or top civil servants. The 'insiders' were content for junior ministers to remain, in effect, little better informed than the 'outsiders'.

Throughout the inter-war years two junior ministers occupied a position which was, at least formally, rather different from that of their colleagues. The Secretary for Overseas Trade and the Secretary for Mines both had a quasi-independent status, in charge of their own small

departments which had a unique 'federal' relationship to other government departments.

The Secretary for Overseas Trade headed the Department of Overseas
Trade, established in 1917 as a compromise between the Foreign Office
and the Board of Trade, both of which had an interest in external trade
policy. The Secretary was simultaneously an additional parliamentary
under-secretary at the Foreign Office (though not counted as such when
calculating the number of under-secretaries capable of sitting in the
Commons) and an additional parliamentary secretary at the Board of
Trade, responsible to the Foreign Secretary and to the President of the
Board of Trade respectively for matters within the competence of each
department. As a Foreign Office minister, the Secretary was responsible
for the appointment and direction of the commercial staffs attached to
embassies; as a Board of Trade minister, he was concerned with
negotiating and securing parliamentary approval for commercial treaties;
as head of the Department of Overseas Trade, his task was to liaise with
traders and to foster exports. On all questions of policy, the Secretary
was supposed to consult with his ministerial chiefs as circumstances
required; his sphere of responsibility was to be the detailed application of
policy. Functions of representation and presentation, such as receiving
deputations and making visits abroad, were also among his duties: 'In
normal times a very large proportion of the time of the Secretary . . . was
occupied with activities other than the administration of the department
– addressing Chambers of Commerce, opening exhibitions, interviewing
industrialists, etc.'[62] The export trade interests saw the Department and
the Secretary as their representative in the government (the Secretary
chaired an advisory council of prominent businessmen), and in 1919 and
1927 business lobbying headed-off attempts to abolish the Department.

The Mines Department was established in 1920 as a device to avoid
nationalization of the mining industry, yet consolidate government
responsibilities and functions towards it and satisfy the demands of the
industry for political representation. The government originally planned
a *Ministry* of Mines, headed by a *Minister* for Mines who would be a
parliamentary secretary at the Board of Trade, directly responsible to
parliament for all the routine work of the department and subject to the
President of the Board of Trade's general directions on questions of
policy. Parliamentary opposition forced the government to change the
title 'Minister' to 'Secretary' and to set up a 'Mines Department' of the
Board of Trade. As a parliamentary secretary at the Board, the Secretary
for Mines was to exercise the powers and duties of the Board of Trade in
relation to the mining industry, subject to the directions of the
President.[63]

Like the Secretary for Overseas Trade, the Secretary for Mines received a salary of £2,000, £500 more than that of under-secretaries of state, placing them alongside the financial secretary to the Treasury, the First Commissioner of Works (sometimes in the Cabinet) and the Minister of Pensions.

In practice, as a junior minister, the authority of the Mines Secretary depended on his ability and competence, his relations with the President of the Board of Trade, the personalities involved and the nature and development of the issues he faced. According to Chester and Willson:

> The President of the Board of Trade was a very real Minister with regard to the Mines Department: he was always concerned with big policy matters and legislation, and would handle such matters in Cabinet and in Parliament. The Secretary for Mines was definitely more than a Parliamentary Secretary, but only dealt with policy matters up to a certain level, above which the President of the Board of Trade took over. Popular opinion, however, probably regarded the Secretary for Mines as the Minister responsible for running the mining industry.

The Secretary for Mines could relieve the President of the Board of Trade of a great deal of the routine work involved in running the Department of Mines. He could meet deputations, attend conferences and make visits, answer questions in Parliament, and deal with much of the day-to-day paperwork. Graham, President of the Board of Trade in the 1929–31 Labour government, told Shinwell, Secretary for Mines, that he could run the Mines Department without constant reference to him: ' "Give me a report on what you're doing", he said, "so that I can let the Cabinet know what's happening. Otherwise the problems are yours. I'll wear the feathers and you can do the scratching." '[64] The reality of the Secretary for Mines's position, then, was not so different from that of other junior ministers. Despite his statutory position, his scope essentially depended on a *personal* delegation of authority to him by his ministerial chief at the Board of Trade.

The problems of the mining industry were acute and often engaged attention at the highest political levels: the President of the Board of Trade or even the Cabinet and prime minister would deal with issues concerning miners' pay and industrial action, though the Secretary for Mines would be found on the relevant Cabinet committees.

The experiment with semi-independent departments and junior ministers was, however, short-lived. In 1942 the Ministry of Fuel and Power took over the Mines Department which had lacked the administrative resources and the political weight to cope with wartime problems. In 1946 the Department of Overseas Trade was formally absorbed into the main Board of Trade, with the Secretary for Overseas Trade keeping his title but now unambiguously a subordinate of the President of the Board of Trade only (even the separate title disappeared when a minister of state was appointed in 1953). Ministers decided that the Foreign Office link could best be made at the level of official committees and consultations, that it was important to integrate fully home and overseas trade policy in the aftermath of war, but that the political sensitivities of the business community meant that it was advisable to retain a junior minister with a special title.[65]

Criticisms levelled against these departments and ministers throw light on the attitudes of MPs and particularly civil servants towards junior ministers in general. MPs expressed disquiet about the responsibilities of various ministers at different times, though they often had motives other than concern for constitutional proprieties (attitudes for or against coal nationalization, for instance, coloured views on the status of the Secretary for Mines). When the Mines Department was created, MPs and peers complained that parliamentary responsibility would be blurred: the Secretary for Mines or the President of the Board of Trade could avoid responsibility by claiming that the other's decision had committed them. In practice, these fears were unfounded. The President of the Board of Trade appeared on major parliamentary occasions and the Mines and Overseas Trade Secretaries had definitely secondary positions. As with conventional government departments and junior ministers, the expectations and behaviour of MPs meant that the Cabinet minister carrying final responsibility had always to be ready to answer to the House of Commons in person.

Civil service criticisms were crystallized during the wartime meetings of the Machinery of Government Committee. The starting point for the civil servants' analysis was the view that the distinction between policy and detailed administration underlying the semi-independent departments was untenable. Detailed administrative questions might raise issues of policy, and it was undesirable that acquaintance with day-to-day administration should be separated from responsibility for formulating policy. Some officials thought that the division of functions might lead Cabinet ministers to neglect the subjects concerned, and not give them full weight in the overall policy they developed. Others argued that the semi-independent junior ministers relieved their superiors only on minor points, and that all major political burdens had to be borne by the senior ministers. Officials also feared that blurring responsibility to parliament entailed confusing authority relationships within departments. The department's permanent secretary may not be able to keep completely in touch with business in the wing of the department under the junior minister, and so not properly perform his role as the top minister's chief policy adviser and departmental manager. There could be uncertain signals on policy as officials could never be sure where they stood with the semi-independent minister because he in turn had a potentially difficult relationship with his superior. The final responsibility of the senior minister for policy meant that officials working to a semi-independent junior minister had a prior loyalty to his supervising minister – there was thus an implicit appeal route built in to these arrangements.

Whitehall doubts about semi-independent ministers also arose from views about the general contours of the machinery of government. Officials were anxious to avoid having a large number of small departments, each with a narrow view. The optimum size of a department was held to be neither so large that one minister could not be effectively in charge, nor so small that the limited views of departments created problems of coordination. As early as 1919, Board of Trade officials wondered whether the Department of Overseas Trade, instead of being a coordinating link between the Foreign Office and the Board of Trade, would become a body itself needing to be coordinated, thus increasing the burdens on ministers.[66]

There were, of course, presentational aspects to each department. In each area of policy – overseas trade and the mining industry – there were groups seeking government action or support. They saw 'their' department and minister as a point of access into the government machine. Business groups opposed the abolition of the Department of Overseas Trade; the Labour movement actually wanted a Mines minister in the Cabinet. Such channels of access are doubtless useful for the groups concerned, but it is a fine question how far such narrow departments with limited power are able to serve as vehicles of the public interest, or whether they are in danger of being 'captured' by their clients. Despite those entrenched interests, the interlocking political, constitutional and administrative objections to semi-independent departments and junior ministers carried more weight with ministers and their senior civil service advisers.

After 1945 the semi-independent junior minister, heading his own department 'federally' linked to its parent department, disappeared. For a few brief years from 1961 to 1964 there existed a minister and department similar to the earlier Overseas Trade and Mines ministers and departments – the Minister for Technical Cooperation – but (as we shall see below) this was essentially a transitional device *en route* to the creation of a distinct Ministry of Overseas Development. The demise of the semi-independent ministers confirmed among other things the status and authority of junior ministers as they had developed over the previous hundred years. Just as the position and work of junior ministers in the inter-war period, and the career paths of ministers, would have been familiar to Victorian politicians, so, as will be seen in the following chapters, the contemporary office of the British junior minister has been decisively shaped by its long history.

2

Appointment and Careers of Junior Ministers

Ministerial appointments and careers in Britain today follow a pattern first discernible in the Victorian era: a backbench apprenticeship in the House of Commons, leading to one or more junior posts on the ministerial hierarchy before promotion to the Cabinet or (more likely) a return to the backbenches or retirement from politics. Today, as in the nineteenth century, MPs continue to win office primarily for political reasons and because of their skills as parliamentarians, and not because of specialist subject expertise or extraparliamentary executive experience. Similarly, successful ministers continue to be generalists, typically serving in a number of quite different departments and posts over the course of their careers in government. Despite sharp criticisms of this traditional model since the 1960s, it is almost certain that the ministers who will carry responsibility for the conduct of government as Britain enters the twenty-first century will have been selected and trained for office in a way familiar to Sir Robert Peel or Gladstone. Later in this chapter the rationale for this system of ministerial recruitment is discussed. The final chapter of this book looks at the ways in which other states appoint and promote ministers and considers the feasibility of changing British practices significantly in these respects. But first it is necessary to examine the way in which junior ministers receive their posts in modern governments and the varied influences and criteria which lie behind their appointment.

The Appointment of Junior Ministers

There has been a tremendous increase in the number of junior ministers since 1945. In July 1945 Attlee's government included a Cabinet of 20 ministers, a further 11 full ministers who were not in the Cabinet, and 32 junior ministers (29 parliamentary under-secretaries, or equivalent, and three with a higher status: the financial secretary to the Treasury, the minister of state at the Foreign Office and the Secretary for Overseas Trade). This total of 63 ministers had grown to 82 by February 1986, with the number of junior ministers almost doubling: Mrs Thatcher's government of that month included a Cabinet of 22 ministers and 60 junior ministers (32 parliamentary under-secretaries and 28 at minister of state rank). While the top and bottom echelons of the hierarchy have been reasonably stable over the post-war period, the middle layer has expanded dramatically. Almost the entire increase in the total number of junior ministers is due to the proliferation of ministers of state. This development has been accompanied by the disappearance of those ministers who were in charge of departments but not members of the Cabinet, changing the nature of the career ladder which successful ministers scale and perhaps also (as shall be seen in a later chapter) affecting in important ways the conduct of government business and the relations between the political and bureaucratic elements in Whitehall.

Table 2.1 shows the size of post-war governments and indicates that, despite the reduction in the number of government departments, the total number of junior ministers has increased, reflecting the enlargement of the ministerial complements of departments. Until the late 1950s, most departments had only one junior minister but nowadays ministerial teams are larger. In February 1986, nine departments had four or more junior ministers (the Department of the Environment and the Department of Trade and Industry each has six junior ministers; the Foreign Office, the Northern Ireland Office and the Department of Health and Social Security each had five; and the Home Office, the Scottish Office, the Ministry of Defence and the Department of Transport each had four), four departments had three junior ministers (the Treasury, the Ministry of Agriculture, Fisheries and Food, the Department of Education and Science and the Department of Energy), two departments had only two junior ministers each (the Welsh Office and the Department of Employment, which had, however, two Cabinet ministers) and a solitary junior minister at the Privy Council Office had responsibility for the Office of Arts and Libraries and represented the Management and Personnel Office. Only the Welsh Office and the Department of Employment had no ministers of state, and eight departments had more than one; the Foreign Office actually having four ministers of state and only one parliamentary under-secretary.

While the number of junior ministerial appointments has increased sharply since 1945, the way in which these appointments are made and

TABLE 2.1 The size of post-war governments

Government and year	Total junior ministers	Parl. secs.	Ministers of state	Junior ministers in House of Lords	Cabinet ministers	Non-Cabinet ministers	No. of depts with junior ministers
Labour							
1945	32	29	3	2	20	11	24
1951	33	28	5	5	17	13	23
Conservative							
1951	32	26	6	4	17	14	23
1957	35	28	7	5	18	9	22
1964	50	35	15	14	23	3	20
Labour							
1964	54	36	18	12	23	7	24
1970	49	26	23	8	21	5	16
Conservative							
1970	38	24	14	7	18	6	15
1974	48	25	23	9	21	2	15
Labour							
1974	53	31	22	7	21	2	18
1979	57	33	24	8	24	1	20
Conservative							
1979	58	31	27	10	22	–	17
(Feb.) 1986	60	32	28	10	22	–	16

the factors influencing them are remarkably similar to the methods and considerations which produced governments in the early years of the twentieth century and even in the nineteenth century.

All ministerial appointments and assignments are decided by the prime minister. Junior ministers are usually given office after a telephone call from the prime minister, or after a brief meeting with him or her at No. 10 Downing Street. ('This tends to be a jovial backslapping occasion', said a private secretary to a former Labour prime minister in interview.) On some occasions the telephone call or meeting is with the chief whip. One junior minister recalled reading of his appointment in a three-day-old copy of the *Sunday Times* while holidaying on a remote Aegean island.

The prime minister's power to appoint ministers appears to be untrammelled. It has become a central tenet of the 'prime ministerial power' thesis, explaining how the prime minister dominates the government and disciplines his or her parliamentary party. In reality, the appointment of junior ministers is less an exertion of prime ministerial power and more an essay in political bargaining. Prime ministers do not usually impose junior ministers on Cabinet ministers in an arbitrary or imperious manner; appointments are made after soundings, consultations and mutual accommodations. It is common for a handful of senior and trusted colleagues to discuss appointments with the prime minister. In 1951, for example, Churchill was heavily influenced in his junior appointments by his chief whip and two senior ministers, James Stuart (a former chief whip) and Harry Crookshank. In 1979 Mrs Thatcher consulted with William Whitelaw, Lord Carrington and her outgoing chief whip, Humphrey Atkins.[1] The chief whip is particularly influential in junior appointments. Inevitably aware of the talents, specialisms, 'representative' quality or nuisance value of MPs, his powers of recommendation or disapproval can be decisive. Concerned with the passage of the government's parliamentary business, and with the opinions, moods and behaviour of MPs, the whips are obliged to listen to and report back on backbencher's speeches on the floor of the House of Commons and during the committee stage of Bills. Consultations within the Whip's Office can thus supply vital intelligence to the prime minister, who may not personally know a great many backbenchers.

Individual Cabinet ministers have varying degrees of influence over junior appointments. Senior figures may be able to include their political allies or clients in the government, and lend a general support, or express a general opposition, to appointments across a range of departments. Harold Wilson recalled that 'Colleagues . . . tend to offer unsolicited advice about backbenchers whom they think should be brought into the government, almost invariably failing to suggest who should be dropped to make way for them.'[2] A former prime minister described reshuffles, 'Hardly a minister doesn't write and say that his parliamentary private secretary is the best in the House and should be promoted.' In most cases, Cabinet ministers have only a limited say in junior appointments in their departments. There may be consultation, a possible veto or a restricted choice offered. Attlee would admit no more than:

> It's generally best to have a talk with the minister concerned in choosing an under-secretary, not just foist someone on him. But you can't necessarily accept the man a minister wants. He's the only one who doesn't know his own deficiencies. You may have picked a minister who is awfully good but, although he doesn't know it, rather weak on certain sides, so you must give him an under-secretary who fills in the gaps.[3]

Harold Wilson has written that in 1974 James Callaghan, the Foreign Secretary, and Roy Jenkins, Home Secretary, virtually picked their own teams of junior ministers.[4] A former prime minister said in interview that it was important for the Treasury team to be united in the face of its civil servants and so the Chancellor of the Exchequer must be given the junior ministers for whom he asks.

Prime ministers do sometimes appoint junior ministers without the knowledge of the relevant Cabinet minister. In 1952, for instance, the Minister of Civil Aviation was surprised by the creation and filling of a parliamentary secretaryship in his department. The new junior minister, Reginald Maudling, recalled the scene:

> 'Hello, Reggie . . . what can I do for you?'
> 'Well, Jack . . . I am your new Parliamentary Secretary.'
> 'Oh, . . . are you?'[5]

A former junior minister described in interview how, on the first evening of the new government, he went straight from Downing Street to his department, went up to the ministers' floor and padded along a gloomy corridor, peering into empty rooms. Finally, he flung open a door on a surprised and solitary Tony Crosland and announced, 'I am your new minister of state.' Crosland simply replied 'Good God, are you?' At that very moment, the telephone rang – it was the Prime Minister to tell his Secretary of State for the Environment the news! A Cabinet minister's experience was typical:

> The prime ministers I served were both willing to discuss appointments. You would get a choice between 'A' and 'B' – twice I indicated preferences, but was told that the chap was going elsewhere, wasn't ready for the move or for a job yet, or wouldn't be getting a job at all. The prime minister would consult you if making your under secretary a minister of state. Of course, if you moved into a department in a reshuffle, the other ministers were already there.

The prime minister's position in relation to individual candidates for junior office is even stronger than in relation to their Cabinet superiors. Gerald Kaufman believes that 'If the prime minister makes you an offer and you are not in an exceptionally powerful position, take what you are offered or be ready to return to the backbenches; dozens will be ready to accept what you have rejected.' Several former ministers agreed, saying, 'Never refuse anything.' However, some MPs were reinvited to join the government after initially refusing office. Enoch Powell turned down the post of parliamentary secretary to the Ministry of Housing and Local Government in October 1954, only to accept it in December 1955. Michael Foot and Eric Heffer both refused office in the 1960s, but accepted it in 1974, the former in the Cabinet. In February 1974 John Smith declined the post of Solicitor-General for Scotland, but the following October became under-secretary at the Department of Energy, reaching the Cabinet in 1978. Neil Kinnock, fearing that he would be silenced, refused a junior post at the Department of Prices in 1976, becoming Labour Party Leader in 1983 with no ministerial experience at all.[6]

The major constraint on the prime minister offered by backbench candidates is not their bargaining capability but the fact that he or she must appoint so many of them. Richard Rose has convincingly demonstrated that as the size of governments has grown, together with the increasing proportion of posts filled by MPs rather than peers, the premier's scope for selectivity has diminished. Excluding the very old and very young, inexperienced parliamentarians and those disqualified on personal grounds or for extreme political views (altogether between one-third and two-fifths of the parliamentary party will be ineligible for these reasons), one in two of the remaining MPs must be given jobs – a limited pool, perhaps allowing the prime minister more choice as to which department an individual will be assigned rather than whether he will be appointed at all. Given the troubles of consultation and pressures to appoint or exclude, the number of posts to be filled and the diverse factors to be considered (competence, loyalty, party balancing, geography and others), it is not surprising that prime ministers often seem to regard appointing junior ministers as a problem rather than a power. Harold Wilson has likened forming a government to a 'nightmarish multi-dimensional jigsaw puzzle, with an almost unlimited number of possible permutations and combinations.'[7]

From July 1945, when Attlee formed his first government, to May 1983, the end of Mrs Thatcher's first term in office, 481 junior ministers were appointed. Of these, 84 (17.5 per cent) were peers (including 15 who had some service either as backbenchers or as junior ministers in the Commons before their appointments in the Lords); 397 served as junior ministers entirely in the House of Commons. The average age on appointment to junior office was 46 years; those ministers in the Commons had served an average of 7.3 years on the backbenches before appointment. Only three (0.6 per cent) junior ministers were under the age of 30 on appointment; all were Labour, one was a young hereditary peer (Lord Melchett, appointed under-secretary in the Department of Industry in 1975), one had been elected to parliament at the age of 26 (Ted Rowlands, appointed under-secretary to the Welsh Office in 1969), the other had been a wartime official and was well connected with the party leadership (Harold Wilson, appointed to the Ministry of Works in

1945). Equally exceptional were the two junior ministers appointed in their seventies: Sir Peter Bennett, who had become an MP at the age of 60 and who was a Conservative Party expert on industry, appointed to the Ministry of Labour in 1951, serving only seven months, and Lord Mitchison, appointed by Harold Wilson to the Ministry of Land and Natural Resources at the age of 74, after being in the House of Commons since 1945 and a Labour frontbencher since 1955; after 18 months' 'reward' for services rendered, he left office.

In general, extreme youth and extreme age disqualify: 50 per cent of all junior ministers were aged between 30 and 45 years on appointment; only 12 per cent were over 55. One of the reasons why youth disqualifies is the requirement that junior ministers have several years' backbench experience. Only three 'freshmen' MPs have received junior office in this period, making their maiden speeches from the front bench, all in the 1945 Labour government. There have been eight 'freshmen' appointments from the Lords, in the sense that individuals were simultaneously granted a peerage and given junior office. Only 15.7 per cent of all junior ministers had served two years or less in the Commons, while 18.3 per cent had 11 or more years experience in the Commons.

The prime minister must take care that younger MPs, who will move up into the Cabinet in years to come, are brought forward to be given their apprenticeship on the lower rungs of the ministerial ladder. At the same time, more MPs have become full-time professional politicians, and are eager for office. New 'intakes' of MPs must be accommodated after each general election. The 1964 intake found its first posts in 1966; the 1966 intake in 1969; the first of the 1979 intake were appointed in 1981 and 1982; the first of the 1983 intake in 1985. Harold Wilson once insisted that Richard Crossman relinquish a junior minister with the words, 'He's over sixty-eight, we want young blood. You must trade him in.' In 1969 the average age of ten retiring junior ministers was 60; their replacements were on average 38. Older junior ministers may have been given office for past political services, loyalty or seniority in the party, and eventually make way for the push of younger talent. Crossman described these as 'People who should be given three years of fat ministerial life as reward for services rendered but whom one shouldn't keep longer than that.'[8]

The administrative ability of new junior ministers is often conjectural, so relevant subject expertise and, most important of all at this level, parliamentary skills must be looked to. Bruce Headey has written that 'There is probably no other country in the world in which assessments of politicians are based so heavily on their parliamentary performances.' Moreover, a parliamentary reputation is won not through zealous Select

Committee investigations (though since 1979 the most able young backbenchers on Select Committees have soon succumbed to the lure of ministerial office), but on the floor of the House of Commons, where it is the sum of an MP's contributions that are weighed: speeches, questions, interventions over several years. Ambitious MPs seek to display their talents before their peers, party leaders, influential ministers and the whips, and must do so for a period longer than the life of a single parliament.[9] Inasmuch as parliamentary duties are an important component of the work of junior ministers, the anxiety of MPs to demonstrate parliamentary ability and of government leaders to look for it is understandable.

The stress on parliamentary ability encourages a generalist attitude among MPs. One MP told Anthony King, 'it is not the narrow specialists who get to the top.' Bruce Headey found that half of the Cabinet ministers he interviewed felt that the intelligent layman/parliamentary politician was best suited for office, while 23 per cent emphasized the importance of specialist subject knowledge. At the junior minister level senior politicians explicity recommend the generalist. Sir Edward Boyle believed that 'There are few Departments where any normally intelligent Parliamentarian couldn't do the junior job all right.' A former chief whip agreed: 'Basically any MP ought to be able to do the job', he told Bruce Headey. To a certain degree, specialist subject knowledge is considered, but its extent and nature must not be exaggerated. A former parliamentary under-secretary said, 'Prime ministers look for experienced specialist types now, if they're available. Nearly all MPs today do specialize, concentrating on two or three subjects. MPs just cannot cover the whole sweep. Prime ministers do try to get political balance or shut up a nuisance, but they need specialist knowledge to add strength to the team.' In the late 1960s and early 1970s Conservative Leader and Prime Minister, Edward Heath, emphasized 'professionalism', appointing shadow spokesmen who had specialized in their subjects in debates, allowing a pronounced continuity between Opposition and government teams, and recruiting junior ministers on the basis of demonstrated subject knowledge and specialism. David Judge found that in the early 1970s nearly half of all MPs concentrated on no more than three subjects in debates, with twice as many Conservative as Labour MPs doing so. But, he stressed, the overall level of backbench specialism was 'relatively low', varying from session to session and always quite dispersed.[10] Specialization in debate may often be a consequence rather than a cause of a junior shadow or government post. Those MPs identified as 'specialists' in the eyes of their colleagues and leaders are not narrow technicians. For instance, attendance at, and especially an officership in, a backbench subject committee is recognized as 'specializing' in a subject, but these committees deal with many different issues each session, so that the *depth* of specialist knowledge of members and officers may be limited, and there is frequently no close correspondence between party committee assignments and ministerial postings.

The growth in the number of MPs appointed to government posts is often ascribed to the requirements of party management: by attaching individual MPs and factional groupings to the government, trouble in the Commons can be averted. Whereas only one Conservative MP in ten had a government post in 1900, in 1974 one in three Labour MPs, and in 1983 one in four Conservative MPs, had a job as a minister, whip or unpaid parliamentary private secretary. However, the increased size of governments since the early 1960s has been accompanied by, rather than prevented, signs of the relative decline of parliamentary party cohesion.[11]

Nevertheless, party leaders and managers do seek to ensure that the ranks of the administration are broadly representative of the strands of opinion within the party and contain MPs representative of its different social and geographical groups. The different ideological wings of the party – 'left' and 'right' or 'wet' and 'dry' – are represented in the government as a whole, and sometimes even balanced within individual departments. In 1976, for example, despite a pronounced right-wing tilt in his appointments, James Callaghan was anxious to include left-wing MPs at junior level. Neil Kinnock and Norman Atkinson refused posts, but Leslie Huckfield and Robert Cryer accepted under-secretaryships at the Department of Industry, under a right-wing Secretary of State, Eric Varley. Mrs Thatcher appointed the 'dry' Sir Keith Joseph and the 'wet' William Waldegrave as, respectively, Secretary of State and Under-secretary of State to the Department of Education and Science in 1981, to join Dr Rhodes Boyson, a particularly 'dry' under-secretary who had been in the department since 1979 when he and the 'dry' Baroness Young (Minister of State until 1981) had balanced the 'wet' Secretary of State, Mark Carlisle. Similarly, from 1983 to 1986 Mrs Lynda Chalker, who is reputed to have said 'I am as dry as I need to be', served as minister of state in the Department of Transport, under the uncompromisingly 'dry' Nicholas Ridley. Significantly, only committed supporters of the government's monetarist economic policies have been given Treasury appointments – in the Cabinet or at junior level – under Mrs Thatcher; for instance, successive financial secretaries (Nigel Lawson, Nicholas Ridley, John Moore and Norman Lamont) have all been drawn from the right of the party.

Labour prime ministers must find posts for MPs with a trade union background. A former Labour premier said in interview that it was essential to have a miner at the Department of Energy; in 1947 miners' MPs complained when Attlee posted a former university lecturer and civil servant, Hugh Gaitskell, to the Ministry of Fuel and Power. Attlee in fact tried to engineer social balances within departments: 'if you have a rather obvious member of the intelligentsia it's quite useful to give him a trade unionist to correct his outlook. In the same way it may be useful to a trade unionist to have someone who's got a different background.'[12]

Geographical considerations are important too. Conservatives with Scottish or Welsh seats have, because of their comparative rarity, better chances of securing posts (at least in their respective national offices) than those from the south-east of England, not least because of the convention that if possible ministers in the Scottish and Welsh Offices have seats there (in 1970 neither the secretary of state for Wales nor his minister of state had Welsh seats, though the secretary of state had sat for Conway 1951–66). It has become the practice to appoint a Scottish MP to the Energy Department because of the symbolic importance of North Sea Oil. A former minister of state said that a London Labour MP (he was one) would not be trusted at the Industry Department because of the regional employment effects of its programmes. A Scottish parliamentary secretary described how he qualified for his first appointment (in a 'UK' department): 'The minister was English, one junior minister was Welsh, the other English, so the third pretty well had to be a Scot.' In the period 1945–74 31 per cent of all MPs held some government office, but 36 per cent of Scottish MPs and 43 per cent of Welsh MPs held office. This 'over-representation' is partially due to the 'reserved seats' in the Scottish and Welsh Offices, but the more ambitious MPs may seek to avoid 'ghetto' posts – half of all the ministerial appointments secured by Scottish MPs since 1945 have been in departments other than the Scottish Office.[13]

Prime ministers seek to broaden the 'representative' nature of their teams by recruiting some women ministers: every government since 1945 has included a few female ministers; since 1964 there has always been at least one in the Cabinet. Of the 24 female junior ministers serving between 1945 and 1983 four were peeresses and one served part of her career in the Lords. Those from the Commons were recruited after an average of 6.8 years on the backbenches and at an average age of 46 (the same as for men). Fifteen of the 24 were Labour appointments, and nine Conservatives, reflecting both the greater number of women Labour MPs and the willingness of Labour prime ministers to appoint women to their governments. It is striking that women have tended to be assigned to a very narrow range of departments. Two-thirds of the women's assignments have been to domestic social departments; 40 per cent of all postings were to Education, Pensions/Social Security or Health departments. Up until 1983 there had been only three Foreign Office appointments, only one Transport, only two Trade (including the Minister of State for Consumer Affairs, 1979–82) and no female Defence or Treasury appointments.

The research of Robert J. Jackson and Philip Norton suggests that occasional dissenting votes, speeches or actions are no bar to appointment, but that persistent critics and rebels are likely to be excluded from office. Jackson identified 21 MPs who rebelled at least once in the 1945–64 period before receiving government posts. Harold Macmillan acknowledged, 'Loyalty should be rewarded, but remembering my own past I never felt that sincere disaffection should be held against a young Member.' Francis Pym, a former chief whip, said 'very often a rebel becomes appointed because he's a good chap in his own right and he disagreed for a perfectly legitimate reason.' Norton argues that Edward Heath's appointments were perceived by MPs as reflecting a greater concern for loyalty than for ability. Of the 16 MPs recruited to the government in 1972, 13 had cast no dissenting votes in that parliament and two had cast only one each. Some Conservative MPs known to be strongly opposed to EEC entry were kept out of office in 1970 in case of embarrassing resignations. Genuine mavericks who personally antagonize the leadership are neither forgotten nor forgiven and are usually permanently excluded from office, for instance John Mackintosh.[14]

Of the 397 junior ministers serving only in the Commons in the period 1945–83, 257 (64.7 per cent) had held one or more official positions as a parliamentary private secretary, whip or Opposition spokesman before or between junior ministerial appointments. These non-ministerial positions provide a pool of talent and furnish an apprenticeship for departmental junior ministers. Since 1945 43 per cent of all junior ministers serving only in the Commons have been parliamentary private secretaries (PPSs) before appointment. The appointment of a PPS is personal to the minister concerned, though 'cleared' with the whips and, through them, the prime minister. Occasionally the whips suggest MPs as likely PPSs to ministers. Selection as a PPS can be seen as a sign of favour and acknowledgement of ministerial potential, though there are some PPSs who are clearly not potential ministers (chiefly because of their age). The role of a PPS can vary between that of a dogsbody (arranging 'pairs', accompanying the minister on visits, pouring the drinks for deputations of MPs) to that of a confidant (seeing official papers, attending meetings, discussing policy and political tactics). It may offer some insight into Whitehall and a taste of ministerial life. One disadvantage for aspiring junior ministers is the convention of discretion imposed by the enveloping of PPSs within the cloak of collective responsibility. They cannot criticize the government, and they have limited opportunities for speaking on their department's subject. Ambitious MPs may take PPS posts for a while, and then leave to build up a parliamentary reputation. The personal and political connections forged during service as a PPS help to qualify for office. Those MPs who have been PPS to the prime minister or Leader of the Opposition almost invariably secure office, often at minister of state level; in 1970 Heath made his PPS, James Prior, a Cabinet minister. PPSs to senior Cabinet ministers can normally expect office. Sometimes a PPS becomes a junior minister in his minister's department. In the 1950s, David Ormsby-Gore, the late Lord Harlech, was PPS to Foreign Office Minister of State Selwyn Lloyd, and then Foreign Office Under-secretary and Minister of State himself when Lloyd became Foreign Secretary. Ivor Richard was PPS to Defence Secretary Denis Healey before becoming a Ministry of Defence under-secretary in 1969. More commonly, service as a PPS is a personal and political qualification rather than a departmental apprenticeship. A link is made with a senior figure who may support a developing career. Merlyn Rees, for example, was PPS to Chancellor of the Exchequer James Callaghan 1964–5, then an under-secretary at the Ministry of Defence until 1968, when he joined his old mentor at the Home Office until 1970, being made Home Secretary by Prime Minister Callaghan in 1976.

In the period 1945–83, 17.1 per cent (68) of junior ministers had experience as a whip before taking departmental office. Only 12.4 per cent (24) of Labour junior ministers, compared to 21.6 per cent (44) of Conservatives had this experience. A former Labour Cabinet minister exaggerated only slightly when he said 'The Tories' Whips' Office is the royal road to ministerial office. Our whips will never get office and are chosen for that reason.' Whips are well placed to acquire experience of the legislative system, through whipping Standing Committees especially. They cannot speak in the House and stand outside factional groupings as party managers. Attending backbench subject committees, they may obtain some acquaintance with fields of policy, but a necessarily limited one. Nevertheless, service as a whip affords opportunities to develop skills in persuasion and (private) communication and places an MP directly under the eye of the chief whip, who is so influential in junior ministerial appointments.

Only in 1955 was a formalized Opposition team created, with junior Shadow spokesmen, and only in 1964 did the first of these enter government. Of the 233 junior ministers serving entirely in the Commons from 1964 to 1983, 43.8 per cent (102) had some Opposition experience. The Labour Shadow Cabinet (Parliamentary Committee) is elected by the

Parliamentary Labour Party, but the Leader appoints junior Shadow spokesmen. The Conservative Leader appoints all of his or her team. The Leader's choice is not independent: he or she is constrained by the pressures and preferences of senior colleagues, factional and 'representative' considerations, and the available pool of backbench talent. In opposition, as in government, the chief whip can have a decisive influence in junior appointments. No one can read their political horoscope in the construction of a Shadow ministry. They are usually smaller than government teams, and there is never a perfect match in the distribution of offices before and after elections. People may clamber on board the boat of government, or fall or be thrown off in the mêlée. In 1964 and 1979 prime ministers introduced large numbers of MPs with no Opposition service into the government (see table 2.2). Over half of those junior ministers serving since 1964 have had no Shadow experience: there is a greater continuity of service between the Shadow and government Cabinets, and a greater influx at junior level. Those MPs with Shadow junior posts have not invariably received departmental posts corresponding to their Opposition portfolios (see table 2.3). The subject expertise which spokesmen develop may be dissipated if they are assigned to departments different from the ones they shadowed, and their lack of general experience or breadth of knowledge may then be a

TABLE 2.2 Size of government and Shadow teams (Commons only)

		Shadow posts	Government posts
Labour	1964	43	68
Conservative	1970	37	45
Labour	1974	53	65
Conservative	1979	38	68

TABLE 2.3 Shadow junior spokesmen receiving junior ministerial posts (Commons only)

		Same subject	Different subject
Labour	1964	3	11
Conservative	1970	16	6
Labour	1974	19	10
Conservative	1979	13	7

handicap. However, Opposition service may also be seen as a general training in frontbench techniques (speaking, moving amendments to Bills, media appearances) which would qualify for office, even if it is not a definite preparation for the administrative and policy-making work of ministers.[15] Service in Opposition, like experience as a PPS or whip, thus confirms the generalist and parliamentary character of the British ministerial cadre, and institutionalizes the acquisition of these qualities.

In the period 1830–1914 one junior minister in six was a peer; in the period 1945–83 a similar proportion (17.5 per cent) served in the Lords. Governments in recent years generally have two or three Cabinet ministers with seats in the Upper House, and from seven to ten junior ministers sitting there. (Conservative governments appoint more peers than do Labour ones; see table 2.1 above.) Whereas the average age of *all* junior ministers on appointment was 46 years, the average age of peers appointed to junior office in this period was 50 years; only 12 per cent of *all* junior ministers were over 55 on appointment, but 26.2 per cent of junior ministers in the Lords were over 55. With rare exceptions, it is only on the Conservative benches in the Lords that there are young hereditary peers trying to make their mark and gain office; it is the large number of Labour life peers that pushes up the average age of peers in junior office. Although older than their counterparts in the Commons, peers are more likely to enter junior office one rung higher up the ladder than MPs (though, as noted below, they are less likely to be promoted to the Cabinet): 86.6 per cent of initial junior ministerial appointments in the Commons were to parliamentary under-secretary rank and 13.4 per cent to minister of state rank; in the Lords those figures were respectively 63.1 per cent and 36.9 per cent. In 1979 Mrs Thatcher's ten junior appointments in the Lords included seven at minister of state level. There was press speculation that peers could not afford the lower pay of under-secretaries, especially as they did not receive the MP's allowance paid to ministers in the Commons (though subsequently peers in junior office were to be paid a higher ministerial salary to bridge that gap somewhat) or that they had been appointed because, lacking a political base, they could be safely sacked when MPs challenged for their jobs.[16] However, only two of the ministers of state appointed in 1979 had left the government by the time of the 1983 election, though by 1986 only one was still in the government (along with two of the three under-secretaries appointed in 1979, who had reached minister of state rank in 1983 and 1984). In February 1986 half of the Conservative peers in junior office were ministers of state – a smaller proportion than that found at the end of the 1974–9 Labour government, when six out of eight peers in junior office held that rank. At the beginning of that Labour government, four out of the seven junior ministers in the Lords were ministers of state, so Mrs Thatcher's 1979 appointments did not really mark such a great departure from previous practice as was suggested.

Although it is common for peers to be 'tried out' for ministerial office by first serving for a few years as a lord-in-waiting, carrying out whipping duties and being a spokesman for a department which has no ministers in the Lords, some enter office with little or no previous national political experience. Lord Kirkhill, Minister of State at the Scottish Office 1975–9, had been Lord Provost of Aberdeen 1971–5. In 1979 Mrs Thatcher introduced another figure with a local government background, appointing the Leader of Leeds City Council to an under-secretaryship in the Department of the Environment, as Lord Bellwin. In the period 1945–83 there were eight 'freshmen' appointments in the Lords, with individuals being simultaneously raised to the peerage and appointed to junior office, although the unhappy experiences of some of Harold Wilson's newly created life peers in office after 1964 demonstrate that it can be difficult suddenly to meet the demands of ministerial office without an adequate political apprenticeship. Under Macmillan, but not under subsequent 'middle class' Conservative Leaders, family connections helped some peers gain office: the Duke of Devonshire, Under-secretary at the Colonial office 1960–2 and Minister of State at the Commonwealth Relations Office 1962–4, was the nephew of the Prime Minister's wife; the Marquess of Lansdowne, who held junior office at the Foreign and Colonial Offices, was a more distant relation. The Duke of Devonshire has called his appointments 'nepotism without any doubt'.[17]

The Development of Ministerial Careers

In the eyes of any ambitious politician, an Under-Secretaryship is a grey purgatory between the outer darkness, which is at least exhilarating, and the heaven of Cabinet rank . . . to achieve the heights, the politician must pass through this valley of obscurity, knowing always that, if he puts a foot wrong, he will either stay there or fall from grace.[18]

The career hierarchy of government is constantly moving. Men and women are recruited to fill junior ministerial positions and after a few years either leave the government or receive promotion. In the years 1945–83, 82.5 per cent of all initial junior ministerial appointments (Commons and Lords) were to parliamentary under-secretary positions, and 17.5 per cent to minister of state rank. Of the under-secretaries, 57 per cent rose no higher (and two-thirds of those held only one post for an average of two years), 18 per cent were promoted to minister of state rank and then rose no higher, 9 per cent reached ministerial positions outside the Cabinet (three-quarters of those before 1964 when such offices were more common) and only 16 per cent eventually reached the Cabinet (of whom three out of five passed through the minister of state grade). Only 17.5 per cent of all initial junior postings were to minister of state level; 60 per cent of all ministers of state had first been under-secretaries. Of all ministers of state, 60 per cent rose no higher, 10 per cent reached non-Cabinet ministerial positions and 30 per cent reached the Cabinet. Altogether, over the period 1945–83, 73 per cent of all junior ministers rose no higher in the career hierarchy, and served on average three and a half years before leaving office. The career movements of all junior ministers in this period are summarized in table 2.4. Table 2.5 shows that the small number of female junior ministers in office after 1945 had promotion prospects hardly inferior to those of

TABLE 2.4 Career destinations of all junior ministers, 1945–83

	No.	%
Parliamentary under-secretary and no higher	228	47
Minister of state and no higher	123	26
Minister outside the Cabinet	40	8
Cabinet rank	90	19
Total	481	100

TABLE 2.5 Career destinations of female junior ministers and peers in junior office, 1945–83

| | Women | | Peers | |
	No.	%	No.	%
Parliamentary under-secretary and no higher	11	45.8	32	38.1
Minister of state and no higher	7	29.2	36	42.9
Minister outside the Cabinet	2	8.3	7	8.3
Cabinet rank	4	16.7	9	10.7
Total	24	100.0	84	100.0

men, in a statistical sense, though – until Mrs Thatcher became Prime Minister – none of the women promoted to the Cabinet held a major departmental portfolio. Table 2.5 shows that 81 per cent of peers appointed to junior office rose no higher. This must be due partly to the high average age of those peers given junior office, and partly to the fact that only two or three Cabinet positions are usually filled from the Lords: minister of state rank is really the highest to which most peers in government can aspire.

About two-thirds of all Cabinet ministers have been junior ministers at some time. Table 2.6 shows the number of Cabinet ministers with experience in junior ministerial office in the various post-war governments. Generally, the longer a government is in office the higher the proportion of Cabinet posts filled by those with junior ministerial experience, individuals who have been tested on the lower rungs of the career ladder. The special circumstances of a long period in Opposition

TABLE 2.6 Junior ministerial experience of post-war Cabinets

	Total Cabinet ministers	No. with junior ministerial experience	%
Labour			
1945	20	13	65
1951	17	12	70.6
Conservative			
1951	17	7	41.2
1957	18	16	88.9
1964	23	20	87
Labour			
1964	23	10	43.5
1970	21	10	47.6
Conservative			
1970	18	14	77.8
1974	21	15	71.4
Labour			
1974	21	12	57.1
1979	24	17	70.8
Conservative			
1979	22	13	59.1
(Feb.) 1986	22	15	68.2

explain the unusually 'inexperienced' Cabinets of the Labour government in the 1960s. Altogether, 70 per cent of all Cabinet ministers with junior ministerial experience had passed through minister of state level (76 per cent of Conservatives, 65 per cent of Labour). As William Rodgers has written, the office of parliamentary under-secretary can be thought of as 'a probationary one', while minister of state is the 'career grade': a successful performance at that level particularly qualifies for Cabinet office.[19]

While most junior ministers never rise to higher office and about one in five eventually reaches the Cabinet, others have more chequered careers. In the post-war period five individuals have occupied junior ministerial positions *after* holding Cabinet rank (which they had attained after moving up the hierarchy in a conventional manner) and a further four received junior appointments *after* occupying full ministerial positions outside the Cabinet. In Attlee's government Lord Listowel moved from being Secretary of State for India (on the abolition of his department) to be Minister of State at the Colonial Office and then Parliamentary Secretary at the Ministry of Agriculture. John Godber moved steadily up the ranks from the Parliamentary Secretaryship at the Ministry of Agriculture (1957–60), to be Parliamentary Under-secretary and then Minister of State at the Foreign Office (1960–3), before being briefly Minister for War outside the Cabinet and Minister of Labour in the Cabinet (1963–4); in Opposition he shadowed Agriculture, but in the 1970 Conservative government he was appointed as Minister of State in the Foreign Office, while Heath's PPS James Prior took the Agriculture portfolio, though he succeeded Prior in 1972. More recently, Baroness Young sat in the Cabinet as Chancellor of the Duchy of Lancaster and then Lord Privy Seal (1981–3) in between holding minister of state posts at the Department of Education and the Foreign Office. And a former Labour Cabinet minister, Reg Prentice, was appointed by Mrs Thatcher to a minister of state post in the Department of Health and Social Security (1979–81). Also illustrating the point that the career hierarchy of government is not entirely regular, Michael Alison was successively Minister of State at the Northern Ireland Office and the Department of Employment before becoming PPS to the Prime Minister in 1983; perhaps, though, given its proximity to the centre of power in government, transfer to this office should not be regarded as a move *down* the hierarchy.

Turning to the factors explaining the promotion of junior ministers, it is clear that the ministers who move up through the ranks entered parliament young and started on the ministerial hierarchy early. Whereas the average age on their first appointment of all junior ministers serving

1945–83 was 46, the average age on first appointment of those who eventually reached the Cabinet was five to six years younger: 41 for Labour and just over 40 for Conservatives. Nearly 15 per cent of all those who never rose above the rank of parliamentary under-secretary were first appointed at the age 56 or over; only 1 per cent of those reaching the Cabinet started their ministerial careers at that age. The average age on appointment to the Cabinet for those junior ministers who made it there was 49, at which age one-third of those never rising above parliamentary under-secretary rank and one-quarter of those never rising above minister of state rank had still to be appointed. Perhaps one junior minister in three is thus virtually out of the running for promotion to the Cabinet on grounds of age alone.

There is less difference in terms of parliamentary service and tenure in office between 'successful' and 'unsuccessful' junior ministers. The average House of Commons service of all junior ministers was 7.3 years before appointment; of those who reached the Cabinet it was six years. Tenure in junior office is similar for those promoted and for those not. Those junior ministers who reached the Cabinet held an average of two posts each and had a total of 38 months of service in office for Conservatives and 41 months for Labour (in other words, about 19–20 months per post). Those junior ministers who never left that level averaged 42 months of total service in 1.75 posts each: not significantly different (except about 25 months per post). Of those never promoted above junior minister rank, 52 per cent held only one post and then left the government, and 30 per cent held only two posts and then left; of those reaching the Cabinet, 37 per cent held only one junior post and 41 per cent held two.

These average figures conceal large and interesting variations. Some Cabinet ministers have a lengthy and varied experience in junior office before heading their own departments, others move so fast through the junior ranks that the value of their ministerial apprenticeship must be questioned. We can illustrate this point with two contrasting pairs of Labour and Conservative ministers. William Rodgers held junior posts at under-secretary or minister of state level in five departments for a total of over eight years in the 1960s and 1970s before becoming Minister of Transport (a department he had not previously served in); Peter Shore was PPS to the prime minister and served in two departments as parliamentary secretary for a total of 18 months before entering the Cabinet. Paul Channon was a junior minister in five departments for a total of ten and a half years before becoming Secretary of State for Trade and Industry in 1986; Norman Tebbit served in two departments for 29 months before entering the Cabinet. Overall, as Bruce Headey has written, 'politicians are usually judged to have Cabinet potential, or to lack it, after a relatively short period in junior office. Deviations from this pattern are not all that rare but, generally, a politician who remains in office for more than five years without reaching the Cabinet has missed the boat.'[20]

Just as parliamentary performance secures initial appointments, so it plays a very important part in determining the career success and promotion of junior ministers. Headey reported that junior ministers felt that parliamentary performance was 'the single most important factor that can win them promotion'. A former Conservative chief whip told him that the administrative ability of a junior minister was difficult to judge so that in nine cases out of ten it was parliamentary performance that gained an individual promotion. This observation was confirmed by Harold Wilson, who told Philip Norton:

> Clearly a Prime Minister would give a lot of weight to parliamentary performance whether considering the appointment of a backbencher to junior office, or planning promotion from the most junior ranks to, say, the position of Minister of State . . . In considering junior Ministers for promotion, ability to handle Questions is probably even more important than ability to make a set speech, and no less important is a junior Minister's ability to absorb briefs and handle the kind of matters which are raised in Standing Committee. Probably with the recent development of Select Committees on specific issues, a Minister's performance there could also advance or retard his promotion.

A former Cabinet minister said in interview, 'The despatch box is a lonely place but all ministers are judged there . . . you see whether they're holding their own in front of the Opposition, whether they sound as if they know what they're talking about.' Junior ministers must develop an effective 'House of Commons style' and secure the trust and respect of their fellow MPs: 'For a good House of Commons reputation they must be matter-of-fact, intelligent and well liked', said a former junior minister with over 30 years' service in parliament. Not surprisingly, ambitious junior ministers may be eager to acquire as much parliamentary work as possible. Headey cited a parliamentary secretary who had badgered his minister to let him take over parliamentary work as much as possible and who felt that he had gained promotion ahead of other junior ministers on the strength of his parliamentary performance. George Thomas, Under-secretary at the Home Office 1964–6, was advised by his private secretary to get the general department when the portfolios were shared out among the team of ministers because it involved a lot of House of Commons business. Thomas recalled, 'It was good advice, for the work gave me frequent occasions to speak.' Within 18 months he had reached minister of state rank, and in 1968 became Secretary of State for Wales.[21]

Interviews suggest that the prime minister is alerted to the departmental achievements of junior ministers only haphazardly, on the private office network or through conversations with senior ministers, and usually only in circumstances when junior ministers have made big mistakes or accomplished major successes. Civil servants judge all ministers by what they achieve for their departments in Cabinet and Cabinet committees, and how they cope with their departmental paperwork and administrative tasks. It seems that gossip circulates around Whitehall on whether junior ministers are up to their work, and whether they take decisions that 'stick'. However, a retired permanent secretary cautioned that 'a reputation inside the department for getting the business through isn't terribly important. The Whitehall grapevine can buzz, but it's the political side that really counts.' It is clear that ability in Cabinet committee is a significant factor marking out high-fliers among junior ministers. Gerald Kaufman has written: 'In Cabinet Committee your reputation is at stake every time you open your mouth. Your colleagues will judge your quality by your performance there more than by your achievements on the floor of the House.'[22] And a former Cabinet minister explained: 'At committee, junior ministers learn how to be ministers . . . I chaired the Home Affairs Committee of the Cabinet. You'd see junior ministers come along and learn if they were any good: if they stuck to their brief, or argued well beyond it and were part of the political discussion around the table.'

In interview, ministers of all ranks invariably mentioned 'good luck' or 'bad luck' as affecting careers. Some junior ministers benefit from chance occurrences. In 1963 John Ramsden moved overnight from the under-secretaryship to the head of the War Office after his chief, John Profumo, resigned and the prime minister wished to avoid a major reshuffle. In 1964 he was relegated to minister of state rank in the newly formed Ministry of Defence, after which he never again held office. In 1977 David Owen became Foreign Secretary at the age of 39 on the death of Anthony Crosland, again to avoid a major Cabinet reshuffle. A promising career can be abruptly terminated if an MP loses his seat. In 1979 a lost seat destroyed Edward Taylor's hopes of the Scottish Secretaryship (he was an under-secretary in the Scottish Office in the Heath government), and laid open the way for the advance of George Younger, who could otherwise have hoped only for a junior post. In the 1983 election Iain Sproat, Parliamentary Under-secretary for Trade, lost his seat and his ministerial post, but Hamish Gray, Minister of State at the Department of Energy, who also lost his seat, was raised to the peerage and made Minister of State at the Scottish Office.

Available evidence suggests that resignation is more likely to extinguish than to improve a junior minister's promotion prospects. Collecting and interpreting information on ministerial resignations is difficult. Some resignations signal the voluntary end of a career through age or ill health; others result from moral lapses or scandals; others are difficult to distinguish from sackings. Of the 17 junior ministers who have resigned for political reasons since 1945, six were later reappointed to office, four of whom finally reached the Cabinet (Edward Boyle, Enoch Powell, Reg Prentice, Nicholas Ridley). Three of the four who resigned for moral reasons were not reappointed and one (Thomas Galbraith, who resigned after the Vassall scandal) was subsequently given another junior post in a different department. A junior minister who resigns office has perhaps a one in three chance of returning to the government, but a smaller chance of reaching the Cabinet. In any case, it would be foolish to argue that it was resignation rather than a mixture of abilities and political views which won promotion to the Cabinet for the four resigning junior ministers mentioned here.

A ministerial career in Britain consists of moves up the ministerial hierarchy and service in a variety of departments. There is little evidence of a planned career system for ministers in the sense of recruiting Cabinet ministers from those junior ministers with experience in the same department. Generally, a move up the hierarchy means a move to another department. As Richard Rose has written, 'ministers . . . are often less concerned with their specific tasks than they are with the political status it gives them within the government. Most MPs would rather join the Cabinet, albeit in an unfamiliar department, than remain outside the Cabinet as a minister of state dealing with subjects they know something about.' Moreover, such a system of promotions is explicitly commended by leading politicians. Attlee, for instance, sent young middle-class 'intellectuals' to learn 'the facts of life' outside the central economic and foreign affairs departments, under the supervision of older trade unionist ministers. Harold Wilson and Evan Durbin were sent to the Ministry of Works, Hugh Gaitskell to Fuel and Power.[23] Twenty years later, when Harold Wilson became Prime Minister, some of his appointments were in the same vein. One of his appointees recalled that he had hoped for a Foreign Office post; instead, he was sent to a less-important domestic department: 'the prime minister put on his best hospital matron style, "I had a bad time [as a junior minister], now it's your turn – but it's for your own good." ' Continuity of service within one department is rarely built up, and – as important – appears not to be valued by politicians.

In the period 1945–83, 124 junior ministers moved from parliamentary under-secretary rank to minister of state posts, only 37 of whom did so in the same department (30 per cent) – ten of those in the Foreign Office alone, where there seems to be a definite pattern of trying out MPs as parliamentary under-secretaries before giving them more responsible positions. Of the 90 junior ministers who were promoted to the Cabinet between 1945 and 1983, 52 (57.8 per cent) received non-departmental posts or headed departments they had not previously served in. The corresponding proportion for the 1830–1914 period was 49.5 per cent, and for 1918–39 54.9 per cent. Cabinet ministers are thus more likely to be generalists in recent years than a century ago, despite the fact that the scale and complexity of government business has greatly increased over this period. Thirty-eight of the 90 junior ministers reaching the Cabinet 1945–83 (42.2 per cent) did have some previous experience in the department they had charge of, even if years before promotion, but usually in a career involving several junior and/or Cabinet assignments; only four individuals served in only one department in this period. In the 1830–1914 period 50.5 per cent of Cabinet ministers had had some junior experience in the departments they headed, and in the 1918–39 period this figure was 45.1 per cent (see chapter 1). The generalist character of Cabinet ministers is confirmed by the fact that of 197 different appointments at Cabinet level from 1964 to 1983, in only 32 cases had the minister any prior junior service in the same department (even years before and/or interspersed with spells in other departments) or in a very closely related department; that is, only 16.2 per cent of Cabinet appointments.

There are a number of explanations for this pattern. Prime ministers try to avoid direct promotions within departments in politically controversial circumstances (for example, the replacement of Shinwell by his junior minister Gaitskell at Fuel and Power in 1947) because of the political upset involved. A second reason is that although they are only one or two ranks apart in their department, in the government as a whole a junior minister and his or her secretary of state are much further apart in their political and party seniority. Promotions take place within the hierarchy formed by the government as a whole.[24] Thus, in a reshuffle an outgoing Chancellor will not be replaced by his financial secretary, but perhaps by a more junior Cabinet minister (for example, the energy secretary), who in turn may be replaced by another Cabinet minister, with perhaps the financial secretary taking his place. More dramatic and rapid promotions of junior ministers would disturb the political balance of the Cabinet and top leadership of the party. The third reason has its origins in the idea of collective government by a group of experienced and senior politicians ('Cabinet government'). A junior minister said in interview: 'It is part of the training for the job of becoming a Cabinet minister to be switched from department to department. I did not want to go to the Department of —, but the PM said it would be good experience, that I must broaden my view and learn the wider picture. And it *is* good experience; the system is a good one. It's useful when you get into the Cabinet.'

In interview, former ministers often emphasized the importance of this latter aspect of their junior ministerial apprenticeship: the development of general political skills through an 'all-rounder's' training. The idea of collective or 'Cabinet government' means that the ministerial cadre of the governing party must be well-groomed 'Westminster types', with parliamentary skills and a party standing, and also must exhibit 'Whitehall qualities': ability to keep up with the flow of work and adeptness at the conciliation of conflicting interests and policies in the Cabinet and its committee system. In this light, the career system discussed in this chapter can be seen as calling for and instilling a combination of 'Westminster' and 'Whitehall' abilities – general political experience and capabilities rather than specialist subject knowledge or executive/managerial skills. This system is well adapted to the world of parliamentary and party politics: recruiting junior ministers on the basis of parliamentary ability, promoting them from department to department, and rewarding those who demonstrate talent in collective fora would seem a good way of training the type of Cabinet leaders needed for a party to govern and survive politically. Bruce Headey believed that 'Junior office is . . . [a] good training for the performance of the cabinet, parliamentary, party and public relations roles of a Cabinet Minister. The harder question is whether it provides adequate experience of decision making and a sufficient insight into how large organisations in general, and Whitehall departments in particular, operate.' Headey was aware that the structures of departmental administration and the behaviour of ministers and senior civil servants (see chapter 4) means that in general those junior ministers who eventually reach the Cabinet lack significant executive and policy-making experience. It is in this sense that Richard Rose argued that 'the job of a junior minister was *not* designed as a training ground for Cabinet ministers. The fact that service in such a post is today virtually *sine qua non* for Cabinet office does not assure that the time spent in these qualifying posts necessarily imparts skills useful in higher offices.'[25]

It is now a familiar argument that British Cabinet ministers are not well prepared for the important tasks of the formulation of policy and the managerial control of their departments. These activities would seem to call for qualities and styles rather different from those stressed and developed by the generalist model. Political sensitivity and ability would not be unimportant, but the values of sustained subject expertise and the capacity to manage large organizations should, on this view, be paramount. Half of the Cabinet ministers interviewed by Headey thought that the intelligent laymen/parliamentary politician – the ministerial generalist – was no longer best qualified to run a government department. From this perspective, service as a junior minister is not a particularly useful qualifying experience, as will be seen more fully in later chapters, but the political forces sustaining the present character of the ministerial career system are powerful. As discussed in the final chapter of this book, the reforms suggested by those wanting to see ministers develop specialist subject or executive/managerial expertise fail to appreciate the political aspects of appointments, the constraints of party management and the relations of power between a prime minister and his or her colleagues. Within the system as it exists at the moment it is clear that the ministerial generalist is the dominant type of executive, and the manner in which junior ministers are appointed and promoted plays no small part in upholding that dominance.

3

The Constitutional Position

Basic Constitutional Concepts

As a prelude to the discussion in later chapters of the political and administrative roles of junior ministers, it is essential to establish clearly their constitutional status and authority. Junior ministers have four basic constitutional characteristics, three of which can be put negatively: they are not ministers of the Crown, they neither possess nor exercise any legal powers of their own, they are not individually responsible to parliament, but they do share in the government's collective responsibility to parliament.

Junior ministers are not ministers of the Crown because, formally, they are appointed by their secretary of state, not by the monarch on the advice of the prime minister. In practice, they are selected by the prime minister and their names are submitted to the Queen, but that does not affect their constitutional status. Ministers of the Crown 'kiss hands' on appointment, take possession of special seals and are invariably Privy Councillors (or are made so). They exercise the Crown's prerogative powers and the statutory powers legislated by parliament. All members of the Cabinet are ministers of the Crown, as were those ministers heading departments not represented in the Cabinet who have now disappeared. In contrast, junior ministers do not 'kiss hands', have no seals of office, are not usually Privy Councillors and have no formal powers of their own.

In the twentieth century there has developed some confusion as to whether or not junior ministers are ministers of the Crown. Their numbers and salaries have been regulated by statutes variously entitled House of Commons Disqualification Act (1957, 1975), Ministerial and Other Salaries Act (1972), but also Ministers of the Crown Act (1937, 1960, 1964, 1974). Herbert Morrison thought that, provided a minister of state is a Privy Councillor, he is a minister of the Crown, but the statutory basis for his argument is weak.[1] The 1974 Ministers of the Crown Act defines a minister of the Crown as simply 'the holder of an office in Her Majesty's Government'. A minister of state is defined in the 1957 and 1975 House of Commons Disqualification Acts as 'a member of Her Majesty's Government . . . who [does not have] charge of any public department'. The same legislation defines a parliamentary secretary as 'a person holding Ministerial office (however called) as assistant to a Member of Her Majesty's Government . . . but not having departmental responsibilities'. Thus, it seems clear that, legally, a parliamentary (under) secretary is not a minister of the Crown. While ministers of state do not have so ambiguous a statutory position as their more junior colleagues, the fact that they are not formally appointed by the monarch, and do not 'kiss hands', suggests that they too are not ministers of the Crown. The position of Sir Edward Boyle, Minister of State in the Department of Education and Science, April–October 1964, with a seat in the Cabinet alongside his secretary of state, and therefore a minister of the Crown, was exceptional, and his appointment can be explained on political grounds. That junior ministers are not ministers of the Crown is not merely a legal and constitutional nicety, but involves questions of status and prestige which affect the relationships of office-holders and the workings of government.

Junior ministers neither possess nor exercise their own independent statutory powers. In law the minister or secretary of state *is* the department he heads: its jurisdiction, powers and responsibilities are his. Legal provisions relating to junior ministers are scanty, referring mostly to numbers, salaries and eligibility for membership of the House of Commons. Thus, the total number of office-holders able to sit in the Commons was set at 70 in 1957, rising to 91 in 1964 and 95 in 1974. An Act of 1960 abolished the limits set in 1937 for the number of parliamentary under-secretaries in each department, replacing them with an overall limitation on the total number of persons to whom salaries could be paid as parliamentary under-secretaries. Junior ministers are not the legal deputies of their secretaries of state; in fact, secretaries of state have no legal deputies but are instead personally interchangeable, any one of them able to exercise the powers of any other in his or her absence. Nor can a junior minister formally act in place of his chief in matters where statutes prescribe that the action shall be taken by the minister, unless there is express provision in the Act enabling the junior minister to act. The authority of junior ministers is essentially informal and indeterminate, depending on personal and political, not statutory, factors.

As members of the government, junior ministers share in its collective responsibility to parliament. They must adhere to and defend the decisions of the Cabinet, and of Cabinet committees of which they may not be members, or else they must resign or risk being sacked. In that respect their constitutional position is identical to that of Cabinet ministers, though unlike them they cannot claim a formal right to be consulted before a 'Cabinet' decision is taken. The collective responsibility of junior ministers carries no even tacit claim to formal or prior consultation. For Cabinet ministers, collective responsibility is the title to collective discussion and power; for junior ministers, it is the obligation to solidarity. The convention of collective responsibility is enforced at the prime minister's discretion, and may be relaxed, as in the 1932, 1975 and 1978 cases of an 'agreement to differ'. Just as Cabinet and junior ministers are suspected of contravening this convention by inspiring 'leaks' to newspapers without forfeiting their jobs, so political circumstances may mean that they can in other ways signal dissent from government decisions and retain their posts. On two occasions in 1974 a Foreign Office junior minister, Joan Lestor, was one of three ministers on the Labour Party National Executive Committee who dissociated themselves from government policy decisions. None was sacked, but the prime minister sent each a minute on the requirements of collective responsibility. In April 1984 an under-secretary at the Department of Employment, Alan Clark, was sceptical about a government defence procurement decision when questioned during a television programme, but he was not sacked. In April 1986 Dr Brian Mawhinney, a Northern Ireland junior minister, told a newspaper in his constituency of his conscientious objection to legislation deregulating Sunday trading on which the government had imposed a three-line whip. A backbench revolt quashed the Bill, and Mawhinney did not have to resign, for it was arranged that he would be duty minister in Ulster on the relevant evening and so not required to vote.[2]

From the nineteenth century, a junior minister has been held to be individually responsible to his ministerial chief, not to parliament. The head of a department carries responsibility to parliament for every act that he or she permits his or her subordinates – junior ministers or civil servants – to do. The convention of individual ministerial responsibility involves the simple and powerful equation of the secretary of state's responsibility *for* his department and his authority *within* it, and thus both protects and enfeebles junior ministers. The responsible departmental chief is expected (*a*) to answer in parliament for the work of his department and (*b*) to 'carry the can' for decisions or policies which are criticized. Junior ministers handle a great deal of parliamentary business, and lists of 'Ministerial Responsibilities within Departments' are made available to MPs to help them direct questions and letters, but they are not ultimately responsible in sense (*a*) because the top minister is expected to defend the department on all major or controversial occasions. The individual responsibility of junior ministers in sense (*b*) is more complex. They 'carry the can' for morally culpable actions in that they are expected to resign if involved in private scandals, and not their chiefs, as the resignations of John Belcher in 1949, Ian Harvey in 1958 and Lord Lambton in 1973 indicate. It is also clear that they must accept the authority and defer to the judgement of their superiors: the departure of Ministry of Defence junior ministers for the Navy in 1966 (Christopher Mayhew) and 1981 (Keith Speed) following intradepartmental rows over defence priorities are extreme cases illustrating this point. Difficulties arise when considering policy failures or mistakes. Recent cases suggest that in highly charged political situations MPs do not wish to pin sole constitutional responsibility for errors on individual junior ministers but rather expect to call to account the minister in charge of a department. Political circumstances then determine who, if anyone, resigns. Thus, in the famous Crichel Down case of 1954, although, in Robert Pyper's words, 'his junior ministers Carrington and Nugent were at least as blameworthy, and possibly more so, than Dugdale himself', it was the Minister of Agriculture, Sir Thomas Dugdale, who resigned, and Lord Carrington's offer of resignation was turned down.[3] The crisis following the 1982 Falklands invasion brought down the Foreign Secretary, Lord Carrington, his deputy, the Lord Privy Seal, Humphrey Atkins, and the Minister of State responsible within the department for South American questions, Richard Luce. Luce had in fact handled South American matters only since the preceding September, when he replaced Nicholas Ridley, who had been closely involved in Falklands policy in 1980 and 1981, so his decision to resign shows the convention at its most formal. Arguably, failures and mistakes at Cabinet level led to the war, and Pyper convincingly argues that the Foreign Office resignations were an exercise in limiting the political damage to the Prime Minister and the government as a whole,[4] a suspicion not allayed when Luce was reinstated at the Foreign Office (though with different responsibilities) in 1983. Following the Maze prison break-out in 1983, neither the Northern Ireland Parliamentary Under-secretary responsible for prisons, Nick Scott, nor the Secretary of State, James Prior, resigned, but instead put their department's case while sheltered by collective responsibility.

While the meaning of individual ministerial responsibility in terms of allotting blame thus depends on political exigencies, in terms of conferring power it enfeebles junior ministers because it ensures the formal dominance of the secretary of state over his political and civil service subordinates and also establishes the rights and powers of officials *vis-à-vis* junior ministers. Junior ministers perform their functions and exercise any power they may have not by virtue of constitutional definitions of the scope and authority of their offices, but by dint of their personal and political relations with their superiors who always have the authority to over-rule them and reverse their decisions, or ignore their advice, if they so desire or are so persuaded. As their executive and administrative powers are strictly derivative, junior ministers can claim no special or inherent authority over civil servants, and indeed their decisions can be challenged by officials appealing to the top minister. Constitutionally, junior ministers cannot take final decisions contrary to the recommendations of the most senior civil servants, permanent secretaries, a limitation on junior ministers which is explicitly noted in confidential government documents regulating the conduct of ministers.

The Lynskey Tribunal and Attlee's 1949 Note on Junior Ministers

On taking office, all ministers receive a Prime Minister's Note called *Questions of Procedure for Ministers* which lays down arrangements for conducting business through Cabinet and Cabinet committees and outlines rules for the circulation and clearance of papers and speeches, access to policy papers, arrangements for travel and so on. An early version of this document was circulated as a Treasury minute in 1924 and successive prime ministers have revised and extended its provisions so that it must now be considered to have a quasi-constitutional status. Attlee's 1945 Note ran to four pages (14 paragraphs); the 1976 Callaghan edition was 27 pages long (132 paragraphs).[5] An important development relating to junior ministers was that in 1949 the right of a permanent secretary to appeal to the minister in charge of a department against a decision of a parliamentary under-secretary was formalized and codified in a Prime Minister's Note circulated to ministers and has since been incorporated into the general code of ministerial conduct. This section describes the controversial events preceding that restatement of the constitutional authority of junior ministers and the preparation and contents of the 1949 Note.

In October 1948 a Tribunal was appointed to investigate allegations of corruption at the Board of Trade. Rumours had been circulating in the press that a junior minister and civil servants at the Board had been taking bribes. The proceedings of the Tribunal, chaired by Justice Lynskey, attracted considerable publicity. It reported in January 1949 that the Parliamentary Secretary to the Board of Trade, John Belcher, had received favours and hospitality, though not money, and had made decisions favourable to his acquaintances as a result. He resigned his post and his seat in February 1949.[6]

At the time of the Tribunal the Board of Trade had two junior ministers, and the distribution of duties between them and the President of the Board was recorded in an office notice circulated in the department. Belcher had, *inter alia*, a general responsibility for deciding matters about paper (except newsprint), and the President had given him a special responsibility over football pools. The prosecution of Sherman Football Pools Ltd over the delivery of their coupons, and the general issue of their paper allocation, percolated to ministers in the Board in April 1948. Cases involving prosecutions did not normally go to ministers, and that the Sherman case did reflected an assessment by officials of its unusual and political aspects. The hearing had been completed, but the magistrate had reserved judgement and then died, raising the question of whether to resume the prosecution. There was, as the department's permanent secretary told the Tribunal, 'a fair balance of argument' about it in the Board of Trade. There had been press criticisms over similar prosecutions made under Orders which had then been revoked. The matter was thought likely to arouse parliamentary consideration and 'stir up questions'; indeed, a number of MPs had approached the junior minister on the issue. In general, it was considered a normal arrangement in a number of departments for prosecution issues, when they rose to the political level, to be handled by a junior minister, the top minister not being brought in. The making or revoking of Orders would normally go to ministers, the President of the Board of Trade not usually being involved if the subject fell within a delegated responsibility of a junior minister. The President, Harold Wilson, did not follow football pools business in any detail. At first he thought that he would like a meeting on the Sherman case, but the heavy load of work he faced, Belcher's special delegated responsibility for that subject and his familiarity with the issues, persuaded him to leave the matter in the hands of his parliamentary secretary. Wilson said to Belcher, 'You have been handling this matter of the football pools, and I should like you to decide it and take charge of it.' Belcher subsequently told the Tribunal that he thought that Wilson had delegated to him the decisions on both the prosecution and the revocation of the Order under which it was made, and that the President had intimated that he wished to avoid a repetition of the judicial and parliamentary criticism provoked by a previous prosecution.

The Board of Trade's solicitor had not at first wanted to proceed with the prosecution, but the assistant secretary heading the relevant division held the opposite view, and when the Board's second secretary referred the question back to the solicitor, he modified his position to the extent that he would not advise against continuation of the prosecution. The second secretary then reported to the permanent secretary that the balance of argument was in favour of continuing the case, and the permanent secretary agreed. There had been internal disagreements, but they were resolved by the time the issue reached the junior minister, and a united departmental view and recommendation was put before him. But Belcher personally addressed a minute directly to the department's solicitor, stating that the prosecution should be withdrawn and the relevant Order revoked. When he became aware of this, the Permanent Secretary, Sir John Woods, decided to see the President of the Board of Trade:

> to raise a point of principle with him; not particularly as to the decision upon this particular case, which did not appear to be of very great importance at that time, but merely to say that if the departmental recommendation including my own marked for the President had gone forward through the Parliamentary Secretary I thought that it was wrong in principle that it should be overridden by the Parliamentary Secretary without my having had an opportunity of putting the matter back.

In the football pools prosecution the permanent secretary had had no opportunity of expressing his views to the President before the junior minister had taken his decision. His advice on the revocation of the Order was not sought at all, whereas in the normal course of events nearly all decisions on the making or revoking of Orders would be seen by him. Belcher's decisions were taken without personally consulting any officials other than the assistant secretary, who had opposed them. The civil servants expected either a departmental meeting and discussions with the permanent secretary, President and others, or that the decision would be referred back through the proper hierarchy. Instead, they were bypassed and their advice rejected.

The permanent secretary told the Tribunal that he was less concerned about the substance of the case than the procedure, though he thought that the junior minister could have acted in the way he did inadvertently or through forgetfulness. The Lynskey Tribunal concluded that Belcher had so acted to make some return for the improper benefactions he had received. For our purposes, the chief interest of the episode is what it revealed about the constitutional principles held to govern the relations between junior ministers and civil servants. The civil servants clearly believed that if a junior minister disagreed with officials on some matter, then they had a right and duty to take the issue to the top minister for an authoritative decision. The minister at the head of a department had the statutory powers, the final authority and the ultimate responsibility to parliament. His delegation to a junior minister could only be personal and provisional, and by taking decisions to him, even in the field of the junior minister's delegated responsibility, the civil servants were emphasizing the nature of that delegation and in effect calling upon the minister either to reaffirm it or to set it aside. They believed that by doing so they were acting in the best interests of the minister and of the department. Officials' views were shared by senior ministers. Harold Wilson, President of the Board of Trade, told the Tribunal that if an official felt that a junior minister's decision was 'wrong' then he should discuss the case with his civil service superiors, and then the permanent secretary should meet the junior minister and if they still disagreed the issue should go to the President who would call a meeting of all the officials concerned.

In the parliamentary debate on the Tribunal's Report in February 1949, the Prime Minister, Attlee, explained that since the minister alone was responsible to parliament for the policy and administration of his department, the powers of the junior minister, like those of the civil servants, were derivative. A junior minister may have delegated to him responsibility for a specific section of the work of the department:

> Within this field the Parliamentary Secretary will have power to take decisions on behalf of the Minister; but he should not take final decisions contrary to the advice of the Permanent Secretary and senior officials of the department. Where differences of opinion arise between the Parliamentary Secretary and senior officials, the right course is for the matter to be referred by the Parliamentary Secretary to the Minister for decision.

Sir John Anderson, a former permanent secretary and wartime minister, held that 'Parliamentary Secretaries . . . [should be] under no illusion that they become automatically vested with authority to override permanent officials of experience in matters of administration. That is not the legal position, that is not the constitutional position, and it is not commonsense.'[7]

Immediately after the debate on the Tribunal's Report, the Prime Minister took steps to define precisely the authority of a parliamentary secretary, and to clarify the relations of junior ministers and officials. Sir Edward Bridges, Permanent Secretary to the Treasury and Head of the Civil Service, and Sir Norman Brook, Secretary to the Cabinet, conferred on the issue of the constitutional position of junior ministers, and prepared a draft for the Prime Minister seeking to lay down 'some practical rules on the difficult question of the relative position of the Parliamentary Secretary and the Permanent Secretary'. Attlee made some minor criticisms of their draft, which were taken into account in a final paper drawn up after Attlee, Bridges and Brook discussed the matter. The Note included all the points made by officials in their initial draft, which largely reflected a brief prepared for the Prime Minister for his speech during the debate on the Lynskey Tribunal. The Cabinet paper, *Parliamentary Secretaries: Note by the Prime Minister*, was issued on 16 February 1949.[8]

Paragraph 1 of the paper set out the constitutional position. Parliamentary secretaries are not ministers of the Crown. The powers of a department are those of its ministerial head, who alone carries responsibility to parliament. Civil servants and parliamentary secretaries are alike in that they both exercise the minister's powers, as his agents, and act on his responsibility.

Paragraph 2 noted that historically the primary duties of parliamentary secretaries were parliamentary but 'in recent years' they had played 'a large and increasing part in helping the Minister with the administrative work of the department'. Ministers and parliamentary secretaries had to arrange this work between themselves. If the minister was in the Lords, his parliamentary secretary 'should interest himself in the work of the department as a whole'. If the minister was in the Commons, the parliamentary secretary might concentrate on 'particular aspects of the department's work' and may have delegated to him 'responsibility for supervising the day-to-day administration of certain branches'.

Paragraph 3 observed that a parliamentary secretary could relieve the minister of much administrative work 'which would otherwise come to him', and that he is 'specially qualified to see that due weight is given to parliamentary and political considerations in the execution of approved policy'. He should also lend 'advice and assistance' in the 'formulation of policy'. Ministers were encouraged to bring their parliamentary secretaries 'fully into their counsels in the formulation of policy within departments'. Such a relationship would help hard-pressed ministers, facilitate the work of Cabinet committees and give parliamentary secretaries experience for 'higher responsibilities'.

Paragraph 4 dealt directly with the administrative role of parliamentary secretaries which was noted to vary from department to department, and was a matter for the minister to decide. The relationship of the parliamentary secretary and the permanent secretary was discussed in four sub-paragraphs:

(a) If the parliamentary secretary had responsibility to supervise the day-to-day work of some parts of the department, the final responsibility of the senior minister was not prejudiced. Nor were the permanent secretary's responsibilities for the organization and discipline of the department, and to advise the minister on policy, affected. 'The Minister is entitled to look to a single person who can advise him on policy over the whole range of the department's work, and that duty must be discharged by the Permanent Secretary.'

(b) The parliamentary secretary is not part of the hierarchy of officials in the department, and so not subject to the orders of the permanent secretary. 'But equally, the Permanent Secretary is not subject to the orders of the Parliamentary Secretary. It follows that any conflict between the two can only be resolved by reference to the Minister.'

(c) Papers may be referred to the parliamentary secretary by the permanent secretary, or through him to the minister, 'particularly if they raise Parliamentary or political considerations'. But, 'the Parliamentary Secretary will not be at liberty to make a final decision contrary to the recommendation made by the Permanent Secretary.' If he disagrees with the permanent secretary, he should discuss the matter with him. If they still cannot reach agreement, the issue must go before the minister 'and the Parliamentary Secretary should normally take the initiative in submitting it'.

(d) In the absence of the minister, the permanent secretary 'may seek the advice of the Parliamentary Secretary on the political and Parliamentary aspects of any questions which would normally have been submitted to the Minister.' Disputes between them, or 'matters of major policy', should be referred to the Cabinet minister assigned to be in temporary charge of the department, or postponed for the final decision of the returning minister.

It would be tempting, but incorrect, to regard this Cabinet paper as a civil servants' coup, however much it may have benefited them, for the views of its civil service drafters reflected those of senior ministers, were explicitly endorsed by those ministers and were based on widely accepted constitutional assumptions. What the paper did was to codify and develop notions and understandings already in common currency among officials and politicians. It made explicit what had previously been implicit. Its originality lay in the fact that for the first time government documents laid down the authority of parliamentary secretaries, how they were to act in certain circumstances and how other office-holders were to act towards them. Indeed, the 1949 formulas have been regarded as authoritative and binding by subsequent governments. For instance, asked in 1963 in which departments the parliamentary secretary ranked below the permanent secretary, Prime Minister Macmillan replied, 'None . . . A Parliamentary Secretary is directly responsible to his Minister.' He added:

> Constitutionally, of course, the Parliamentary Secretary, theoretically, cannot give orders to the Permanent Secretary. If there were some division

of opinion, then that must be resolved only by the Minister . . . Constitutionally, the Permanent Secretary is responsible for the organisation and discipline of his Department and he has the right for any question to be settled by the Minister in charge of his Department.

Rejecting suggestions that he create a new rank of 'deputy minister' to replace the tiers of junior ministers and establish a definite political chain-of-command, Macmillan referred to 'a considerable step' he had taken in instructing all departments to print the names of all their ministers before the name of the permanent secretary and other civil servants in official lists; previously, not all departments had followed this practice.[9] The Foreign Office List, for instance, printed the names of the parliamentary secretaries after the name of the permanent secretary until the 1964 edition; the names of the ministers of state were printed above that of the permanent secretary, but below the secretary of state, after 1945. Copies of *Questions of Procedure for Ministers* for the governments of the 1960s, 1970s and 1980s are, of course, still secret (even if extracts periodically appear in the press), but are believed to reaffirm the 1949 rules.[10]

Ministers of state were not mentioned in the 1949 Note (in fact there were only two ministers of state in 1949), nor in the parliamentary statements of 1949 and 1963, but the constitutional precepts that they were based upon effectively place them in the same position *vis-à-vis* civil servants as their more junior colleagues. Ministers of state serve under secretaries of state who have charge of departments; that means that they act under the responsibility of the top minister, and carry no responsibility to parliament themselves; officials have a right of access to the responsible minister on all questions, as a point of principle; hence, disputes between ministers of state and civil servants can only be settled by the secretary of state.

The constitutional conventions and formulas discussed in this chapter are important influences, decisively shaping the work of junior ministers in parliament and in their departments. Indeed, the political and administrative work of junior ministers cannot be fully understood without reference to their constitutional position as it has been defined since the nineteenth century. But constitutional doctrine alone is an inadequate basis for assessing the nature of junior ministers' jobs, as demonstrated in the following chapters. Personalities and circumstances are also critically important factors.

4

The Departmental Role of Junior Ministers

This and chapters 5 and 6 deal with the work of junior ministers: in their departments, on Cabinet committees and in Parliament and as departmental 'ambassadors'. While it has long been clear that Cabinet ministers heading departments must be physical and intellectual prodigies to cope with their jobs, it is also the case that contemporary junior ministers work long hours at varied and often demanding tasks which frequently win them little public recognition. It is difficult to generalize about the nature of junior ministers' jobs for much depends on their rank – minister of state or parliamentary under-secretary – and department, on whether or not the House of Commons is sitting, and because of the importance of political circumstances and of relations with the secretary of state in determining the content of their work and their scope and authority. However, junior ministers' appointments diaries give a good impression of their range of work. No week or day is 'typical'. What is 'typical' about the extracts from the diaries of two junior ministers shown in table 4.1 is the length and variety of the working day.

A 12–15 hour working day is common, often starting in the office or leaving on a visit before 9 a.m., and finishing well after 10 p.m. to vote in the House of Commons. Ministers must switch rapidly from one subject to another, and throw themselves into widely different activities: public speeches, meetings with other ministers, departmental briefings with officials, questions and debates in parliament. A few hours each week must be devoted to going through correspondence with the minister's constituency secretary. Paperwork – briefs for meetings, draft policy papers, letters to be signed – is dealt with between meetings or packed into red dispatch boxes to be worked on in the minister's room in the Commons or at home, late at night or first thing in the morning before starting the new day's work. Ministers in the Commons will usually

TABLE 4.1 Engagement diaries of William Waldegrave (Minister of State for the Environment, Countryside and Local Government, Department of the Environment) and David Trippier (Parliamentary Under-secretary, Department of Employment) for Tuesday 22 April 1986

	William Waldegrave		David Trippier
		8.00	Wages Bill team (Caxton House)
		9.00	Meeting with Peter Morrison (Minister of State, Trade and Industry): management development and training (Dept of Trade and Industry)
9.20	Arr. Ringway, Manchester (shuttle)		
10.20	Arr. Heyside, nr Oldham. Launch of Oldham Countryside Voluntary Projects Prog.		
10.30	Press call	10.30 to 1.00	Standing Committee: Wages Bill (House of Commons)
10.45	Dep. for Rochdale		
11.10	Arr. Healey Dell: 10th anniversary of local nature reserve		
11.30	Press call – stocking of new lagoons, tree planting etc.		
11.55	Dep.		
12.00 to 12.45	TBA Industrial Products Ltd. Reception and buffet lunch		
1.40	Arr. Ringway		
		2.30	First Order Parl. Questions (House of Commons)
2.50	Arr. Heathrow	3.00	Ministry of Defence Small Firms Group: meeting with Lord Young (Sec. of State), Norman Lamont (MoD Min. of State), Peter Levene (Chief of Defence Procurement)
		3.15	Prime Minister's Questions
		3.30	Small business lobby: Dept of Employment Simplification
3.45	Briefing for . . .		
4.00	Meeting with Alistair Goodlad (Parl. Under-sec. Energy): Reprocessing (DOE Marsham St)	4.00	MSC presentation on non-advanced further education: Sec. of State and Chris Patten (Min. of State, Education) (Caxton House)
4.45	Briefing for First Order Parl. Questions (next day)	4.30 to 7.00	Standing Committee: Wages Bill (House of Commons)
5.30	Meeting with Kenneth Baker (Sec. of State): Chairmanship of the Audit Commission		
6.15	Briefing for First Order Parl. Questions		
6.30 for 7.00	Two-line whip on Opposition Day debates: Housing and Transport (House of Commons)	6.30 for 7.00	Two-line whip on Opposition Day debates (House of Commons)
7.15 for 7.45	United and Cecil Club Dinner (House of Commons)	7.00 for 7.30	British Tissues Dinner: Speech (House of Commons)
9.30 for 10.00	Two-line whip on Opposition Day debates	9.30 for 10.00	Two-line whip on Opposition Day debates

travel down to their constituencies on Friday afternoon, and may have some formal engagement or a constituency 'surgery' on Saturday morning. Over the weekend a number of dispatch boxes will be delivered to the minister's house by official car – the private office will expect the work to be done by Monday morning. The burdens on junior ministers are not as onerous as those on their secretaries of state,[1] but even so the routine is gruelling. A parliamentary under-secretary at the Ministry of Defence said: 'Overall I was probably working one hundred hours a week. You *can* cope with that, but you really feel the strain when you stop – at Christmas or Easter, for the holidays. Then it just hits you.'

An Increasing Role

It is indisputable that in the 1970s and 1980s junior ministers in general have played more significant roles and carried more weight in Westminster and Whitehall than in the 1940s, 1950s and early 1960s. MPs and civil servants, not to say Cabinet ministers, have increasingly come to accept an enlargement of the role of junior ministers as inevitable and proper. To some extent, too, junior ministers have moved into the political limelight and acquired named responsibilities and special titles by which they are known to the press and the wider public (such as Minister for Sport, Minister for the Arts, Minister for the Disabled). But, at the same time, modern junior ministers still remain subject to constitutional, political and administrative constraints and limitations similar to those experienced by their Victorian forebears, and which constitute the context within which junior ministers operate, crucially affecting their roles.

Shortly after becoming Minister of Fuel and Power in 1947, Hugh Gaitskell recorded in his diary his views on the general question of the parliamentary secretary's position:

> It is without doubt a very difficult one. I see that even more clearly sitting here as a Minister. You are the boss. The Civil Servants look to you. You naturally turn to them and unless you are careful you just forget about the poor P.S. He comes in as a rule without experience, not knowing the game, and in a small department inevitably tends to get left on the shelf. If his relations are too close with the Minister the Permanent Secretary suspects him. If his relations are too close with the Permanent Secretary the Minister suspects him. So he ends, I think, in many cases by having only tenuous relations with both of them.
>
> Of course, he can be given special jobs, though this is not so easy in a small Department . . . But they are generally not very important jobs and so usually he feels himself excluded from the important decisions. If he

comes in after the Minister, the Minister cannot be bothered because he assumes the P.S. knows nothing about anything. If he is there when the Minister takes office, then the Minister is probably determined not to let the experience of his colleague put him in the position of running the show.[2]

Many junior ministers in the 1940s and 1950s had little to do beyond signing replies to letters from MPs, answering parliamentary questions, occasionally attending debates in the House of Commons and making visits around the country. They might deal also with minor administrative cases, but in only a few departments did the junior ministers have substantial administrative responsibilities, and in all cases the extent to which they were drawn into policy discussions depended primarily on the attitude of the minister and secondly on the calibre of the individual.[3]

At the Ministry of Education, the parliamentary secretary was mainly occupied with Welsh matters and teachers' misconduct affairs, and at least during the 1945–51 Labour government also attended UNESCO Conferences. The team of Florence Horsbrugh and Kenneth Pickthorn (1951–4) was not a close one: the minister had not been consulted on the appointment of her junior, and he had little impact on policy. Junior ministers in small departments like Pensions and National Insurance (merged in 1953) did not have a great deal of work to occupy them except correspondence with MPs on constituency cases and visits to provincial offices and voluntary bodies. At the Ministry of Works there was so little for the junior minister to do that efforts were made in the early 1950s to abolish the job, but the Conservative whips wanted to retain it; the parliamentary secretary from 1948 to 1951 was a peer who spent a good deal of time handling Scottish affairs in the Lords. The Ministry of Agriculture and Fisheries had two parliamentary secretaries, one in each House. They each had specific subjects delegated to them in the department and chaired the relevant advisory committees (for instance, Hill Farming, Smallholdings, Artificial Insemination). The junior minister in the Lords dealt with all departmental business there, the one in the Commons supported the minister *ad hoc* and took adjournment debates and questions on days other than the Ministry's special day. There was also a full programme of visits to County Agriculture Executive Committees, with the parliamentary secretary in the Lords usually liaising with the Country Landowners' Association. Junior ministers in the Board of Trade also had clearly delegated functions, set out in an Office Notice circulated for the guidance of officials. One of the two parliamentary secretaries, known as the Secretary for Overseas Trade, concentrated on export promotion and trade negotiations with individual countries, though the President of the

Board of Trade set the general strategy here and handled trade relations with major states (the USA in particular). In 1951 Harold Wilson told Attlee:

> there has been for a long time much more devolution of work to Junior Ministers in this department than in most others. The large number of the Board's administrative staff, and the heterogeneous nature of its work, makes it essential to have a division of labour between Ministers . . . In general I leave all the day to day decisions which are half way between the political and purely administrative to the Junior Ministers and reserve to myself the main policy direction, together with a small group of subjects which are . . . of special . . . national or political importance . . . I find it useful, indeed essential, whenever there is sufficient time, for papers to come to me through the appropriate Parliamentary Secretary: or for a copy of the submission to be sent to him so that he can give me his advice.

The Ministry of Food provides a good example of the importance of the top minister's personality in defining the junior minister's job. Attlee was told in 1951 that the parliamentary secretary had his share of parliamentary business (mostly adjournment debates and prayers against Orders, in addition to questions), and was given responsibility in the department for food hygiene and standards, the Ministry's regional organization and ration book distribution. From time to time he had special assignments, such as looking into the question of price controls on rabbits. In the period 1951–4, though, the Minister, Gwilym Lloyd-George was, according to Anthony Seldon, 'essentially only a front man', delegating a great deal to his ambitious and hard-working junior minister, Charles Hill, who not only had a heavy load of parliamentary speaking but also had a major influence on policy. Lloyd-George's relaxed style gave Hill the chance to show his worth; in 1955 he was rewarded by promotion to Postmaster-General, and reached the Cabinet in 1957.

At the Home Office in this period all advice to the secretary of state was channelled through the permanent secretary, a practice which effectively excluded the junior ministers from significant parts in the making of policy. From 1952 there were two parliamentary under-secretaries: one was responsible for Welsh affairs, the other had general oversight of the Home Office departments dealing with aliens, children, the Fire Service, Civil Defence and Northern Ireland. The Home Office was always in the parliamentary firing line, and ministers made a great many visits too. The Conservatives had made the political gesture of adding responsibility for Welsh affairs to the Home Secretary's portfolio in 1951, and this increased the workload: the Secretary of State, Maxwell Fyfe, made about 25 visits a year there, and his junior minister made trips sometimes more than once a week and had an office in Cardiff to receive deputations. Despite the great breadth of its responsibilities, even up until the early 1960s decision-taking in the Home Office was highly centralized, and the junior ministers on the whole did not count for much. C.M. Woodhouse, who served as parliamentary under-secretary 1962–4, recalled his time there as 'an opportunity for insight into a system of great subtlety and complexity without really taking part in it. Policy is made in the Home Office by the Home Secretary and senior civil servants. There must be ways in which a junior minister can make himself useful, but I never discovered them.'[4]

In 1945 the Foreign Office had one minister of state and one parliamentary under-secretary; a second under-secretary was added in 1948 and an additional minister of state in 1953. Office Memoranda indicated which junior ministers supervised which divisions: in 1951, for instance, the Minister of State, Selwyn Lloyd, had responsibility for the United Nations, disarmament and the Middle East, one under-secretary dealt with Latin America and the Far East, as well as having protocol responsibility, and the second took on European questions. The secretary of state's private secretary had the responsibility for seeing that the junior ministers, if available, were invited to be present at important policy meetings in the foreign secretary's room. Senior staff were also urged to send copies of policy papers intended for the foreign secretary to the junior ministers.[5] In practice, the foreign secretary relied on his junior ministers for assistance and decisions as he saw fit. Eden, according to Anthony Seldon, delegated widely to Selwyn Lloyd but 'on matters which Eden considered of prime importance, Lloyd played little or no part.' Eden's parliamentary under-secretaries, apart from Nutting, for whom he had a high regard, actually saw little of the foreign secretary and had no influence on his policy.

Treasury junior ministers carried heavy loads of parliamentary and administrative work. The financial secretary dealt with parliamentary financial procedure, home finance, control of government expenditure, administration of the civil service and the revenue departments (Inland Revenue and Customs). The post of economic secretary was created in 1947 to handle overseas finance and the work of the Central Economic Planning Staff, transferred to the Treasury when Cripps became Chancellor. This office was left vacant for eight months in 1950 when Gaitskell, styled Minister for Economic Affairs, became in effect Deputy Chancellor of the Exchequer. For the first year of Churchill's 1951 government Sir Arthur Salter held the post of Minister of State for Economic Affairs, responsible for overseas finance, but his appointment was not a success – the Chancellor, R. A. Butler, told Anthony Seldon:

'[He] was very trying, because he didn't really agree with very much I did' – and in December 1952 the office of economic secretary was revived. As Chancellor 1950–1, Gaitskell encouraged his junior ministers to decide as much as possible without reference to him. He made it clear that they had 'the Chancellor's authority to take final decisions on his behalf where this can be done by agreement'. Reference was to be made to him whenever: a minister heading another department was involved and took a different view; agreement could not be reached within the Treasury; a memorandum was to be circulated to the Cabinet or to a committee on which the Chancellor sat; or where a decision would have 'an important impact on any of the matters which are the Chancellor's direct responsibility for general policy' (defined as: the Budget, general financial policy, general defence policy, general economic policy, the investment and import programmes, and issues raised at the Cabinet's Production Committee). Anthony Seldon describes Butler's junior ministers (1951–5) as having on the whole little influence on his economic policy, though he obviously depended greatly on them for parliamentary speaking and day-to-day administration.

The extremely wide-ranging and varied functions of the Scottish Office, together with the necessity for ministers to travel between London and Scotland, meant that the junior ministers had delegated responsibility for dealing with the day-to-day work of the different Scottish departments. In 1951 one of Labour's parliamentary under-secretaries covered agriculture, forestry, fisheries, housing and town and country planning, while the other dealt with education, health and the Home Department. Hector McNeil, the Scottish Secretary, informed Attlee that they dealt with 'the general run of Departmental questions', received deputations, shared the burdens of parliamentary business and questions, and represented him at various Cabinet committees. The 1951–5 Conservative government appointed a minister of state and three under-secretaries; to some extent, the appointment of extra ministers was a response to nationalist sentiments. Although Churchill called the new minister of state the secretary of state's 'deputy', and he was to exercise a general oversight of all the Scottish departments, it was clear that he could not give orders to the parliamentary under-secretaries, that differences of opinion between the junior ministers would go to the Scottish Secretary for decision, and that the parliamentary under-secretaries would deal directly with the secretary of state and not work to him *through* the minister of state.[6] The first Minister of State, Lord Home, spent much of his time in Scotland and was particularly concerned with industry and development, the Highlands and Islands and aspects of local government and education. He recalled to Anthony

Seldon that the Scottish Secretary, Stuart, told him, 'Do what you like provided you don't get me into trouble.' The three under-secretaries were responsible for housing, health and local government; agriculture and forestry; and education, fisheries, law and order and Home Department services, respectively. Stuart expected his political subordinates to deal with the detailed work coming up from the departments, while some issues would go direct to him (for instance capital decisions) and he would personally handle politically sensitive subjects (housing, unemployment) and those he was interested in (fishing).

Writing in the 1950s, Herbert Morrison, concerned that the life of the parliamentary secretary could be 'uninteresting and rather empty', particularly if, 'departmentally, he is left out in the cold or given little or nothing to do', set out 'A Parliamentary Secretaries' Charter' and described the problems he had experienced with Foreign Office officials in giving his junior ministers clear, delegated functions. Morrison felt that parliamentary secretaries should have a real role in the department to make their jobs less frustrating, to train them for possible future Cabinet responsibilities, and to lighten the burden on the top minister.[7] The issue of the burden on senior ministers prompted Harold Macmillan to appoint an all-party group of senior Privy Councillors, under Lord Attlee, to advise him whether there was scope for a fuller and formal inquiry into the problem. The committee apparently recommended to the prime minister that, short of major changes in the structure of government, little could be done except to make fuller use of junior ministers. Macmillan agreed, but was aware that it required the cooperation of MPs, appealing to the House to be more ready to accept ministers of state and parliamentary secretaries taking an increasing part of the work on Bills and other matters, not only answering questions. In response *The Economist* argued:

> If Parliament is to have to make do with junior ministers, it will be entitled to expect that the juniors will no longer be simply extension loudspeakers, but will have been put fully into the picture by their seniors, and should have been given more direct administrative responsibility inside the departments; as a corollary, juniors may have to 'carry the can' more often for mistakes.[8]

In this context it is significant that the total number of junior ministers increased from 35 to 50 between 1957 and the end of the Conservative government in 1964. Ministers of state doubled from seven to 15, indicating a perceived need for subordinate ministers of a higher status than that of parliamentary under-secretaries (whose numbers rose from 28 to 35) to handle parliamentary business and represent departments in public as well as taking a full part in departmental administration. Responsibility for Welsh Affairs was transferred to the Ministry of Housing and Local Government in 1957 and a minister of state, who was a peer, appointed to deal with the relevant business; in 1961 a second parliamentary under-secretary was added to the department. Ministers of state were appointed for the first time to the Commonwealth Relations Office in 1959 and to the Home Office in 1960; in 1962 a second minister of state was added at the Board of Trade. The Ministry of Education had only one parliamentary secretary until 1964, when a major reorganization left the Department of Education and Science with a secretary of state, two ministers of state (one actually in the Cabinet – Sir Edward Boyle – and the other a peer) and two parliamentary under-secretaries (one in each House). The Defence reorganization of that year left the total number of ministers in that area unchanged at seven (the second Admiralty junior minister disappeared in 1959), but downgraded the former heads of the separate service ministries to minister of state status, giving each of them a supporting parliamentary under-secretary, and placing all under the control of a single secretary of state in the Cabinet.

Although Harold Wilson appointed a handful of junior ministers more than had been in office under Sir Alec Douglas-Home in 1964, and by 1970 the total of Labour junior ministers had fallen to one less than the Conservative total in 1964, standing at 49 (see table 2.1 above), a significant development of the mid-1960s was the greater size of ministerial teams in departments due to reorganizations and amalgamations, and the consequent reduction in the number of ministerial departments. This was reflected not only in the large teams found in the so-called 'giant departments', but also in the virtual disappearance of what had been the common pattern before the mid-1950s, namely one minister and one junior minister per department. The 'giant departments' had up to half a dozen ministers: in 1970 the Ministry of Technology had, under the secretary of state, two ministers of state and three parliamentary under-secretaries; the Foreign and Commonwealth Office had three ministers of state and two under-secretaries; the Ministry of Defence had two ministers of state and three under-secretaries; and the Department of Health and Social Security had two of each type of junior minister. The 'giants' had absorbed a number of the departments that had had only one junior minister, for instance Health, Aviation and Power, and, generally speaking, by the end of the 1960s only minor departments like Overseas Development, Public Building and Works and Posts and Telecommunications merited only one junior under the minister in charge. Even only medium-sized departments increased their complement of junior ministers.

Before 1964 the Conservative government had a single parliamentary secretary at the Ministry of Labour; in 1964 Labour appointed two; in 1968 the restyled Department of Employment and Productivity (with a wider remit) had three under-secretaries, though by 1970 only one minister of state and one under-secretary. Edward Boyle was not alone in wondering what all those ministers found to occupy their time: 'There were far too many junior Ministers appointed by the Labour government – top civil servants had great difficulty in finding anything for them to do.'[9] Of course, if the growing number of government non-jobs is to be ascribed to the needs of party management – satisfying backbench demands for office, buying off dissent – then Labour prime ministers do not have a monopoly of cynicism. One would be neglecting an important dimension of political life if the large increase in the number of appointments between 1957 and 1964 was explained solely in terms of the burden on senior ministers! It is significant that although Heath sharply cut back the number of junior ministers he initially appointed, by 1974 the number had crept back to that found in the outgoing Wilson administration of 1970.

Headey's study of governments in the late 1960s and early 1970s reported 'highly variable experiences' for junior ministers. A minister of state 'may be given *de facto* responsibility for the preparation and passage of a quite important Bill, or for managing a large segment of departmental business ... Less frequently, a Parliamentary Secretary may be invested with real authority.' Starting his ministerial career as a parliamentary under-secretary in 1964, William Rodgers was dismayed to discover that there were 'top-dogs and dogs-bodies, the insiders and those who fetched and carried'. Looking back in 1980 he said: 'I am sure that some Parliamentary Secretaries still have little work of their own and that some Permanent Secretaries prefer it that way (and would prefer fewer junior Ministers). But this is very much less the case than fifteen years ago ...' Jeremy Bray, a parliamentary secretary 1966–9, considered that 'some ministers make a point of building up their junior ministers in the department, while a few ministers, like some civil servants, regard the job of a junior minister as merely signing letters to MPs, dealing with minor business in Parliament, and deputising for the minister on public occasions.' Some parliamentary secretaries complained to Headey of their frustration with 'processing routine cases' or 'translating civil servants' letters into ordinary English'. However, on the positive side, from 1964 the prime minister increasingly appointed a number of junior ministers with specific responsibilities for subjects which he thought 'had not been given an adequate priority in the past'. A Minister for Sport and another for the Arts were appointed, a Foreign Office minister of state was given a special responsibility for disarmament, a London MP was designated as specially responsible for London housing at the Ministry of Housing and Local Government. And the Wilson government also saw experiments with 'mixed committees' of junior ministers and civil servants working together on particular subjects, for instance science and technology.[10]

Jeremy Bray thought that:

> if the anomalous position of junior ministers were cleared up and they were made proper deputy and assistant ministers with recognised functions and a place in departmental hierarchies, the quality of ministers would improve, their appointments would be a less hit and miss business, and the government would have greater continuity and a firmer grip on its own machinery. It is not a question of having more or less junior ministers, but of expecting however many we have to do a proper job of work in government.

In the 1970s a major step was taken in this direction when it became the practice to assign to named junior ministers specific areas of departmental work to oversee, rather than delegating to them miscellaneous duties on an *ad hoc* basis. The allocation of responsibilities inside departments was made available first to MPs, via their party whips' offices, to help them with parliamentary questions and letters to ministers, and then published in standard reference books such as *Vacher's Parliamentary Companion*. Regularly updated by the Civil Service Department and then the Management and Personnel Office, this 'map of the public face of government' identifies which junior ministers are formally dealing with which subjects or divisions in a department, and usually describes the secretary of state as having 'overall responsibility for the work of the department'.[11] There are frequent adjustments as ministers enter, leave or change their posts, and as changing circumstances push issues up or down the political agenda, as can be seen from table 4.2, which shows ministerial responsibilities in the Department of Employment, and table 4.3, describing the allocation of work in the Foreign Office. The secretary of state in charge of a department lays down the division of responsibility. Usually this is done in consultation with the permanent secretary, who can advise on the administrative implications and feasibility of a particular division of labour. Sometimes ministers and permanent secretaries discuss frankly the strengths and weaknesses of individual junior ministers before distributing departmental jobs. Departmental responsibilities may reflect not the administrative logic of particular combinations, but the desire to give individual junior ministers more or less important jobs (for instance if the secretary of state

TABLE 4.2   Ministerial responsibilities in the Department of Employment

Labour government	Conservative government	
October 1978	July 1979	February 1986
Secretary of state	*Secretary of state*	*Secretary of state*
Albert Booth	James Prior	Lord Young
Overall responsibility	Overall responsibility	Overall responsibility
Minister of state	*Minister of state*	*Paymaster-general* (in the Cabinet)
Harold Walker	Lord Gowrie	Kenneth Clarke
Industrial relations (including collective bargaining, terms and conditions of employment, workers' rights); industrial democracy; incomes policy; employment agencies; industrial respiratory diseases	EEC and overseas matters; work permits; youth (including careers service, youth opportunities prog., vocational preparation); social security issues relating to unemployment; race relations; equal pay and women's general employment questions; disablement; wages councils; job satisfaction (the Work Research Unit); employment agencies; statistics	Jobs strategy; industrial relations strategy; Manpower Services Commission; financial management initiative; deregulation; city action teams
Parl. under-secretary	*Parl. under-secretary*	*Parl. under-secretary*
John Golding	James Lester	(Vacant)
Liaison with Manpower Services Commission; vocational training; employment services; youth opportunities prog.; special temporary employment prog.; job subsidies; job release scheme; redundancy payments; short-time working compensation; unemployment benefit; statistics	Manpower other than youth and disabled, and including employment services; training; special temporary employment prog.; special employment measures; redundancy payments; pay, other than low pay	Industrial relations legislation; ACAS; wages councils; docks; Health and Safety Commission; redundancy scheme; disabled; equal opportunities; employment agencies; research; international matters; the careers service

Labour government	Conservative government	
October 1978	July 1979	February 1986
Parl. under-secretary	*Parl. under-secretary*	*Parl. under-secretary*
John Grant	Patrick Mayhew	Ian Lang
Liaison with Health and Safety Commission; occupational safety and health (excluding industrial respiratory diseases); employment of disabled people; wages councils; incomes policy in relation to low pay; job satisfaction; sex discrimination; work permits and overseas workers; race relations; EEC; overseas matters (including ILO)	Industrial relations, including legislation; health and safety at work	Unemployment benefit service; social security issues affecting employment; job-centres; long-term unemployed; community programme; voluntary projects prog.; special employment measures; local/ regional employment issues; statistics; pay and work permits
		Parl. under-secretary
		David Trippier
		Small firms; enterprise; deregulation; enterprise allowance scheme; tourism; training

Sources: *Ministerial Responsibilities within Departments*, 1 October 1978, 1 July 1979; *Vacher's Parliamentary Companion*, no. 1041, February 1986.

TABLE 4.3   Ministerial responsibilities in the Foreign Office

Labour government	Conservative government	
October 1978	July 1979	February 1986
Secretary of state	Secretary of state	Secretary of state
David Owen	Lord Carrington	Sir Geoffrey Howe
Overall responsibility; supervises the work of the planning staff	Overall responsibility	Overall responsiblity
Minister of state	Lord privy seal (in the Cabinet)	Minister of state
Frank Judd	Sir Ian Gilmour	Baroness Young
Western and southern Europe (including Gibraltar, Malta, Cyprus); EEC; North America; Middle East defence; economic and associated matters	Deputy to the Sec. of State and principal Commons spokesman for the full range of subjects covered by the department; EEC; western and southern Europe; Eire; the Commonwealth and Africa (policy aspects); economic matters relating to the industrialized world	Deputy to the Secretary of State and spokesman in the Lords for the full range of the department's work; the Commonwealth; western and southern Europe; North, Central and South America; West Indies and the Atlantic; Falkland Islands; South Asia and South Pacific; Eire
Minister of state	Minister of state	Minister of state: minister for overseas development
Lord Goronwy-Roberts	Douglas Hurd	Timothy Raison
Parliamentary matters in the Lords; East/West relations; Eastern Europe; South East Asia; Far East (including Hong Kong); Australasia; Pacific Dependent Territories; disarmament; personnel and administration (policy aspects)	Defence; arms control and disarmament; Middle East; North Africa; United Nations; economic matters relating to the developing world; personnel; administration; security	Overseas development and aid; certain overseas pensions
Minister of state	Minister of state	Minister of state
Edward Rowlands	Nicholas Ridley	Lynda Chalker
Africa; Latin America; Central America (including Falkland Islands and Belize); Caribbean (including Dependent Territories); aid (general FCO interest in matters within the responsibility of the Minister of Overseas Development)	North Central and South America; Caribbean; Dependent Territories; economic matters relating to the developing world	EEC; East/West relations; Central, East, Southern and West Africa; trade; economic; UNLOSC

Labour government	Conservative government	
October 1978	July 1979	February 1986
Parl. under-secretary	*Minister of state*	*Minister of state*
John Tomlinson	Peter Blaker	Timothy Renton
EEC; security; personnel and administration	Eastern Europe and Soviet Union; East/West relations and the Conference on Security & Cooperation in Europe; Asia; Australasia; Pacific Dependent Territories; Commonwealth (general); information and cultural matters; immigration	Near, Middle and Far East; South East Asia; Hong Kong; defence; arms control and disarmament; nuclear energy; government hospitality fund
Parl. under-secretary	*Minister of state*	*Parl. under-secretary*
Evan Luard	Neil Marten	Timothy Eggar
United Nations (including UNLOSC); East/West relations; Eastern Europe; Indian sub-continent; general Commonwealth questions; parliamentary unit; information; passport office; immigration and nationality; general consular questions; overseas labour adviser; overseas police adviser	Overseas development and aid	Immigration and nationality; general consular questions; information and cultural affairs; United Nations; energy, science and space; maritime, aviation and environment; Commons spokesman for Baroness Young's responsibilities
	Parl. under-secretary	
	Richard Luce	
	Africa; overseas labour adviser; overseas police adviser; passport office; immigration and nationality; general consular questions; parliamentary unit	

Sources: as table 4.2

especially trusts one member of his team) or to share out the burdens of parliamentary questions and correspondence. The pattern of civil service responsibilities and the boundaries of the department's divisions may not exactly match the junior ministers' areas of concern: report lines can be complex. What junior ministers then make of their jobs cannot be gleaned from organization charts or from a perusal of documents setting out formal responsibilities: relations with other office-holders, political and official, are of major importance.

The Importance of Political Relationships

The relationship between a junior minister and his or her ministerial superior, the secretary of state, is the single most important factor influencing the junior minister's role and influence. In interview, a former minister of state said, 'Personalities are vitally important in office. Junior ministers are only as effective and as good as their boss wants them to be.' Another junior minister thought that 'It depends enormously on personal relations with other people in the department – primarily with the secretary of state. If you two are close, then you are a powerful person. If he hates you, wants you out, won't listen to you, then you can almost be less powerful than a junior official.' He added, 'If you are a pal of the prime minister you can do a lot even if the secretary of state doesn't like you.'

Secretaries of state treat junior ministers differently. Some are reluctant to delegate and prefer to employ their subordinates on administrative trivia and parliamentary chores. Others may delegate widely and support their juniors, have an open style and avoid detail. The secretary of state's own personality and conception of *his* job are thus important determinants of the content and nature of the junior minister's job. Two examples indicate the range of possible styles. A former minister of state described how his chief centralized decision-taking:

> — was adamant that he took all the major decisions and that his junior ministers only vet them and indicate their views on the way up to him. If he liked and trusted the junior minister he would normally assent to his advice. But for the last twelve months I was there he just vetoed anything controversial I sent up . . . he just stopped it. So I did nothing. It was like Siberia on my corridor; no one came to see me, no one would talk to me. I couldn't get to see the secretary of state unless it was very urgent.

At the other end of the spectrum, Anthony Crosland had a clear view of his role as a Cabinet minister, which was to concentrate on a limited number of issues and delegate others to civil servants or junior ministers, who were left free to conduct business unless it engaged wider interests and was likely to go before the Cabinet or arouse parliamentary passions. ' "That's not for me", he said, waving away whatever it was he couldn't be bothered with. "Let one of my junior Ministers deal with that." ' But even his delegation had limits: he told Maurice Kogan that 'of course all *major* policy decisions have in the end to be taken by the Minister himself.'[12]

To some extent, the personal relations of secretaries of state and junior ministers may be unsatisfactory because of the manner of appointment of junior ministers. As noted in chapter 2, Cabinet ministers may not always have much influence over the appointment of their subordinates, who may in fact be very different from them in personality, experience and political background. 'The majority of ministers may hardly know their junior ministers and hardly get to know them', said a civil service deputy secretary who had been a private secretary earlier in his career. Despite the small and enclosed world of Westminster and party politics, ministers may not be friends or know and trust each other sufficiently to allow real delegation of responsibility for policy. Another source of tension is the nature of career politics. All politicians are competitors for public support, office and power. They watch each other with what a former permanent secretary at the Foreign Office called 'the wary eye of self-regard and self-preservation'. This atmosphere may not be conducive to smooth and amicable working relations, or delegation if it affords others opportunities to shine. Lord Crowther-Hunt, a former minister of state, wrote that 'your ministerial boss . . . may want to cut you down to size if there seems to be any danger of your building up a more attractive public image than the minister himself.' Underlying tensions and rivalries can affect the conduct of business. In interview, one senior civil servant said, 'Ministerial teams don't often work together well. There's a certain amount of jostling for position.' The ability of a junior minister, and his secretary of state's perception of that ability, affect the extent of delegation. Crosland thought, 'How far you . . . delegate *decisions* depends partly of course on the Minister's own desire to delegate, but mainly on the calibre of the junior Ministers you have. One simply can't generalise. I've had junior Ministers to whom I would delegate a great deal, others to whom I wouldn't delegate anything but routine trivia.'[13] MPs receive junior office for many political reasons other than their (largely unknown) executive ability. In such circumstances, it is not surprising if some secretaries of state, at least initially, do not allow them much discretion. As the junior minister's experience increases, and particularly if he has successfully weathered some political or parliamentary storm, a secretary of state may feel he can rely more on his junior, who may then acquire more business and carry more weight. A long-established patronage relationship and a close political or personal affinity between a senior and junior minister may increase the latter's stature in the department. On the other hand, embarrassing mistakes, or a failure to achieve (or maintain) a political or personal rapport, may consign a junior minister to the sidelines.

Departmental structures also affect ministerial relationships. In interview, some officials and former ministers suggested that small departments with one minister and one junior minister – the common pattern until the 1950s – allowed easy, informal contacts, facilitating delegation and close working relations. The junior minister could become an *alter ego* and be brought in to important matters frequently. Enoch Powell believes that such an arrangement is a model:

> it would be an unusually abrupt minister who came to major decisions in his department, especially if he was taking a line other than the traditional line or the departmental line, without putting all the problems through another political mind as well as his own, namely that of his junior minister. It's a tremendous asset to have another politician or two as a longstop in the department . . . But I think it's a mistake to assume that just because it is essential to have at least one other political mind applying itself to the policy problems, one would be helped by multiplying the political minds. After all, if your parliamentary secretary is going to help you in this, he must be very closely in touch with all that you are doing and thinking. It very soon becomes difficult to do this if the number increases. I personally would sooner operate in a department with one junior minister than with more than one. It's astonishing how much more difficult it is to keep even two people in touch with what you're doing and thinking than one. . . . I'm very much opposed to [increasing the number of junior ministers] because I think it would result in the junior ministers ceasing to be political longstops or political understudies of the minister, which I believe is their true function in the machine. They would start to become departmental sub-heads divorced from the minister . . . in helping the person who is the minister, you want a political mind that is as near as may be his double, so that he doesn't bear the burden unshared.[14]

However, such views may idealize a set-up in which the junior minister had only a limited role, as was often the case in the 1940s and 1950s, as we have seen. A retired permanent secretary, who had been a private secretary in the late 1950s, disagreed with the Powell analysis:

> One of the minister's preoccupations was finding something for the parliamentary secretary to do. You could hive off general responsibility for a number of executive functions which didn't throw up great problems,

and in that way the parliamentary secretary was identified with certain areas of the department's work. But I didn't detect much talk of a political character between the minister and the parliamentary secretary when I was a private secretary. In my experience, there is now much more discussion of the politics of a problem and of parliamentary tactics between ministers in a department than in the 'one plus one' days.

Modern 'giant departments', like the Department of the Environment (DOE) and the Department of Trade and Industry, require substantial delegation of ministerial functions to junior ministers to allow the secretary of state to meet all the demands on his time. One observer of the DOE noted that second-tier ministers carried heavy loads of executive responsibility and, so far as the secretary of state was concerned, 'It was necessary to work collaboratively, with give and take on both sides . . . Often he had to leave his ministers to get on with things and to accept many of their conclusions.'[15] The top minister would concentrate on major trans-departmental business (such as resource allocation), take on one or two subjects chosen as priorities and interfere in the functional fields of his subordinates as the political situation demanded. At the Scottish and Northern Ireland Offices, junior ministers can play a significant administrative role by virtue of supervising departments dealing with particular segments of the wide span of responsibilities facing the respective secretaries of state. Here, as in the 1940s and 1950s in the Scottish office, the ministerial heads must leave much of the detailed and day-to-day work to their juniors, themselves handling overall policy, Cabinet issues and political problem areas.

Political controversy gives meaning to the constitutional convention of ministerial responsibility. Secretaries of state must deal personally with issues with major political repercussions. If an issue is going to Cabinet, the secretary of state must be involved, for only he or she can argue it at that level, even if a junior minister has done the preliminary work or is normally concerned with the details. Parliamentary pressures may divert work from a junior minister to his chief. Sir Patrick Nairne, a retired permanent secretary at the Department of Health and Social Security, has written: 'when there is something important to be answered or anything goes seriously wrong, the House of Commons will insist on an answer from the Cabinet Minister in charge.' In interview, a former permanent secretary acknowledged, 'Patterns are imposed by parliament of suction-pumping things up to ministers. There is no escape from the pressures. If a political row erupts, hitting the newspaper headlines, then the minister must go himself.' In such cases the usual distribution of business between ministers is set aside. And William Rodgers has emphasized that 'on all major issues the head of the department must stand at the despatch box and a major issue is any issue with real political steam behind it, even if it is a minor one in policy terms.'[16] When there is political credit involved, secretaries of state may step in and take business away from their juniors. A minister of state in the Department of Health and Social Security described his superior:

> — originally left a lot to me. His job was seen as being the big policy decisions, mine as running the National Health Service on a day-to-day basis. After a few months it was becoming obvious that the interesting NHS stories were not the major policies (for example, regional growth rates or the dispersal of resources), however important they may be, but instead public excitement was about the individual hospital closures and openings – which were supposed to be my concern. That was what was attracting publicity in newspapers, on television and with the public. — became a bit jealous and took more of that work towards himself.

Not only are relations with secretaries of state problematic, but individual junior ministers may not work well together. Some departments – Defence, Health and Social Security, Trade and Industry, and Environment – have teams in which parliamentary under-secretaries are designated as assisting ministers of state on particular subjects. Ministers of state may not allow *their* subordinates much scope. One parliamentary under-secretary who had worked to a minister of state said in interview, 'It is fatal to have to report through a minister of state. They are inevitably power-hungry, ambitious men, who won't give anyone credit. It leaves you with no real job.' At the Department of Health and Social Security, 1968–70, Richard Crossman, for instance, persuaded one of his ministers of state to arrange a 'precise slab of work' for her parliamentary under-secretary, but found it difficult to induce his other, David Ennals, to delegate to his. Ennals, he wrote in his diaries, 'is determined to get on. He always does what he is told in the end but he won't be generous to his subordinates.'[17]

Where a parliamentary under-secretary assists a minister of state, it seems that in practice he or she may make only a limited contribution to policy: issues and decisions are directed to the more senior of the two, and the under-secretary handles parliamentary or routine administrative chores, or stands in for the minister of state at public engagements. Some parliamentary under-secretaries who have felt uncomfortable or under-employed have complained to their secretaries of state and achieved some clarification of their position and separate responsibilities working directly to him. Ultimately, a secretary of state will resolve differences of opinion between members of his team, but of course 'appeals' to the top minister are infrequent. A parliamentary under-secretary who had to report through a minister of state explained:

If the minister of state and his private secretary and officials questioned too much, my private secretary would get to work to massage the minister of state's PS, and ask him not to stir him up . . . If the worst comes to the worst, you can go to the secretary of state about it, but he wouldn't thank you. He'd think that colleagues ought to be able to sort it out between themselves.

It seems that one secretary of state at the Northern Ireland Office refused to discuss disputes between his junior ministers, and left his permanent secretary to resolve issues when the juniors disagreed:

This was very odd but simply his way of doing things. We all lived together most of the week, saw a lot of each other, had meals together, spent little time in parliament and saw little of other colleagues in different departments. We all had to get on and trust the secretary of state, and he didn't want to take sides between us.

Parliamentary under-secretaries feel that subordination to a minister of state weakens them against civil servants. In interview one said, 'The hierarchical system suits the civil servants – they have two or three goes at getting it back to the line they want.' Another recalled what happened when he secured a set of functions of his own, separate from those of the minister of state: 'That affected the civil servants. Now I mattered, and they had to come to me.' The civil servants' attitude also depends on the competence of the junior ministers concerned. A former permanent secretary contrasted a parliamentary under-secretary in his department – 'he was a good junior minister: he listened to advice, he gave decisions' – with a minister of state – 'a bad minister: unreliable, temperamental'. And officials clearly look to see how the secretary of state regards his ministers. Interviews provided examples of teams in which good personal relations with the secretary of state further strengthened a minister of state's formal position, and also cases in which the top minister felt more empathy towards a parliamentary under-secretary than to a minister of state and, whatever the formal delineation of functions, in fact relied on the more junior when delegating decisions and consulting on policy.

Some commentators have claimed that parliamentary private secretaries (PPSs) provide governments with junior ministers 'on the cheap'. Such a claim is unjustified. The role of the PPS is variable: some are shown important policy papers and consulted on decisions, but most are parliamentary go-betweens, keeping their secretary of state in touch with backbench opinion. Much depends on their personal relation with their chief, but in important respects the work of a PPS is quite different from that of a junior minister. PPSs do not have executive responsibilities delegated to them. During the Second World War some hard-pressed

ministers left their PPSs to answer letters from MPs, and on some
occasions PPSs took responsibility for dealing with the cases involved
without ministers having seen the letters, a practice criticized by MPs.
Junior ministers' work in overseeing departmental administration,
deciding cases and replying to parliamentary correspondence thus
distinguishes them from PPSs. By convention, PPSs do not speak in
parliament on matters affecting the department to which they are
attached; they have also to exercise discretion in speeches they make
outside the Commons. In contrast, junior ministers appear in parliament
on behalf of the department and represent it on visits and inspections, to
say nothing of attending Cabinet committees to put its case – an arena
completely closed to PPSs. Officially, PPSs are not members of the
government, and so the information given to them should be limited to
what is necessary for their parliamentary and political duties.[18] Their
access to Cabinet and departmental policy papers depends on their
secretary of state's predilections. As shown in a later chapter, junior
ministers see departmental papers in their field of responsibility and
papers for those Cabinet committees they attend, but whether they see
the most sensitive departmental papers and Cabinet papers on subjects
other than their own depends on their chief. Unequivocal statements are
difficult on this point: *some* PPSs may have access to more information
than *some* junior ministers, for political and personal reasons, but this
would not be the general rule.

The secretary of state's PPS usually has an office in the department. His
master *may* use him as a confidant, discussing policy, political, party and
even personality problems with him. In this role a very small number of
PPSs are more influential than the general run of junior ministers. The
fact that a PPS is personally appointed by the secretary of state may
facilitate such a close relationship. A junior minister said in interview
that when he had been appointed a PPS his secretary of state had 'claimed
that I'd be able to function as a junior minister, but that was tripe – you
can't and the civil servants make sure you can't.' It seems that officials
will not send papers to a PPS and will not inform him of meetings unless
instructed to do so by the top minister. Such behaviour is, of course,
perfectly understandable, and firmly supported by his chief a PPS will not
find officials hindering his work. A former PPS said, 'I had only one or
two problems with officials – nothing serious. They took their cue from
the close relationship the secretary of state had with me – his clear
intention that I should be involved.'

The proliferation of special advisers in recent governments has been
interpreted as evidence that Cabinet ministers are failing to use their
existing resources of political support as fully as they might. Some junior

ministers clearly resent advisers' privileged access to information and to the secretary of state, and their opportunities for influence over policy. David Owen, while in favour of a *cabinet* style unit of personal policy advisers for ministers, wrote from personal experience in the Department of Health and Social Security when he described the role of special advisers as 'acting as an extra pair of arms and eyes for the minister – sometimes in this role clashing with junior Ministers'.[19] And in interview a permanent secretary recalled a special adviser who 'cut much more ice with the secretary of state' than a parliamentary under-secretary whom he named. He continued, 'Sometimes the junior ministers did feel that the advisers were against them. The minister of state had strong views and he didn't take kindly to the special adviser arguing a different case . . . It's best when people at the top are open with each other – with their cases and their points against each other.' However, as a rule, open antagonism did not mark relations between junior ministers and special advisers. A deputy secretary said of the advisers in his department:

> They had an incentive to keep on the right side of ministers. I think that they were sensitive to the secretary of state/department/junior minister relationships and were concerned to smooth away friction. Advisers must identify a role not filled by junior ministers. They should try to make themselves useful to them, and not appear to step into the junior ministers' shoes. Writing junior ministers' speeches may help them win their confidence.

A parliamentary under-secretary explained:

> I made it clear with the special advisers that I'd welcome comments and I saw that they got copies of papers that I'd circulate to them and that I'd be willing to discuss issues. They didn't always agree with me, nor I with them, but the arrangement worked well. They wanted to advise the secretary of state – I'd been a PPS so I knew and understood their position well.

Special advisers are an understandably attractive option for secretaries of state. Chosen by their chief, they owe their position and influence to their *personal loyalty* to him. Another contrast with junior ministers is the sheer *availability* of advisers: 'I think that I didn't do a thing that couldn't have been done by the right Junior Minister. Except that I had more time. In the end all of them have to go to the House of Commons. Also they have constituencies and all of that.'[20] While some special advisers offer general political assistance, others contribute impressive *subject expertise* not likely to be found among junior ministers. But again it is important to note that, in the words of a former special adviser, such aides 'were in no sense junior ministers or took over essential ministerial functions'.[21] If some of the activities of junior ministers are chores then, equally, special advisers can never be certain of influence. In any case, not all Cabinet ministers have special advisers (over half the Labour Cabinet did, 1974–9, but only about one-third of current Conservative ministers) and instead may rely on their junior ministers for political advice, informally or in specially convened ministers' meetings.

With small ministerial teams, few Cabinet ministers before the 1960s felt the need for formal ministers' meetings. In the 1964–70 Labour government several ministers called weekly meetings of their juniors 'to check things through and see how they are going', in Richard Crossman's words, and often meeting on the day the department faced parliamentary questions. The practice became common in the 1970s. At one extreme, Peter Walker at the Department of the Environment 1970–2 emphasized the collegiate nature of his team by holding half-hour meetings each morning of all ministers and PPSs, with no officials present. At the other extreme, Tony Crosland thought 'meetings with all junior Ministers, which sounds the obvious way of going about things, were always rather a shambles, with one person talking too much of the time. So in fact you talk to them separately.' Crosland told his wife, 'What they really want is for one to be their psychoanalyst.'[22] Other Cabinet ministers differed according to whether they called meetings daily or (more usually) weekly, whether or not they also invited along civil servants, and the degree of formality they encouraged (some meetings appear to have had papers and minutes, others were less structured).

Walker's meetings have attracted most press and academic attention. They reflected his ideas about how the Department of the Environment should be run. As a deputy secretary commented:

> Walker ran the DOE at its most mammoth. He worked extremely well with his junior ministers. He deliberately fostered a team image to manage the department, and his was the most successful team. He wanted to be like a company boss with his junior ministers as the Board. Other secretaries of state lacked his business experience and that had something to do with it. They didn't have the habit of including other members of the 'Board' of the department in decision-taking.

However, Walker's meetings were not forums for decision-taking, with papers and minutes, but rather opportunities for the DOE ministers to gossip, keep in touch and exchange information and views. One of Walker's former parliamentary under-secretaries said that participants could have 'a real *tour de horizon* – filling in on what was happening, and picking up things that one didn't otherwise know about.' One observer of the DOE wrote, 'At the morning meetings, Ministers talked about their own work rather than deliberated as a body of collective decision-makers.' Walker's successors at the DOE discontinued his 'morning prayers', to the chagrin of the junior ministers, but continued to hold regular ministers' meetings, the frequency varying according to the secretary of state's inclinations and the press of other business (for instance a clash with a regional visit). The importance of the top minister's style is also brought out by a comparison of two successive Chancellors. According to Joel Barnett, Denis Healey was 'too much of a "loner" to be a good leader of a team'. He would delegate to his junior ministers, back them up and read papers they wrote for him, but held meetings only rarely. It seems that Labour's Treasury team had lunch together once a month, but the sessions were not a success, and one of Healey's junior ministers felt 'we were too much at our individual grindstones because of the Chancellor's style rather than "the system".' After 1979 Sir Geoffrey Howe held a meeting each morning with his junior ministers and special advisers, with no officials present. One of his special advisers said 'there were almost literally no occasions, except for these morning meetings, when the five ministers got together.' The difference between Healey and Howe in this respect perhaps partly reflects personalities, but also the Conservative Chancellor's desire to maintain the impetus of his innovative economic policies against supposed civil service scepticism.[23]

Some ministers felt that the presence of civil servants at these meetings was inhibiting, especially of discussing political and party points, and personality clashes with officials. However, in several departments the permanent secretary attended the ministers' meeting, in others officials might be called in for information on specific issues, and in others the secretary of state's private secretary would take a note of the meeting so the department knew what went on. One permanent secretary recalled, 'I wasn't there, but I'd learn about the meetings. The secretary of state would want me to be told. They weren't secret meetings, but politicians' meetings, looking at things that way.' A former junior minister told of sandwich lunches held by Tony Benn, to which the permanent secretary and his senior colleagues went. 'They disliked the meetings. Permanent secretaries have lunches and contacts planned months in advance, and to disrupt their plans for poor food at meetings which weren't well-organized didn't go down well.' One style is to have a 'politicians only' meeting first, followed by a meeting including top officials, as practised by Barbara Castle at the Department of Health and Social Security 1974–6. This type of arrangement, said one permanent secretary, meant that 'the civil servants joined in the meeting with their hearts in their mouths. The ministers had all whooped it up together, and we had to go in and say, "I'm sorry, but did you think of this, and this and this?" '

Interviews with participants point to five functions of these sessions, depending on the secretary of state's attitude: (a) to discuss parliamentary business and tactics; (b) general discussions of Cabinet business and wider issues (for instance the Budget); (c) departmental matters: ministers could brief colleagues on developments in their areas, float proposals and the top minister could elucidate his general themes and strategies; (d) to discuss personality problems with officials; (e) and, from the top minister's perspective, to prevent 'empire building' (as a minister of state said, 'One view is that they were designed to see that no one was stepping out of line'). Such meetings are useful for ministers, who spend a great deal of time with civil servants and relatively little time with each other, and they are particularly valued by junior ministers as a way of keeping in touch. Their real effect depends on the secretary of state and what sort of relationship he wants to establish with subordinates, how seriously he takes their time together and the role he sees for junior ministers.

The Bureaucratic Embrace?

Civil servants take their cues from ministers. The relationship between a secretary of state and his junior minister(s) shapes the relations between civil servants and the junior minister(s). Malcolm Rifkind, appointed a junior minister in 1979 and promoted to the Cabinet in 1986, has noted that:

> in the case of junior Ministers, the civil servants want to assess the extent to which the junior enjoys the confidence of his Secretary of State or whether he is merely a transit lounge that must be passed through before the actual decision is taken on any matter of substance by the Secretary of State himself. If the Secretary of State is seen to prefer the judgement of the junior Minister to that of the department the message is soon taken and appeals . . . become relatively infrequent. If, however, in the first few weeks the junior Minister is regularly over-ruled by his boss the officials would be less than human if they did not file that away for future use.

Lord Crowther-Hunt has argued that civil service appeals are more likely if officials know that the ministerial team is not cohesive: 'if there was any division between yourself and the top civil servants this would be fully exploited if the civil servants believed that your personal relationship with the Secretary of State was in any way "shaky".'[24] In interview, a minister of state summarized the position succinctly: 'The whole civil

service machine is geared to not taking junior ministers seriously if they
know that they'll be over-ruled.'

Two officials hold positions of great importance in the departmental
machine: the private secretary and the permanent secretary. A minister's
private secretary is his personal assistant, whose tasks include keeping his
diary and making appointments, processing papers to and from him, and
accompanying him on visits and to meetings. The private office of a
secretary of state will be headed by a principal or an assistant secretary
and, including clerks, will number eight or nine staff; that of a junior
minister will probably be headed by a 'fast-streamed' higher executive
officer and contain only about four officials. In interview, junior
ministers often said that when first appointed they relied a lot on their
private secretaries to get to know their jobs: 'Your private secretary tells
you how to be a minister – what to do, how to go about it, how the
system works.' 'My private secretary had prepared a job description, a
brief telling me how the department worked, how the committees fitted
together – a useful child's guide to the department.' The best private
secretaries can be sounding-boards for the minister's bright ideas and
advisers on the internal politics of Whitehall: 'The private secretary is a
source of intelligence within the department – what's going on, the
people, the issues. He can give you an early warning on things –
problems, where we'll be defeated on a thing unless we bring in other
ministers or talk it through with other civil servants.' But there is no
doubt that, while they service and advise ministers, private secretaries
owe their ultimate loyalty to the civil service. As Richard Crossman put
it:

> The Private Secretary's job is to make sure that when the Minister comes
> into Whitehall he doesn't let the side or himself down and behaves in
> accordance with the requirements of the institution . . . The Private Office
> is the Department's way of keeping a watch on me, of making sure that I
> run along the lines they want me to run on, of dividing my time and getting
> the department's policies and attitudes brought to my notice.[25]

Ministers' private secretaries see senior departmental officials, including
the permanent secretary, every day, at meetings or for casual chats and
contacts. Consequently, civil servants in the department have an intimate
knowledge of the competence and views of the junior minister.
Facilitating the work of junior ministers, the private office network can
thus also serve to control or thwart them.

One symbolic indicator of the relationship between junior ministers
and permanent secretaries are the arrangements made for them to meet
each other in the course of their work. Permanent secretaries used to

behave condescendingly towards junior ministers. A retired permanent secretary recalled: 'There used to be a time when permanent secretaries would see it as an affront to be "called in" by junior ministers – *they* would "call in" junior ministers.' According to Gerald Kaufman, when they first take office and arrive at the department, junior ministers go along to the permanent secretary's room to see him; the permanent secretary, however, goes to see the secretary of state. After that, junior ministers may 'call in' any rank of civil servant to their offices. Lord Crowther-Hunt recorded his experience as a minister of state:

> As number two minister it would be most unusual for you to chair a meeting at which the Permanent Secretary was present. That would be *infra dig* as far as the Permanent Secretary was concerned. Nor, if you wanted to talk with the Permanent Secretary, would you 'send' for him. If *you* wanted to see *him*, it would be arranged by the two private offices that you would go to his office at a convenient time; and if he wanted to see you, then it would be arranged for him to call on you at a convenient time. You would normally call Deputy Secretaries and below to your office. But only the number 1 Minister would 'send' for the Permanent Secretary.[26]

Such conventions indicate the *amour propre* of permanent secretaries, but also make the important point that they are not the servants of junior ministers, but the servants of secretaries of state.

A permanent secretary has four main responsibilities: he is the secretary of state's chief official adviser on policy; as departmental accounting officer he has a special concern for financial business; he heads the official machine and is responsible for the management and efficiency of the department; and finally he has a role in inter-departmental consultations and on official committees. These responsibilities have a highly centralizing effect in departments. They mean that the permanent secretary should be conversant with all the department's actions and policies, and in a position to advise the secretary of state on all issues. Increasing pressure of business has meant that the permanent secretary now presides over a collegiate team of officials at the top of the department, rather than monopolizing the advisory function: indeed civil servants right down to assistant secretary level may deal direct with ministers in their different fields. However, it is still the case that the position and powers of the permanent secretary are not matched by those of the junior minister. The top official has an overview of the whole range of the department's policies and problems and, constitutionally, cannot be over-ruled by a junior minister (see chapter 3). As table 4.4 indicates, the tenure and experience of the permanent secretary relative to the junior minister, and even the secretary of state, are factors increasing his influence. The average tenure of a permanent secretary is twice that of the secretary of state he works with, and junior ministers hold office for shorter periods of time than their superiors. The rapid turnover of ministers gives some advantage to officials by enabling them to delay or fight back against proposals they oppose, and by giving them a background of enduring expertise and familiarity with policy subjects ministers lack and have to rely on.

TABLE 4.4 Tenures of departmental office-holders

| Department | Average tenures 1945–83 (in months) | | | |
	Cabinet minister	Minister of state	Parl. under-secretary	Permanent secretary
Foreign Office	27	27	21	49
Home Office	35	22	24	77
Treasury	30	25 (financial sec.) 21 (economic sec. or min. of state)		65
Education	24	19	26	65
Scottish Office	41	31	36	92

At the Treasury, the chief secretary has the same average tenure as the Chancellor – 30 months. At the Foreign and Home Offices tenures of permanent secretaries start in 1938, and at the Scottish Office in 1937, to give accurate figures.

In many ways the relationship between the secretary of state and the permanent secretary is the central axis of the department. A former permanent secretary said:

All secretaries of state talk more frankly to their permanent secretaries than to most of their ministerial colleagues, even on highly political matters, and especially if the permanent secretary enjoys the secretary of state's confidence, and his advice, experience and judgement are good and known to be so (and he shouldn't be a permanent secretary unless that is the case). The permanent secretary can be a sort of political neuter and 'father-confessor' figure, and he is not a parliamentary and party politician, which helps their relationship. A junior minister is ambitious and younger and wants to be a secretary of state, so among ministers there is a rivalry relationship rather than a strict hierarchical one ... A junior minister is generally less aware of what is in his secretary of state's mind than is the permanent secretary. The permanent secretary will see the secretary of state usually once a day at least, and sometimes more often; with junior ministers there may be two or three days between meetings with the secretary of state, unless their subject is on the boil. So junior ministers feel a bit cut off.

In interview, other permanent secretaries confirmed that they and their secretary of state would discuss candidly the personalities and actions of junior ministers, to say nothing of other Cabinet ministers and even the prime minister. It seemed that junior ministers themselves were unlikely to confide in the permanent secretary in this way, and in any case he would find it difficult to be as frank with a junior minister as with his secretary of state.

Life in Whitehall is not lived in a state of permanent conflict and struggle between ministers and civil servants. Analyses of policy-making which focus on adversarial confrontations between ministers and the civil service oversimplify and distort. Relations are complex and fluid, and the lines of division are more often than not to be found not *between* the political and bureaucratic elements in government but *within* them, as alliances of ministers *and* officials compete with each other to advance particular goals or defend common interests. Hence, it is not surprising that comments like the following are frequently heard from former ministers: 'You should over-rule civil servants only if you know your job and your facts. The civil servants do, so you should normally align with them' (Cabinet minister). 'I usually said "Yes" when I saw the papers – their analysis was always pretty good' (Treasury junior minister). However, on the other hand, there are complaints from former ministers that civil servants regard junior ministers as of no importance and regularly appeal to the top minister against their decisions. Herbert Morrison noted 'the unwillingness . . . of the higher civil servants to bring the Parliamentary Secretary in', and Richard Crossman also detected 'a determination to freeze out your Parliamentary Secretary . . . Unless you lay down that your Parliamentary Secretary will receive a certain paper he will automatically not receive it.'[27] Symbolically, PUSS is the unflattering Whitehall acronym for the most junior ministers, but in interview ministers of state also gave examples of civil service appeals from them to the secretary of state.

Civil servants may appeal, as Malcolm Rifkind suggested, because they are not sure that the secretary of state will back up the junior minister. A retired permanent secretary was adamant:

> The only man who can take decisions is the minister. You should be absolutely clear what he delegates to the junior minister, and the civil servants will go along with that. But if the junior minister thinks that he has a brief of his own, or can do things differently from the minister, it is the

minister who stands in his way, not the civil servants. Some things cannot be done unless the minister wants them done, and not on the say-so of a junior minister who is out of step. So you ask the minister, 'He's doing this; do you want it done?'

In particular, officials say that they want to involve the top minister in controversial issues with inter-departmental (i.e. Cabinet) and parliamentary repercussions and in matters that deeply divide different sections of the department. Thus, the reason for going to the secretary of state is not necessarily an attempt by civil servants to reverse a decision they dislike, but rather a sensible move to alert the secretary of state, who after all carries full constitutional responsibility, of a sensitive issue. The secretary of state is involved so that any decision will – in civil service parlance – 'stick'. As a minister of state recalled:

> Civil servants sometimes circumvent you and go to the senior minister, even if he knows nothing at first hand of the question, because he has the ministerial responsibility in Cabinet and in parliament. They would say, 'We have to be sure that your views are reflected by the senior minister.' It is deep in the behaviour patterns of Whitehall, and also seen when civil servants go to the Treasury, prime minister or Cabinet against their own secretary of state –to make sure that the political weight of the government supports the line to be taken.

A parliamentary secretary described what happened when civil servants alerted their permanent secretary of a dispute with him:

> The civil servants would take things to the permanent secretary, and he would come along and we'd have coffee and a chat. He would point out the problems for the department, and you would have to ask yourself whether it was big enough to have that sort of battle. You want conditions to be such that you have a chance of winning.

Rather than such open and explicit appeals, issues may be steered to the secretary of state as a junior minister's views become known. In interview, a deputy secretary described how the private office system may be used to inspire intervention or to keep the secretary of state informed about his junior ministers. Papers could be sent up or meetings called and junior ministers blocked almost without them realizing the fact. A permanent secretary said that he would be kept in the picture by his deputy secretaries and, if a junior minister was doing something which the secretary of state would not be in favour of, he would informally raise the matter with the secretary of state. Alternatively, he might suggest that the secretary of state ask the junior minister for a progress report or for a paper at the next ministers' meeting. 'Perhaps it does look as if you're going behind the junior minister's back, but you don't allow that to become apparent. There are ways of doing these things. But you are not simply slapping down the junior minister – you're making sure that he's not doing something without the authority of his secretary of state.'

Assessing the frequency of civil service appeals is difficult. Evidence is anecdotal, patchy and sometimes self-serving. Some examples seem absurd, but are possibly indicative of more general relations: thus Jeremy Bray, junior minister in the Ministry of Power 1966–7, arranged to have lunch with an outside oil expert, but the permanent secretary complained to the minister, Richard Marsh, that Bray was to meet 'an undesirable character'. However, Marsh insisted that Bray could have lunch with whomever he liked! More seriously, in 1976 Michael Meacher, Parliamentary Under-secretary at the Department of Health and Social Security, rejected drafts of an answer to a parliamentary question about hypothermia deaths in Britain, wanting to release more information than officials thought wise. The matter was handled at successively higher stages of the civil service hierarchy before the secretary of state was persuaded to over-rule Meacher and authorize the original suggested answer. A well-known case is that of Alex Lyon, sacked as Home Office Minister of State in 1976, who claimed that officials had bypassed him and taken decisions to the Home Secretary. One writer described officials in the Department of the Environment 'calling on subordinate ministers for support if necessary, or by-passing them if convenient, and competing for the ear of the Secretary of State'. It seems that 'it was not un-known for a second permanent secretary to be telling a Secretary of State the grounds on which he should disagree with his subordinate minister.'[28]

However, appeals are not continuous. Junior ministers and civil servants will establish some *modus vivendi* based on an assessment of the other's position, support from above and past relations. The knowledge that officials have a right and the ability to appeal may be a factor in the adjustment of junior ministers' relations with them, without open appeals being made. As a Treasury junior minister said, 'You should try to take your own decisions and not get into a position where you or they are appealing. If my stuff was going to the Chancellor all the time to decide, he'd soon get fed up. You can't allow that.' At the Board of Trade in the 1960s, Anthony Crosland faced hundreds of decisions each year on Industrial Development Certificates, which he left entirely to a junior minister and civil servants, refusing to look at them unless there was 'a violent disagreement on a major case between the junior Minister and the officials, which happened perhaps twice a year'. It is clear that civil service appeals come to naught if the top minister supports his juniors and refuses to allow civil servants to bypass them. Edward Heath has admitted that a minister's delegation to his junior 'needs to be reinforced the whole time', and that:

> It is always open of course, for a Permanent Secretary to go to the Secretary of State and say, 'I think that this is a matter which really cannot be decided only by the Parliamentary Secretary but ought to come to you personally.' The Secretary of State can reject that advice and say, 'No, I have complete confidence in him. Let him get on with it.'

But, for reasons discussed above, secretaries of state may not trust or support their subordinates, a factor which moved William Rodgers to write, 'the complaints that junior Ministers have about officials should sometimes be directed to their own senior ministerial colleagues who do not always give them support.'[29]

Finally, we turn to the administrative implications of the disappearance of those ministers in charge of departments but not members of the Cabinet and of the recent shift in the ratio of ministers to senior mandarins. We noted earlier that Attlee's government included 13 of these non-Cabinet departmental ministers in 1951, but that they have since departed the Whitehall scene and, in effect, been replaced by ministers of state. Along with this development, there has been a trend towards departmental amalgamations: the 24 departments with junior ministers existing in 1945 had fallen to 16 by 1986 (see table 2.1 above). Conventionally, these changes are justified as producing a more tidy and efficient set-up which allows a manageable Cabinet, inclusive of all departmental interests and perspectives, and reduces overlap, confusion and the need for cumbersome inter-departmental coordination. However, for constitutional and political reasons, there must be some doubt about the extent to which the modern arrangement permits adequate ministerial control of the bureaucracy. The ratio of ministers to senior civil servants may not have worsened significantly as smaller departments were merged into 'giant' ones, but the constitutional status of ministers of state is definitely inferior to that of the non-Cabinet departmental ministers they have replaced. The latter figures carried full individual responsibility to parliament and were thus able to issue authoritative commands to their officials; as we have seen, ministers of state have no such inherent authority – their power depends upon delegation from, and relations with, their chiefs. The reduced number of responsible departmental heads may mean, then, that political control of Whitehall has, constitutionally, become less assured. And politically, the status and weight of ministers of state may be less than that of the now extinct non-Cabinet minister. In career terms, both sorts of office were and are a jumping-off point for promotion to the Cabinet. But the non-Cabinet minister

frequently attended Cabinet meetings for items concerning his department, and in parliament and elsewhere he was the minister responsible
for a particular subject in a way which only those second-tier ministers of
state from major departments who have clearly delegated functions, and
who are firmly supported by their chiefs, are today. As William Rodgers
has said, 'A junior Minister is a junior Minister whatever his salary and
however he is dressed up.'[30] This too affects the balance between
political and bureaucratic elements in government. These remarks are
necessarily tentative, for hypotheses about ministerial control of Whitehall can only be properly tested by detailed historical analysis or case
studies, but nevertheless there are grounds for concern about the effects
of the demise of the non-Cabinet minister and the changed shape of the
ministerial hierarchy in the post-war period.

A little-noticed development of recent years has been the shift in the
ratio of ministers to senior civil servants in favour of the politicians.
Table 4.5 gives the 'minister : mandarin ratio' for government departments in 1971 and 1985. The number of civil servants at under-secretary
and above is conventionally taken as a good indicator of the volume of
important work in departments and of the burden on ministers (in the
Foreign Office the total of officials reflects the large number of
ambassadors overseas). Departments differ greatly in terms of their size,
the nature of their activities and their political and parliamentary
salience. But the number of ministers appointed to each department
depends not on a scientific calculation of the work to be done and the
number of senior bureaucrats to oversee, but instead on traditional and
political considerations.

In interview, a retired permanent secretary said, 'Frankly, there are too
many junior ministers. Many of my former colleagues would prefer fewer
junior ministers rather than more. The ones left could then have a real
job to do. The tendency is, if there are too many, for them to find things
for idle hands. So you actually create more work.' Another permanent
secretary considered that his department, and a number of others around
Whitehall, had one junior minister too many. It is true that there may be
a form of 'Parkinson's Law' operating here, with more ministers dividing
the work into smaller and smaller pieces, and busying themselves on
visits around the country, administrative trivia and so on. Nor must we
forget the patronage calculations of prime ministers anxious to assuage
backbenchers' demands for office. Cutting the number of ministerial
posts, as Heath did in 1970, may simply make the job of managing the
parliamentary party more difficult. But junior ministers *can* find useful
work to do. As noted in a later chapter, there is no doubt that the volume
of parliamentary business has increased since the 1960s, and some

TABLE 4.5 Minister : mandarin ratio for government departments

	1971			1985		
Department	Total ministers (1)	Officials (under-secs and above) (2)	Ratio (1) : (2)	Total ministers (1)	Officials (under-secs and above) (2)	Ratio (1) : (2)
Foreign Office	7	250	1 : 35.7	6	160	1 : 26.6
Treasury	4	119	1 : 29.7	5	75	1 : 15
Defence	6	154	1 : 25.6	5	76	1 : 15.2
Health and Social Security	4	72	1 : 18	6	61	1 : 10.1
Trade and Industry	7	118	1 : 16.8	8	63	1 : 7.8
Environment	8	109	1 : 13.6	6	53	1 : 8.8
Agriculture	2	42	1 : 21	4	31	1 : 7.7
Employment	4	35	1 : 8.7	4	31	1 : 7.7
Education	4	38	1 : 9.5	3	18	1 : 6
Home Office	4	38	1 : 9.5	5	26	1 : 5.2
Scottish Office	5	40	1 : 8	5	36	1 : 7.2
Welsh Office	2	8	1 : 4	3	13	1 : 4.3
Civil Service Dept	2	39	1 : 19.5			
Post and Telecoms	1	5	1 : 5			
Northern Ireland Office				5	47	1 : 9.4
Transport				4	24	1 : 6
Energy				4	15	1 : 3.75
Total	60	1067	1 : 17.8	73	729	1 : 10

additional junior ministers have been appointed for that reason (for instance, to help steer a major Bill through the Commons or to meet the burden of parliamentary correspondence). Inside the government machine, extra junior ministers, with designated responsibilities, have surely made a difference for the better in terms of bringing more areas of departmental activity under political supervision at an earlier stage in the policy-making process than was the case in the 1960s or earlier. Ministers are very much part-time departmental administrators and decision-takers because of the multiplicity of other tasks they face, but it would seem, even comparing 1985 with 1971, that Whitehall departments are now potentially subject to more pervasive ministerial control and influence. Perhaps, too, the greater availability of junior ministers has helped government to become politically better coordinated: as noted in the next chapter, junior ministers play an important role on Cabinet committees.

Between 1971 and 1985 the number of departmental ministers rose by 22 per cent, and the number of senior civil servants was cut by 32 per cent; Mrs Thatcher has contributed greatly to both these changes, appointing more junior ministers than her Labour predecessors and pushing through large reductions in civil service numbers. An important factor in the success of the Conservative government in implementing its policies has been the shift in the balance of power in Whitehall this has engendered. During the post-war period as a whole, the greater role played by junior ministers has also affected the balance of power inside government. Junior ministers now cut much more substantial figures than in the 1940s and 1950s. The disappearance of the non-Cabinet minister heading a small department means that it is more important than ever for junior ministers to make a real contribution to the process of government; that they are doing so is both necessary and desirable.

5

Junior Ministers and the Problems of Collective Government

On the inter-departmental level, collective responsibility does not entail collective decision-taking. As one minister said, 'It is often very frustrating. You see the big decisions made elsewhere, and you must accept collective responsibility even if you have doubts. You don't have the Cabinet minister's power and you don't have the backbencher's freedom to have his say.' Junior ministers have only limited opportunities to acquire information or to participate in collective deliberations and decisions.

Access to Information

There is no such thing as 'open government' even within Whitehall. Information is rationed on a 'need-to-know' basis. Among Cabinet ministers the circulation of papers, telegrams and information is carefully limited, and Cabinet ministers and civil servants husband their power by restricting access to information on the issues and options they are considering. Some junior ministers do not know what is going on in their departments outside their own sphere of responsibilities; so far as the 'wider picture' or other departments are concerned, a Cabinet minister put the position bluntly: 'Many junior ministers read in the newspapers what's going on in the government.' Tessa Blackstone has written that, 'One aspect of official secrecy is that junior ministers are often denied access to papers which quite junior civil servants may see.' Cabinet Office doctrine is extremely restrictive. In 1944 Sir Edward Bridges, then Secretary to the Cabinet, noted that, 'Parliamentary Secretaries should see only those Cabinet papers which their duties require them to see, e.g. (a) papers to be taken at a meeting at which the Parliamentary Secretary is representing the minister; (b) papers concerning some aspect of the work of the Department which has been allotted to the Parliamentary Secretary.' After the war Attlee instructed his Cabinet colleagues that parliamentary secretaries 'should be fully informed of the work of the Department and kept in general touch with all Cabinet matters affecting it, so that when called upon to attend a meeting in place of the Minister [they] understand the subject and do . . . not merely recite a brief.' But he then laid down rules controlling access to official information which are still affirmed in the government's confidential handbook *Questions of Procedure for Ministers*:

> It is within the discretion of Ministers to decide which of their advisers or subordinates should be shown Cabinet and Cabinet Committee documents . . . Ministers who share the collective responsibility for the Government's programme must be kept generally aware of the development of important aspects of Government policy. But outside this limited circle knowledge of these matters should be confined to those, whether Ministers or officials, who are assisting in the formulation or execution of the particular policy concerned or need to know what is afoot because of its effect on other aspects of public business for which they are responsible.[1]

The way in which official guidelines are framed means that the attitude of the secretary of state chiefly determines whether junior ministers see only those departmental papers that directly concern them, or whether they are shown a wide range of policy documents and Cabinet papers. In 1967 Richard Crossman met some junior ministers and discovered that there was 'an amazing variety in the amount of information they had about government policy'. Barbara Castle's junior ministers at the Ministry of Transport saw 'all the Cabinet minutes'; Anthony Greenwood's juniors at Housing had 'nothing'.[2] It is well known that at the Department of Trade 1976–8 Edmund Dell insisted that his junior minister, Michael Meacher, was not shown certain sensitive policy papers. In interview, a former parliamentary secretary said that he saw all Cabinet and committee papers and a number of official committee papers; he saw all the papers his chief saw, but had more time to read them and felt that they helped him play a useful role on Cabinet committees. But others commented that they did not have a clear view of what was happening elsewhere in the government, because it was difficult to do anything but keep abreast of departmental work: 'I had all the papers, but the sheer volume of the stuff is fantastic. You're cut off by your utter inability to pay attention.'

It seems that whether or not a junior minister is a Privy Councillor also determines his access to information. All Cabinet ministers are Privy Councillors, but only a minority of junior ministers. In October 1978, 16 out of 26 Labour ministers of state were Privy Councillors, but none of the 32 parliamentary under-secretaries. In February 1986, ten out of 28 Conservative ministers of state were Privy Councillors, but no under-secretaries. Ministers of state are admitted to the Privy Council either as a political honour or for what Harold Wilson called 'operational reasons'. John Gilbert, Minister of State at the Ministry of Defence during the Callaghan government had been seeing top secret documents before he became a Privy Councillor, but afterwards, 'I found myself seeing a lot of material in fields in which I was interested that I had no idea heretofore had existed.' As a civil servant said, 'politicians will not allow themselves to be positively vetted . . . [so] the Privy Councillor's oath is all we have got – the nearest thing to a Boy Scout's oath for ministers. So of course Privy Councillors get more documents.'[3]

Some prime ministers hold sessions to keep junior ministers informed of important matters affecting the government and to foster some collective spirit. Macmillan (after 1961) and Heath instituted weekly meetings at which a Cabinet minister briefed junior ministers on policy developments; an ex-minister reported that similar meetings were called once or twice a month after 1979. Heath also asked for reports on the discussions following bi-annual Central Policy Review Staff presentations to junior ministers. Callaghan met junior ministers as a group two or three times a year, a practice which Thatcher has apparently continued. These conferences would last one and a half to two hours, and would cover specific but broad subjects like public expenditure, the Budget or election timing.[4] But, while these meetings helped junior ministers propagate more effectively the government's line on policy issues and kept the Prime Minister and senior colleagues aware of opinion in the lower ranks of the administration, they did not provide meaningful opportunities for concerted influence over policy. The meetings took no decisions, but rather conveyed opinions. One former junior minister said, 'the general pep-talks with the prime minister weren't much use'; another dismissed them as occasions to 'let off steam at having no say at all in broad policy'.

Only two junior ministers have been Cabinet ministers in their own right, and each case was exceptional. From May to August 1923, Stanley Baldwin was both Prime Minister and Chancellor of the Exchequer, and he made the Financial Secretary to the Treasury, Joynson-Hicks, a Cabinet minister and in charge of day-to-day Treasury business. Baldwin hoped that Reginald McKenna would find a parliamentary seat and become Chancellor, but he failed and Neville Chamberlain was appointed in his place. Joynson-Hicks then became Minister of Health and a new financial secretary, outside the Cabinet, was appointed. From April to October 1964, Sir Edward Boyle served as Minister of State at the Department of Education and Science alongside his Secretary of State, Quintin Hogg. This expedient was born out of the creation of the new department, and the political need of the Prime Minister, Sir Alec Douglas-Home, to keep Boyle (the former Minister of Education) in the Cabinet. When John Selwyn Gummer, Parliamentary Under-secretary at the Department of Employment, was promoted to be Minister of State and made Chairman of the Conservative Party in October 1983, he attended Cabinet meetings, but did not become a member of the Cabinet.[5] The limited time he could devote to departmental duties occasioned some controversy, especially as the Department of Employment already had a minister of state and two under-secretaries, and in September 1984 Gummer was reshuffled to the post of Paymaster-General, outside the Cabinet, which he held for another year before giving up the Party Chairmanship and moving to be Minister of State at the Ministry of Agriculture. Apart from these instances, junior ministers usually attend full Cabinet only as substitutes for absent secretaries of state, and then only for particular agenda items affecting their department. Normally, it is the senior minister of state in the department who stands in for his chief. Thus, even though they may have day-to-day charge of the detailed work, the top minister must be involved in junior ministers' subjects in order to present proposals to Cabinet.

Some Cabinet ministers have afforded rather more access to Cabinet for their subordinates. Apparently George Brown, when Foreign Secretary 1966–8, used to insist that one of his ministerial team attend throughout Cabinet meetings when he was away or indisposed – and this might happen once or twice a month. In the 1970–4 Conservative government, Peter Walker (1970–2) and Geoffrey Rippon (1972–4), Secretaries of State for the Environment, would occasionally take their second-tier ministers responsible for defined sections of the DOE's work, along to Cabinet to help put the department's case, but their successors did not continue this practice. Prime ministers evidently discourage this sort of arrangement. When Foreign Secretary, Tony Crosland wanted to take his Minister of State for European Affairs, Roy Hattersley, to a Cabinet meeting in 1976 for an EEC item, James Callaghan objected. Crosland argued, 'I understand the economic side. He understands the institutional side. It will save everybody's time.' But the Prime Minister retorted, 'It would set up the most endless precedents.' And there is certainly no right of appeal for a junior minister from his secretary of state to Cabinet. At the Ministry of Defence the Minister for the Navy, 1964–6, Christopher

Mayhew, wanted to speak at Cabinet 'on an issue dividing him and Denis Healey, Defence Secretary. Healey blocked the effort. 'No bloody fear. I'm the boss ... I didn't forbid other Ministers going before Cabinet – they had no right. People like to feel that the Minister is in charge.'[6]

A considerable volume of inter-departmental business is carried out by correspondence between ministers. A letter sent by one minister to another will often be copied to a number of other interested ministers. William Rodgers, when Parliamentary Under-secretary at the Department of Economic Affairs dealing with regional policy, once wrote direct to Richard Crossman, Minister of Housing, as he had known him personally for many years. No reply came, and when Crossman's private office was contacted to discover what had happened, the answer came back that Crossman would be writing to George Brown, the Secretary of State, because Cabinet ministers could only correspond with ministers of the same rank. Interviews suggest that since the 1960s this rigid sense of hierarchy has been broken down somewhat. Kaufman explains that ministers generally correspond with ministers of their own rank, but that a junior minister may write to a secretary of state and even direct to the prime minister, though the reply will often be through the private office.[7] A great deal of business is also transacted in bilateral meetings between ministers in different departments. It is quite common for one junior minister, with a small group of officials, to meet another junior minister to sort out an inter-departmental issue. There is an elaborate protocol governing where these meetings are held. Parliamentary secretaries go to ministers of state's offices; when ministers are of the same rank, the meeting is held at the department whose chief is higher in order in the list of Cabinet ministers issued by Downing Street. If ministers cannot reach agreement this way, the matter may go before a Cabinet committee. One former junior minister recalled that she had once wanted to meet a colleague from another department to discuss a common problem. When her officials heard, 'they were up in arms. They said, "What status will this have? Who will be in the chair? What's the agenda?" They are determined to keep ministers separate and apart.' However, civil servants' concern for the enduring arrangements and interests of government is understandable. They prefer decisions that are properly arrived at and agreed to by all affected departments to casual encounters between politicians. Hence, if a matter engages the interests of a department sufficiently, or if agreement is difficult because of departmental or ministerial stakes, it will sooner or later be channelled into the formal Cabinet committee system.

Cabinet Committees

Cabinet committees reflect the needs of coordination or arbitration between departments. The prime minister, working with the cabinet secretary and other Cabinet Office civil servants, determines the structure of the committee system. There are standing and *ad hoc* committees. Standing committees are identified by letter-combination titles, and cover the main functional fields of government policy: economic policy (EY under Callaghan, EA under Thatcher), defence and foreign policy (DOP under Callaghan, OD under Thatcher), home and social affairs (HS under Callaghan, H under Thatcher), the government's legislative planning and programme (LG under Callaghan, L under Thatcher) and so on. *Ad hoc* committees are identified by a general code and a number; the code being GEN or MISC depending on the prime minister in office. These committees are established to deal with particular problems and then disbanded, although some may exist for lengthy periods. Both types of Cabinet committee may have sub-committees, which are identified by letter-combinations in brackets after the parent committee designation, and which usually report to the parent committee, though some report direct to the Cabinet. Each committee is shadowed by a committee of officials drawn from the same departments as the ministerial members of the Cabinet committee, and chaired either by a civil servant from the 'lead' department or by one from the Cabinet Office. These official committees service ministerial committees by preparing papers and briefs, clearing away minor points to throw major issues into sharp relief, and considering questions delegated to them by ministers.

The membership, like the existence and operations, of Cabinet committees is private to the government. It is known that the prime minister, advised by the Cabinet Office, decides the membership of committees. Irrespective of whether they are standing or *ad hoc*, membership is normally a reflection of departmental interest, but the membership of some committees, and some of the membership of many more committees, owes more to personal and political than to *ex officio* factors. Cabinet Office doctrine apparently has it that a Cabinet committee is formally made up of Cabinet ministers, and that junior ministers attend only as the representative of a Cabinet minister. In practice, some committees are composed only of Cabinet ministers, while others are composed predominantly of junior ministers or Cabinet and junior ministers mixed together. The main standing committees of the Cabinet tend to be composed of Cabinet ministers only, with occasional appearances by junior ministers as substitutes for absent ministers.

However, the Industrial Policy committee in the 1976–9 Callaghan government, titled EI, though composed mostly of Cabinet ministers included as members the ministers of state from the Industry Department, as well as their secretary of state in the chair. The Home and Social Affairs committee and the Legislation committee are usually attended by a number of junior ministers standing in for their chiefs. A participant said that the Callaghan government's Prices and Incomes committee included the Secretary of State for Prices in the chair, three or four Cabinet ministers, three or four ministers of state and three or four parliamentary secretaries at a typical meeting. An example in the same government of a committee manned mostly by junior ministers was GEN 38, an *ad hoc* committee on inner-city policy, chaired by the environment secretary.[8]

Several factors determine the membership of Cabinet committees. The workload of Cabinet ministers and the sheer number and frequency of meetings make junior ministerial attendance necessary and desirable. Then there are tactical considerations. In interview, a Cabinet minister said that he may want to stall and so may send a junior minister to a meeting, knowing that his presence may hold up matters or make a decision harder to reach. Junior ministers tend to attend committees where the department is not fully involved but has an 'interest'. If a department is centrally involved in a crucial subject, the secretary of state will go; if it is a more 'peripheral' matter, a junior minister may attend instead. At some meetings of some committees, the prime minister will allow only secretaries of state to appear, at others he or she will allow substitutes. In the 1964–70 Labour government, so many Cabinet ministers sent their junior ministers to the Home Affairs committee that the chairman asked the prime minister to send round a note objecting to the practice. According to one minister, Harold Wilson was 'free and easy on allowing junior ministers to appear at committees for their secretaries of state, and even at meetings at No. 10 . . . Callaghan stopped all that. He made a rule that the secretary of state had to go, unless he had a good excuse, to important committees. And if the prime minister chaired a meeting, he wanted the secretary of state there.' Similarly, a junior minister reported that 'if the Chancellor is in the chair, the ministerial pecking order is important: not as between a minister of state and an under-secretary, but that on major issues a Cabinet minister is needed to get the department's view across.' Kellner and Crowther-Hunt were told by a junior minister that civil servants manipulated Cabinet committees by, among other things, picking their members:

> Briefs always arrived late. Complaints were useless. There was always an explanation. Perhaps some crucial information couldn't be obtained till the

last minute. It was not, they maintained, the well-known ploy of keeping ministers uninformed until the last minute. Often I would get a box at midnight and find I was due to be at a Cabinet committee at nine the next morning on a subject I knew nothing about. I would be there instead of X (another junior minister) whose subject it was, even though he might be available. The next morning he might be at another meeting instead of me. Switching ministers in this way was common. There was never any notice of Cabinet committees; and the Permanent Secretary decided who went to them . . . Ideally they wanted people at . . . meetings who knew nothing except what was in their briefs.[9]

In interview, a former Treasury junior minister said, 'Often the Chancellor couldn't go to a Cabinet committee and I would get a note the night before, "Can you go?" Things like that always came late. You're supposed to have 48 hours, but you never do.' The late arrival of briefs, or the sudden summons to a committee, were often mentioned in interview, but Cabinet ministers insisted that *they* decided who attended on behalf of the department, not the permanent secretary.

The load of committee work varies between ministers and departments. Headey calculated that Cabinet ministers spend three or four hours each week in Cabinet and four to six hours in committees (assuming about three or four meetings each week), a total of about one-tenth of their working time.[10] Interviews and examination of engagement diaries suggest that junior ministers spend less time in committees or meetings with other ministers: two or three hours each week, at perhaps two meetings, is typical; six hours at four meetings would be unusual. Some departments are relatively free-standing in Whitehall and do not generate much committee work for ministers. The Foreign Office and the Ministry of Defence legislate infrequently and do not much overlap with other departments. They are represented at only a few committees, and then the secretaries of state usually appear. The Foreign Office minister of state concerned usually appears at the EEC policy committee. Ministry of Defence single service parliamentary under-secretaries went to very few committees. Conversely, the Treasury is represented on almost every committee, and Treasury junior ministers have a heavier than average load.

A former Scottish Office junior minister complained that:

Scottish Office Ministers have a weakness in committees: that they're one rank below the UK ministers they're dealing with. At a committee on my subject, I [a parliamentary under-secretary] could be there against a minister of state or a secretary of state. It's the same for the civil servants too. They're a grade below their English counterparts. That difference presents problems. People can pull rank at the political and civil service levels.

A retired permanent secretary admitted, 'There is rank consciousness. One art of committee work is to cut down the junior to you in rank. A department represented by a lower rank chap gets trodden on.' However, in interview, many ministers imply that there is little difference between a minister of state and a parliamentary under-secretary in terms of committee weight, and some assert that there can be little difference too between a junior and a Cabinet minister. A minister of state said, 'You must stand your corner and do your piece. You're there as an equal so get on with it.' Gerald Kaufman wrote, 'No one will pull rank on you in Cabinet Committee. You may be there as a Parliamentary Secretary surrounded by senior Cabinet Ministers, but they will judge you not by your seniority but by the quality of your arguments. Similarly they will have no mercy on you just because you are a junior. It is a meeting of equals.'[11] A Treasury junior minister said, 'A Treasury minister of state at a committee can virtually over-rule a Cabinet minister – especially if he and the others know that he does so on the Chancellor of the Exchequer's authority and is unlikely to be overturned.' Treasury ministers are always in a stronger position on committees than ministers from other departments, unless they are from the 'lead' department speaking to their own paper.

Junior ministers attend Cabinet committees with detailed briefs to put their department's point of view. Richard Crossman complained of the Prices and Incomes committee in 1966, 'It's an enormous public meeting with endless Parliamentary Secretaries reading aloud briefs from their Departments.' He and two other Cabinet ministers attended: 'We were the prefects. The rest were the schoolboys.' Crossman felt that if too few senior ministers attended a committee, junior ministers would stick to their briefs and no adequate discussion or decision would follow. For instance, at a committee meeting on planning appeals policy he failed to stimulate a discussion of general policy as 'they were mostly Parliamentary Secretaries with small departmental points' to make, sent along to 'join the queue and make the right noise at the right moment'.[12] In interview, junior ministers agreed that their first job at Cabinet committees was to represent their departments, but said that experience, knowledge and a desire to shine and make a reputation led some to join in the discussion around the table of wider political issues and governmental interests.

Critics such as Edmund Dell argue that the practice of sending junior ministers to committees 'with instructions to vote one way or the other without having heard the arguments orally presented at all' subverts rather than strengthens collective government. Another problem is that – if the argument is going against them – junior ministers may be obliged to 'reserve the position' of their secretary of state by seeking to defer a decision or by insisting on his right to re-open the question in Cabinet, thus slowing the flow of business or congesting the machine. And a former Cabinet minister said in interview, 'If a secretary of state turns up and finds he is outvoted – or rather outvoiced, as formal votes aren't taken – by junior ministers, then of course he'll reserve his position and take it to Cabinet.' The Cabinet committee system exists to take decisions and relieve the Cabinet of much of the burden on it. If committees cannot act as sieves because ministers challenge their decisions, the system fails. Hence the reminders that Cabinet ministers should attend important committees, and also edicts like those issued in 1967 and 1975 that only if the committee chairman agreed could a minister take a matter from a committee to full Cabinet. Barbara Castle complained about the 1975 ruling: 'it is too facile to assume that if a Cabinet committee decides a matter, this necessarily reflects the view of Cabinet. The trouble, as I well know, is that desperately busy Cabinet Ministers tend to skip Cabinet committees if they can and send their juniors.'[13]

On balance, however, the involvement of junior ministers in Cabinet committees is beneficial. They can play a useful, if limited, role there. Edmund Dell appears to overestimate the collegiality of Cabinet government. Headey's study showed that Cabinet ministers give their first priority to their departmental roles, and see the Cabinet as an inter-departmental battleground, not a forum for collective discussion and decision. But it is important to note that from the perspective of junior ministers, collective forums are transient and segmented: committees covering specific subjects rather than having an overview of the whole range of government policy (which the Cabinet, at least nominally, has). With narrow departmental horizons, junior ministers must accept that they will acquire influence commensurate with their collective respons-ibility only on promotion to the Cabinet.

Mixed Committees

All governments use mixed committees of ministers and civil servants together. Indeed, ministers, officials and military officers intermingled on the prototype of the modern Cabinet committee – the Committee of Imperial Defence, established in 1903. During the Second World War and its immediate aftermath it was not unusual for junior ministers to be found chairing committees of civil servants reviewing technical subjects or deciding priorities in areas such as shipping space, food distribution, oil requirements, the distribution of raw materials and the allocation of coal supplies. The technical detail of the work pointed to civil service membership, but their political implications and arbitral manner called for ministerial oversight. In the last resort civil servants needed ministers to sort out disputes among them. It was the practice for these mixed committees to report to the Cabinet, or to one of its major committees, or even direct to the prime minister. Hugh Gaitskell's work as chairman of official committees responding to the 1947 fuel crisis helped to make his ministerial reputation. He thought them:

> among the most business-like and useful bodies I have ever been connected with. At Ministerial Committees there tends to be too much bickering, talking, wooliness, ignorance, and personal feelings. At purely official committees there tends to be too little drive. The combination of a Minister and officials may give you the drive combined with the expertise, and without the personal feelings and ambitions being too prominent.[14]

There was a mixed committee on science and technology in the 1960s, which Shirley Williams served on when a junior minister at the Department of Education. It seems that there was also a mixed committee on statistics policy and reform in the same government, with junior ministers and officials from the Treasury, Department of Economic Affairs, Ministry of Technology and Department of Education, among others. There appears to have been a similar committee on statistics in the 1974–9 Labour government. In that government the Minister of State at the Department of Industry, Gerald Kaufman, was three times put in charge of inter-departmental groups of civil servants, which met to review particular areas of policy. In early 1979 he worked under the Home Secretary in the Cabinet Office during public service strikes, and had meetings with civil servants from many departments – that ministerial supervision of a Cabinet Office responsibility was exceptional, he claims. The 1970–4 Heath government apparently made extensive use of mixed committees of ministers and officials, but this approach to problems was not entirely successful. According to one participant, 'It had a slightly forced atmosphere. Officials would not disagree with their Ministers.'[15]

As mentioned above, each Cabinet committee is shadowed by an inter-departmental committee of civil servants. There is a lively controversy surrounding the work of these committees. Some observers describe their role as simply servicing and complementing ministerial committees. Others point to civil service predigestion of business to the extent of removing the power of decision from ministers. A frequently canvassed proposal in this context is to involve junior ministers in the deliberations of these committees, to ensure that options are not foreclosed and to give a political steer. Harold Wilson, when Prime Minister, professed to be in favour of mixed committees with junior ministers in the chair: 'Junior ministers who are keen, energetic, and perhaps with a little more time than senior ministers to look at the problems involved, can press some of the problems . . . much more thoroughly than could be done by the old system, under which you have a committee of officials bringing it up to ministers.'[16]

Despite their supposed advantages in allowing a greater role for junior ministers and equipping the political element in government better to oversee the operations of the permanent bureaucracy, mixed committees remain very much the exception rather than the rule in Whitehall. Chapter 8 will give more attention to this proposal and examine the feasibility of a more extensive system of such committees, along with other ideas for strengthening the position and influence of junior ministers in the government machine.

6

Junior Ministers in Parliament and as Departmental Ambassadors

A substantial proportion of the time of junior ministers is spent not sitting behind their desks in their departments or around the tables in the ministerial conference rooms of Whitehall, but on their feet in parliament, and in making public speeches and visits, receiving deputations and attending formal social functions. Bruce Headey calculated that Cabinet ministers spent, on average, one-sixth of their time in parliament and one-third on visits, meeting deputations and going to receptions, luncheons and so on. Perhaps one full day a fortnight would be devoted to a regional visit. Many Cabinet ministers wished to spend more time on major policy issues and thought that their parliamentary and public relations work absorbed too much time. Ministerial appointments diaries and interviews with junior ministers suggest that, in recent governments, they have devoted between one-tenth and a half of their working time to parliamentary duties (including being briefed for questions or debates) and from one-third to a half of their time to a variety of 'ambassadorial' tasks.

Departments differ in the volume and nature of work of this kind they impose on their ministers. Those which generate a heavy load of parliamentary business for ministers include the Department of the Environment, Department of Health and Social Security, Home Office, Scottish Office, Department of Transport and the Treasury. The Ministry of Defence, the Welsh Office and the Ministry of Agriculture do not in general throw up long hours of work in parliament for their ministers. These differences between departments depend on a number of measurements: the extent to which they legislate, the number of questions, letters from MPs and adjournment debates they attract and the number of general debates on departmental policies. The Foreign Office does not impose a heavy parliamentary burden, but its ministers spend a great deal of time travelling and visiting overseas.[1] Compared with their colleagues in domestically orientated departments, Treasury ministers tend to make few visits.

Parliamentary Duties

Constitutional convention and the attitudes and behaviour of MPs, ministers and officials define the secretary of state as the principal parliamentary spokesman of a department. That junior ministers do not carry final responsibility to parliament is neatly symbolized by the form of words they use in their speeches or answers to questions. They do not say, 'I decided . . .', or 'I believe . . .', but 'My Rt Hon. Friend decided . . .', and 'My Rt Hon. Friend believes . . .'.[2] The convention of ministerial responsibility forces the secretary of state to concentrate on those matters which are most politically controversial and contentious in the House of Commons. Secretaries of state normally open set-piece debates lasting all day, speaking in mid-afternoon, while a junior minister winds up before the 10 p.m. vote. They will thus initiate the second reading of major Bills, whereas junior ministers conduct the later stages. It is also usual for secretaries of state to lead for the government during debates on Opposition motions. Junior ministers handle delegated legislation and adjournment debates. The full ministerial team will normally be on the frontbench when the department is top of the rota for answering oral questions – this happens once a month, and is called 'First Order Questions' in ministers' diaries. Ministers' designated departmental responsibilities indicate which junior minister will answer which question or speak at which debate, but the final decision on this matter is the secretary of state's. Junior ministers, however, answer the bulk of written questions, and sign most of the replies to letters from MPs on constituency cases.

The Opposition, and even the government's own backbenchers, may complain if a secretary of state leaves too much to his junior ministers. A former Cabinet minister explained:

> The ministers of state in the department may be identified with specific areas of policy, but they are still not the men to make major statements. The departmental machine is geared to putting up the secretary of state as the premier spokesman. The House of Commons can be intolerant of junior ministers making policy statements, as they are not in the Cabinet and not aware of the Cabinet considerations that went into them. MPs feel the issue is demoted. The presence of the secretary of state signifies that the government attaches importance to the matter.

Another ex-Cabinet minister agreed: 'You spend all your time in Opposition trying to get the top man out in the open. The whole pressure is on trying to get the secretary of state into the firing line.' A recent example involved the then Secretary of State for Transport, Nicholas Ridley, who, because of an engagement elsewhere, could not in person make a statement to the Commons the day after the High Court set aside his decision to increase tolls on the Severn Bridge. MPs complained that his Minister of State, Lynda Chalker, appeared for the department, a Labour MP describing her as 'a surrogate for someone who is involved in illegalities'. Mrs Chalker replied, 'I am no one's surrogate. I am the Minister of State at the Department of Transport.' This prompted Enoch Powell to ask a question of the Prime Minister whether the status of ministers of state in relation to their secretaries of state had been redefined; he was told that it had not! A secretary of state may damage his reputation with MPs if he tries to avoid parliamentary flak by using his junior ministers to announce bad news. The former Defence Secretary, Michael Heseltine, was criticized for tending 'to push subordinates into the breach'. In December 1985 he was in Brussels when his Minister of State John Stanley faced MPs' anger over the Cyprus spy trial acquittals; in that month too, his other Minister of State, Norman Lamont, was left to make an important announcement on the government dockyards. In January 1986 Heseltine's preoccupation with the Westland crisis meant that an apparently ill-briefed Lamont made a poor performance announcing changes in defence spending.[3]

The career interests of professional politicians normally dovetail with the convention of ministerial responsibility and the demands of the House of Commons. If a minister gives too many opportunities to his subordinates, they may shine at his expense, or he will at least forsake some opportunities to consolidate or improve his own personal political position. These ego-calculations are particularly apparent in the parliamentary arena. In the late 1940s, Emanuel Shinwell, Minister of Fuel and Power, prided himself on his virtuoso performances at question time, and allowed his junior minister, Hugh Gaitskell, to take questions only once in his first year of office.[4] A retired permanent secretary said in interview, 'The relations of a secretary of state and his junior ministers can improve or deteriorate depending on how well each performs in the House.'

The device of 'double-banking' a department with two Cabinet ministers has sometimes been used when the secretary of state has been a peer and it has been felt that the Commons would not be satisfied with junior ministers alone representing the department. In selecting Harold Macmillan rather than Lord Salisbury as Foreign Secretary in 1955, Anthony Eden considered:

the very serious difficulties which must arise if the Foreign Secretary were to be a member of the House of Lords, in present times. The House of Commons would never take an important statement on foreign affairs from a junior Minister. A member of the Cabinet would therefore have to be the spokesman of the Foreign Office in the House of Commons on all major issues. This could only be the Prime Minister.[5]

In 1960, however, Harold Macmillan felt able to appoint a peer, Lord Home, Foreign Secretary, providing a Commons spokesman in the person of the Lord Privy Seal, Edward Heath, a Cabinet minister designated as deputy to the Secretary of State and responsible for European questions. When the foreign secretary was again a peer, from 1979 to 1982, the department was also 'double-banked', as was the Department of Employment after 1985, a particularly sensitive department given high levels of unemployment. However, this arrangement is not invariably adopted when the departmental head is a peer: the Colonial Office 1965–6, the Ministry of Defence 1970–4 and the Department of Trade 1982–3 all had secretaries of state in the Lords and were represented in the Commons by junior ministers.

Junior ministers usually lead for the government on Standing Committees, shepherding Bills through a time-consuming process of detailed scrutiny and attempted amendment. Given the state of parliamentary procedure, junior ministers perform an essential role here. As S.A. Walkland has put it, 'Without a ministerial initiative the committees would be at a loss as to how to proceed.'[6] If junior ministers did not appear for the government, there would be a gross misuse of the time and energies of secretaries of state. Standing Committees usually meet on Tuesday and Thursday mornings from 10.30 a.m. to 1.00 p.m., which is also the time of Cabinet meetings (on one or both those days). There is thus a practical matter of simultaneous and irreconcilable demands on the time of Cabinet ministers whose departments are legislating. If they attempt to attend some Committee sessions for important clauses or amendments, they may discover that they do not have a tactical 'feel' for the Committee and may disrupt proceedings. Committees which are not making progress on Bills often start holding additional afternoon or evening sessions, generating burdens incompatible with the pressing duties of Cabinet ministers.

The work connected with what one permanent secretary called 'the legislative treadmill' is time-consuming. One parliamentary under-secretary estimated that legislation could occupy a total of one-third of his time in 'a heavy year' (six or seven Bills), less at other times. 'The invisible part of the legislative iceberg', according to a junior minister, is made up of lengthy discussions with officials on the concepts and contents of measures, with parliamentary draftsmen on the language of legislation and with interested pressure and lobby groups who are affected. Ministers also generally consult backbench subject committees about pending legislation, and may hold sessions with their backbenchers to discuss progress on a Bill during its committee stage. The minister taking a Bill through Standing Committee is carefully briefed. A parliamentary secretary said, 'You must know your legislation inside out, and you get extremely detailed briefing and speaking notes for all amendments.' A senior civil servant described the department's preparations: 'Amendments may be made overnight and Bill teams [of officials] may work overnight to write notes. The minister taking the Bill through has to burn a lot of midnight oil, so it would be a waste of a senior minister's time.' Ministers have to understand the general purpose of the Bill, but also the meaning of particular clauses and the legal language they are couched in. Richard Crossman, as Minister of Housing:

> was spoilt by having Jim MacColl [as parliamentary secretary]. As a result of his presence I never bothered to read any of the Bills I got through. I glanced at them, and I read the briefs about them, and I also knew the policies from the White Papers, and I therefore knew exactly how the briefs and the White Papers corresponded with the clauses of the Bills. But I never bothered to understand the actual clauses, nor did many Members, not even the spokesmen for the opposition. Both sides worked off written briefs to an astonishing extent.

In committee, civil servants will send notes to guide ministers on questions and amendments. One observer of a Standing Committee described the junior minister in charge: 'Sometimes ... he is forced simply to read his instant instructions. "It should be clear when you read it in print." ' Not surprisingly, in 1974 a junior minister appearing for the government less than two weeks after his appointment opened the proceedings with the words, 'This is the sort of occasion where I can hardly wait to hear what I am going to say.'[7]

Many government Bills are uncontroversial administrative measures, the committee stage of which tend to be 'brief, smooth and businesslike'. But others arouse a deeply partisan 'war of attrition in committee over detail'. The minister in charge of a Bill in committee will be assisted by a whip, his PPS (if he has one) and perhaps by other ministers. (The 1980 Housing Bill, for instance, was steered through Standing Committee by John Stanley, Minister for Housing and Construction in the Department of the Environment, Geoffrey Finsberg, a parliamentary under-secretary in the DOE, and Wyn Roberts, Parliamentary Under-secretary for Wales, responsible for housing.) Griffith found that ministers comprised 10 per cent of the membership of Standing Committees, but made 28 per cent of the speeches. Whereas backbenchers will typically wander in and out of the committee rooms, and on the government side at least contribute relatively little (the whips prefer government backbenchers to occupy themselves with their constituency correspondence), the junior minister in charge faces continuous involvement: 'You can't drift in and out – you're the man on parade the whole time.' In truth, as a means of considering and amending the details of legislation, Standing Committee proceedings are often, in Crossman's words, 'utterly futile . . . and . . . utterly debilitating'. More important is their value for scrutinizing ministers as they explain and defend government policies:

> For hour after hour and for week after week a Minister may be required to defend his bill against attack from others who may be only slightly less knowledgeable than himself. His departmental brief may be full and his grasp of the subject considerable but even so he needs to be constantly on the alert and any defects he or his policy reveals will be very quickly exploited by his political opponents.[8]

Civil servants testify to the value of junior ministers who 'have safe hands and can be relied upon not to land us in trouble'. This aspect of the junior minister's job calls for knowledge of the details of the legislation, combined with an understanding of the mechanisms of committee procedure and a tactical feel for MPs' attitudes on both sides of the party divide.

The load of Standing Committee work varies depending on a junior minister's rank and department, and whether or not it is legislating. In the 1983–4 session of parliament, for instance, the Home Office was responsible for the Police and Criminal Evidence Bill, the Data Protection Bill and the Prevention of Terrorism Bill. Minister of State, Douglas Hurd, attended 71 meetings of Standing Committees, Parliamentary Under-secretary, David Mellor, went to 69 meetings, and Minister of State, David Waddington, to 37. The Secretary of State, Leon Brittan, attended only 17 Standing Committee meetings. The Department of Employment's sponsorship of the Trade Union Bill meant that the two parliamentary under-secretaries, John Selwyn Gummer and Alan Clark, attended 32 and 40 sessions respectively, while Minister of State, Peter Morrison, went to only one session and the department's Secretary of State, Tom King, attended none at all. At the Scottish Office, two parliamentary under-secretaries went to 12 and 14 sessions, but the third notched up 60 appearances because of a spate of Scottish and UK housing legislation, which was his departmental responsibility. Junior ministers at the Department of Education and the Northern Ireland

Office attended only eight and six Standing Committee meetings in total. Treasury junior ministers faced 13 Standing Committee meetings on the Finance Bill, considering its detailed provisions; this is also subject to several days general debate on the floor of the house.[9]

While most Standing Committee work is delegated to junior ministers, Cabinet ministers do sometimes attend sessions. The Opposition may attempt to waste time (their only weapon unless the government's majority is slim) by protesting about the absence of the secretary of state. In 1970 Richard Crossman was concerned that his minister of state and parliamentary secretary were getting credit for their work on the Social Security Bill. When he attended a meeting of the Standing Committee, the Conservative MPs seized the opportunity to debate with the secretary of state, and a whole morning was occupied with a matter that would otherwise have taken 20 minutes. Walter Harrison, the government whip on the committee, told Crossman, 'That very often happens. Senior Ministers make it too political and we don't like them to come. It's easier for us to have the number two's and to get into a quiet routine, just plugging along and reading the briefs.'[10] Governments know the utility of the humdrum. In a Standing Committee, debate and argument waste time. The work is detailed and laborious. Hence, it is perfectly understandable that, in the words of a senior civil servant, 'junior ministers do virtually all the donkey work.'

Junior ministers also relieve their chiefs by taking as a matter of routine certain classes of parliamentary business such as MPs' correspondence, adjournment debates and written questions. These tasks may be the small change of parliamentary life, but without the assistance of junior ministers, Cabinet ministers would be hopelessly overloaded by them.

Junior ministers answer the bulk of letters sent in torrents by MPs to departments, and deal with the related casework. Philip Norton has calculated that between 3,000 and 16,000 letters a week go from MPs to ministers, mostly on constituents' problems, but also on questions of policy. The Home Office, the Department of Health and Social Security and the Department of the Environment receive most parliamentary mail – these are departments which directly affect the daily lives of MPs' constituents. In 1970 the Department of Health and Social Security was dealing with 15,000 letters a year from MPs to ministers; by 1975 that had risen to 25,000 a year; Norton found that the department received over 2,000 a month in 1979–80, with the weekly figure rarely being less than 500. Most of those letters concerned social security problems. The Home Office receives many letters from MPs on immigration, police and prisons. In 1982 about 13,000 letters were sent on immigration, with

1,243 sent to the relevant minister of state alone in July 1979. MPs also make representations to the Home Office, often telephoning the minister of state's private office, after visitors to the UK have been refused entry: in 1982 there were 1,000 cases of this nature, which had risen to 5,700 in 1985, and it was estimated that the number would exceed 7,000 in 1986. In contrast, other departments have much lighter loads. A Foreign Office minister of state told Norton that he received only four or five letters from MPs each day; in the early 1970s, a Foreign Office parliamentary under-secretary reported receiving only 120 letters in four and a half months. The Civil Service Department minister of state told Norton he answered about 2,000 letters a year, mostly on pensions, recruitment and pay. The three ministers at the Welsh Office received a total of 1,137 letters in 11 months in 1980 – less than the DHSS can receive in a fortnight![11]

Historically, there has been a great increase in this volume of correspondence to ministers, reflecting an enlargement of the sphere of government activities, the greater willingness of citizens to write to their MPs and for those MPs – taking on the role of 'local ombudsman' – to pass the letters on to ministers. A Cabinet Office note of January 1949 recorded the increase in volume, over 'comparatively recent years', of letters from MPs to ministers. It seemed that before 1914 it was quite common for MPs to write direct to, and see, civil servants about constituency cases, but that it was now accepted that MPs should write to ministers and not see officials, and ministers were reluctant to allow MPs to deal directly with civil servants. The note explained that MPs considered that their cases would be considered more intelligently, speedily and perhaps more favourably than they would otherwise be. The housing division of the Ministry of Health was singled out as the target of a great many letters and complaints.[12]

The departmental responsibilities of junior ministers generally serve as signals for the direction of letters, though if one minister's load is especially burdensome, or if he or she is unavailable, other ministers will lend assistance. A DHSS junior minister described a departmental exercise, involving calculation of the volume of letters, questions and adjournment debates, which led to a redistribution of responsibilities to even out loads. Usually the secretary of state replies to letters from Privy Councillors (including Cabinet colleagues, leading Opposition figures and the Speaker) as a matter of courtesy and prudence. Occasionally, the top minister considers letters from ordinary MPs if they raise major questions or are very sensitive. Individual junior ministers at the DHSS (called 'the Department of Stealth and Total Obscurity' by one rueful minister) may see 150 letters a week pass across their desks, and can spend up to 20 hours a week on the related work. A former parliamentary under-secretary there complained, 'The letters never end. They go on and on. I never want to go back there.' Officials, often at assistant secretary rank, prepare draft replies to letters, but ministers have to read them, perhaps amend and sign them, 'which, when the letters can run to several closely argued pages about complex rules or calculations, represents a considerable expenditure of ministerial time and energy.' As a minister of state at the Department of Education, Lord Crowther-Hunt signed 300 letters a month on individual cases (not all to MPs). Two or three hours a day were spent in this way, and he felt that 'If you say "Yes" to your officials' proposals in the ceaseless flow of files into your in-tray, it can all be relatively quick and straightforward.' To amend or question a draft led to delay and more work. Reports of the workload of the Home Office junior minister responsible for immigration in 1978 mentioned that she had to work until 2.00 a.m. to do the paperwork, or else start work on it at 6.00 a.m., on top of the normal day's work.[13] The element of discretion allowed to ministers on immigration cases means that papers have to be carefully read and considered. It is not surprising that many former ministers consider this volume of casework a major constraint on policy thinking.

Dealing with MPs' letters constitutes an important part of a junior minister's apprenticeship. As a former Cabinet minister said:

> Junior ministers have a lot of correspondence with MPs. It is an important part of the job. But there is a lot of it. You must be selective – recognize the routine case and deal with it rapidly. You develop a nose for it – you recognize the exception to which to devote time and attention. I couldn't have coped with the load I carried at the DHSS if I hadn't had that knack . . . This style marks off the successful and the unsuccessful minister, the amateur and the professional politician.

Norton noted that ministers' reputations are affected by the helpfulness and sincerity of their replies, and certainly many junior ministers take enormous pains with this work: 'I'd try to see every colleague's letter when it came in, before it went into the machine, and use my personal knowledge to see his problem and suggest an answer or later amend a draft. I, as a minister, knew the individual MPs – or should. Also, I had a short list of really awkward chaps, and I'd see their letters straight away.' 'At first I didn't see MPs' letters – the draft reply was the first glimpse. So I insisted that xeroxes of all MPs' correspondence be on my desk each morning to glance through. It was useful – I could smooth things, say in the Lobby [of the House of Commons] "Oh, I've seen your letter . . ." '

Employing junior ministers to vet official replies to MPs' letters shows that the redress of individual grievances continues to be considered a proper concern of high-level government institutions and personnel. Administratively, letters may alert ministers and their officials to the practical effects of policies and to problems of which they may not otherwise become aware. The attention given to these letters also reveals the sensitivity of British government to political embarrassment. MPs' letters receive high-level attention not merely because of the merits of their cases, but because of the possibility of adjournment debates or questions tabled by dissatisfied MPs, and consequent press outcry. Junior ministers, in this light, are political filters and mollifiers – functions which civil servants could not perform – supporting their own ministerial superiors.

MPs pursuing constituency cases or, less frequently, minor policy points, who feel dissatisfied with replies to letters or questions, often attempt to raise the matters at adjournment debates, which take half an hour at the end of the day's parliamentary business, at whatever hour that is. Members ballot for the right to raise an issue on an adjournment debate, with the Speaker choosing one additional backbencher each week. Junior ministers reply to virtually all of them, making a 15 minute speech in reply to a similar length speech from the backbencher, often in the presence of the occupant of the Chair, a whip and perhaps only one or two other MPs. The late hour of the debates and the fairly narrow substantive focus point to their delegation to junior ministers. A study of adjournment debates in the 1976–7 session (chosen at random) revealed that 54 of the 141 debates ended after midnight (38.3 per cent); 24 ended only after 2 a.m. (three of which ended after 6 a.m.!). A secretary of state's life would become impossible if he or she had to appear in parliament at such hours of the night. Of the 141 debates, only three were answered by ministers other than junior ministers. Among junior ministers, parliamentary under-secretaries carried a heavier load than ministers of state; 36 were answered by 12 different ministers of state; 102 by 28 different parliamentary secretaries. As with MPs' letters, domestically orientated departments attract most adjournment debates. The Department of Health and Social Security had most, with 34 adjournment debates in that session. Altogether, the DHSS, the Department of the Environment, the Home Office, the Ministry of Transport and the Department of Education between them accounted for 98 debates, two-thirds of the total. Eight individual junior ministers took seven or more adjournment debates each, totalling 79, or 56 per cent, of all debates. Eric Deakins, parliamentary under-secretary at the DHSS held the (dubious) record for adjournment debate attendances, replying to 17, closely followed by John Horam of the Ministry of Transport with

14 debates. An adjournment debate is a face-to-face encounter with an MP who has a grievance to air. The junior minister will have to defend his department's actions or promise to investigate further and modify them. His reply is normally polite, factual and reasoned: the terse or evasive style of answers at question time would be inappropriate.

Since the mid-1960s the number of written questions has risen dramatically: averaging about 20 a day for most of this century up to the 1950s, over 50 a day by the mid-1960s, over 100 a day by the early 1970s, and 150–200 a day by the 1980s. As the number of written questions has increased, junior ministers have answered an ever-growing proportion. Behind the explosion in the number of written questions are factors such as the pressure on time available for oral questions, MPs' greater appetite for information, the use of questions to mount campaigns on particular topics and the use of research assistants to devise them and use the answers. Table 6.1 shows the greater volume of written questions between 1956 and 1986 and demonstrates that junior ministers have been used to answer most of them. One-quarter of written answers went out in the name of a junior minister in 1956, three-quarters in 1976 and five-sixths in 1986. Departments which usually face large numbers of questions for written answer are the Department of the Environment, Department of Health and Social Security, Home Office, Department of Education and the Scottish Office – domestic departments which also usually have substantial parliamentary work of other sorts. In the week studied in 1986, for instance, these five departments together accounted for 445 or 47.7 per cent of all written questions. It is not unusual to find a parliamentary under-secretary in the DHSS answering 40 written questions each week; some draft answers can be rapidly disposed of, others require more attention. According to Gerald Kaufman, there are civil service 'formulas' for answering some written questions, which ministers may be advised not to reject in case they set a precedent.[14] Table 6.2 makes the contrast with oral parliamentary questions, which secretaries of state are less inclined to leave to their subordinates, not least because, while MPs regard written questions as a means of gathering information and are happy to deal with the appropriate junior minister covering the subject, oral questions are seen as a party political point-scoring exercise and Opposition MPs want to 'get at' the top man. Comparing the first three months of 1977 with the equivalent period in 1985 shows that the number of questions answered has declined, reflecting the growing number and the length of supplementary questions asked and the length of ministers' replies.

In these various, and perhaps unexciting, ways junior ministers perform an essential role in representing their departments in parliament.

TABLE 6.1   Written questions

One week in year	Total no. of questions	Answered by (%)		
		Departmental head	Minister of state	Parliamentary under-secretary
1956	206	72.3	8.7	18.9
1966	516	45.7	26.5	27.7
1976	933	27.3	41.6	31.1
1986	934	13.9	37.2	48.9

Figures exclude written questions answered by the prime minister, non-departmental ministers, law officers. The weeks chosen were 5–9 March 1956; 28 February–4 March 1966; 1–5 March 1976; 3–7 March 1986.

TABLE 6.2   Oral questions

Year	Total no. of questions	Answered by (%)		
		Secretary of state	Minister of state	Parliamentary under-secretary
1977	869	40.3	24.3	35.4
1985	666	35.9	30.8	33.3

Figures exclude questions answered by the prime minister, non-departmental ministers, law officers. The periods chosen were 10 January 1977–31 March 1977; 9 January 1985–28 March 1985.

They act in the name of, and on behalf of, the responsible secretary of state. They relieve the pressure on his time and energies, allowing him to concentrate on his Cabinet and departmental duties and to represent the department personally on important and politically charged occasions. Like Sherpas on Himalayan mountain expeditions, junior ministers support and sustain the headline-catching activities of leading figures by taking a load they could carry only at the cost of not achieving their ultimate goals.

Representation in the House of Lords

Governments in recent years have had two or three Cabinet ministers and seven to ten junior ministers with seats in the Lords (see table 2.1).

Departments which are usually directly represented in the Lords by junior ministers are the Foreign Office, Home Office, Scottish Office, Northern Ireland Office, Department of the Environment, Department of Education and the Ministry of Agriculture. The extra ministers appointed from the Lords by Mrs Thatcher means that only four major departments have no minister of their own in the Upper House: the Treasury, Welsh Office, Department of Energy and Department of Education (after 1981).

Each junior minister in the Lords deals with all his department's parliamentary business, and not just the subjects for which he has a special departmental responsibility. In addition, he usually speaks for one, two or three other departments. A department not represented by its own minister or junior minister employs a lord (or lady)-in-waiting (government whip) as a spokesman, assisting another department's minister designated as a spokesman for that subject too. Often, a departmental junior minister will be supported by a lord-in-waiting, who will take on some of the parliamentary work. Sometimes up to half of all government departments are represented in the Lords by combinations of lords-in-waiting and ministers from other departments, though only a handful of departments have been in this position since 1979.

Most junior ministers in the Lords face heavy loads of parliamentary work. In interview one peer said he represented in the Lords three departments (in one of which he was a junior minister) which in the Commons had a total of 11 ministers. Although he did not have eleven times the volume of parliamentary business to deal with than the other junior ministers, he still faced what he called 'a long waterfront' and spent half his time on work in parliament and preparing for it. In contrast to the procedure in the Commons, in the Lords all stages of legislation are taken on the floor of the House; there are no Standing Committees. Briefing for, and performance at, debates on legislation and general policy, statements and questions are likely to be demanding: the Lords is less partisan than the Commons, but government spokesmen are perhaps more likely to be tested on the details of their subject matter than in the Commons.

Junior ministers called upon to represent departments other than their own, and lords-in-waiting, often report that their position is unsatisfactory. An ex-minister of state said he did not enjoy the experience. 'I felt that I had enough on my plate already, apart from that as well. I had to mug it up a bit, and used to get down to it with a heavy heart. There was nothing in it for me, and a lack of cooperation from the department concerned. Civil servants there didn't go out of their way to be helpful to me.' Lords-in-waiting have no executive responsibilities within departments, no officials reporting to them, and apparently do not always have an office in the department. They usually attend the regular ministers' meeting to keep in touch with political and policy developments inside the department. A former lord-in-waiting said in interview, 'I had no influence over the drafting of things from departments I had to present – no power or authority, and no time if I had wanted to.' Another described himself as 'a mouthpiece having no control over content', but he added, 'after a year, with more experience, you might be able to say to officials that you're not happy with a particular aspect and then take it up with the minister.' In theory, spokesmen are well briefed in advance of debates, but in practice briefing often takes place at the last moment. Peers in such a position may not be able fully to satisfy questioners or other peers in debates; often, all they can do is promise to refer matters to their Rt Hon. Friend, whom they cannot commit. A peer who spoke for several departments described his experience:

> You may run into trouble with someone who presses you or who has years of experience of the subject. Then you just draw your breath and trust to your wits to take you along. You have a very good brief. You've got the details, the facts; you know the government's intentions and analysis; you've talked to ministers and officials. If the critics have a strategic advantage, you have the immediate tactical advantage in debate and that's what counts at the moment.

Peers representing the government often have light parliamentary workloads from October to December, apart from questions and a few debates. However, as Bills are passed by the Commons and come to the Lords, their work increases. The last few months of the parliamentary session, when business has to be cleared away before the summer recess, generate heavy demands on the time of junior ministers and lords-in-waiting. The Lords sits for about half the time of the Commons, for only three or four days a week at the start of a session, five towards the end, and adjourning at 8.00 or 9.00 p.m. In addition, peers have no constituencies to visit or correspond with, saving them several hours of work each week.

Departmental Ambassadors

The 'ambassadorial' role of junior ministers encompasses the following activities: attending formal social functions, receiving deputations, making visits and tours inside the UK, and visiting foreign countries and international organizations. The constitutional convention of ministerial responsibility and the political pressures of a Cabinet and parliamentary system of government constrain junior ministers, but their effectiveness in the decision-taking process is further limited by these varied and time-consuming duties.

Ministers make many appearances at luncheons, dinners and receptions organized by the government, local authorities, public organizations, embassies, and private associations and companies. Such functions may open, be fitted into or conclude more substantive occasions such as visits, negotiations or conferences. Ministers may be expected to make a speech. Bruce Headey, in his study of *British Cabinet Ministers*, noted 'the frequency with which even senior Ministers are obliged (or feel obliged) to attend . . . formal engagements. It is no exaggeration to say that one such engagement every day of the week is not unusual.' Men cannot govern on empty stomachs, but there are so many invitations to eat in the course of duty that Cabinet ministers must delegate many of these superficially attractive tasks to their junior ministers. The evidence of interviews and ministers' appointments diaries is that one formal engagement every day of the week is typical. Richard Crossman professed to hating the job of 'shaking hands at the door on behalf of the government'. He tried to give social and official engagements to his junior ministers. However, to avoid some ceremonies risks giving offence to the people or organizations involved. When Crossman's parliamentary secretary, Bob Mellish, was sent to represent the Ministry of Housing and Local Government at the annual lunch of the National House Builders' Registration Council, Crossman came in for some unfair press criticism: at the time he was in Brighton, addressing the annual dinner of the Institute of Sewage Purification! In the mid-1970s a Foreign Office minister of state would have official luncheons four days a week.[15] A Foreign Office parliamentary under-secretary admitted in interview, 'The "social" work is very time-consuming. You do your real work in the office, though occasionally you are taken to one side at a cocktail party. But, it's really just the frills. There is too much of it. You eat and drink too much, and you could spend your time more profitably.'

Junior ministers act as buffers between the public and their secretary of state. They receive a large number of deputations and delegations to save them going to the top minister. These contacts are, of course, only one aspect of the web of consultations developed between departments and their clients. Most contacts take place at official level, but ministers are likely to be involved when deputations arrive at departments to discuss legislation, new policies or major changes in programmes, or at the Treasury before the Budget. Lord Brabazon, a junior minister in the 1920s and a minister outside the (War) Cabinet 1940–2, recalled, 'If the

Minister had decided to say "yes" he would take the deputation himself, but if the answer was going to be "no" it was the [Parliamentary] Under Secretary who had to do the job.' This seems to be a standard wisecrack among former ministers, but may have an element of truth in it. More prosaically, asked in March 1986 by what criteria he met delegations or referred them to other ministers, the then Environment Secretary, Kenneth Baker, replied, 'The decision as to who should meet a particular delegation is taken according to the circumstances of each case and in the light of our respective workloads and the special responsibilities of my hon. Friends.'[16] It seems that deputations from national organizations or groups are more likely to be seen by a Cabinet minister than those from local bodies. At the Department of Education, the secretary of state usually meets the associations of education authorities, the University Grants Committee and trade unions on national issues; junior ministers usually see local authority representatives or groups concerned with individual schools or colleges. Similarly, junior ministers at the Department of the Environment generally deal with deputations from individual local authorities, though on sensitive issues such as Rate Support Grant allocations the secretary of state may also meet some delegations from local councils.

Major national deputations and groups will see the Cabinet minister in charge of the department, either because they have a direct and substantial stake in a politically significant problem or because it would be impolitic to deny them access. The Trades Union Congress and the Confederation of British Industry thus have regular contact with senior ministers. Junior ministers would be seen by them either with the secretary of state or, if alone, as a preliminary move. The authors of a major study of the CBI suggest that the group will have discussions with senior ministers on a 'crucial, wide-ranging policy', such as the general shape of a government's incomes policy, but will see junior ministers and senior civil servants if the matter being discussed is 'the outline of a more specific piece of legislation'.[17] Given the division of departmental responsibilities and the relative weight of a junior and Cabinet minister, this seems perfectly understandable. For other groups, it is clear that to include an MP or two on a deputation is to increase the chances of seeing the secretary of state rather than a junior minister because of possible follow-up action in parliament. Pressure groups and organizations thus value links with MPs and often try to include at least one in a deputation.

Departments and ministers differ in the extent to which they have contact with the public and with deputations. A minister of state in the Department of Employment said that it was not uncommon for him to receive a dozen deputations each week. In contrast, the Foreign Office in the 1970s received an average of five or six deputations which included MPs each week, met by a minister and officials.[18] Ministers who had served in the Northern Ireland Office said that deputations and even attempts to talk directly to ministers on the telephone were frequent. A parliamentary under-secretary said that people in Ulster 'treated us like county councillors'. And a former minister of state said, 'people knew your 'phone number and would ring up. Old dears would ring me at my desk. The private office tries to head off some, but it is a different machine to the British, where ministers are more protected from the public.'

Visits to departmental out-stations, local authorities, schools, factories, prisons, armed forces' bases and elsewhere fill ministerial diaries. Usually, junior ministers spend at least one full day each week on a regional visit when the Commons is sitting, more at other times. In recess, they may spend a couple of days a week on visits. Table 6.3 gives details of visits, receptions and so on from the appointments diaries of two serving junior ministers in 1986. On visits, ministers are usually accompanied by their private secretary and by an official from the relevant policy division. 'The brief covers everything', said a former minister in interview. 'One reads it the night before, or on the train or in the car going up there. The civil service are superb at that – at servicing a minister and on a visit.'

Ministry of Defence single-service parliamentary under-secretaries (1964–81) spent up to half their time on visits. A former defence secretary said, 'A big problem was finding jobs for the service ministers to do. But the services like having their own ministers, and you can have a better rota of visits and get to know people in the services.' A navy minister recalled, 'It was a fascinating job to have – one of the nicest jobs in government. I flew onto the *Ark Royal*, went up in a Harrier, went on exercises with the commandoes, was being lowered down on bits of string to land on ships all the time.' An army minister was rather proud of the fact that 'when one goes out and about, one is received in a manner not accorded to under-secretaries in other departments.' David Owen, an ex-navy minister himself, put it well: 'Some Ministers who serve in the Ministry of Defence "join up" and wholly identify with one service. The Army, Air Force and Navy have developed a system of service indoctrination for their junior Ministers which can make a Parliamentary Under Secretary for the Royal Navy feel like a First Lord of the Admiralty in the old days.'[19] The existence of single-service ministers, even if they were only parliamentary under-secretaries, symbolized and helped to reinforce already well-developed inter-service rivalries which had a deleterious effect on policy for the whole Ministry. In 1981,

TABLE 6.3   Ministerial visits and social engagements of two junior ministers in April 1986

William Waldegrave (Minister of State, Department of the Environment)

21 April	All day visit to proposed radioactive waste disposal sites – Fulbeck and South Killinghole. Evening: address local government conference, Eastbourne
22 April	Morning: visit to Oldham and Rochdale 'Groundwork' Foundation. Arrive Heathrow 2.50. Evening: dinner in the Commons, United and Cecil Club
23 April	Student lobby – House of Commons, 3.30–4.00. Evening: reception to celebrate St George's Day (Mayfair)
24 April	Lunch: City of London. Radio and press interviews: 4.30–6.00. Evening: reception for King of Spain (Spanish Embassy)
25 April	Morning: West Country visit: presentation by Farming & Wildlife Advisory Group, visit to conservation features. Pub lunch. 2.00 depart for Bristol – 5.00 constituency surgery
26 April	9.30 surgery. Lunch: address Federation of Master Builders, Western super Mare

David Trippier (Parliamentary Under-secretary, Department of Employment)

21 April	All day visit and speeches: Blackpool (National Market Traders' Federation) and Newcastle. Arrive Heathrow 5.55. Evening: dinner, British Chambers of Commerce
22 April	Evening: dinner, British Tissues
23 April	All day visit: Torquay (Business Enterprise Conference – speech) and Plymouth (Enterprise Agency). Arrive Paddington 9.29
24 April	Evening: dinner (press/trade night for launch of medieval dinners, London restaurant)
25 April	Morning: CBI conference on YTS, Manchester – speech and lunch. Afternoon: constituency canvassing. Evening: constituency – civic dinner and dance

---

following a much publicized departmental row over naval strategy and force levels, and the dismissal of the navy minister, Keith Speed, 'functional' under-secretaries replaced the service ones. Visits to service establishments continued, but it was hoped that with new patterns of responsibility junior ministers would be less tempted to press sectional service interests.

In interview, ministers and officials argued that ministerial visits provide useful opportunities to gather information and have a beneficial effect on departmental morale. Ministers are able to hear the views of organizations outside central government, can defend their policies in speeches, learn of things that otherwise may not be brought to their attention and make decisions – either on the spot or afterwards – on the basis of what they have learnt. In other words, visits are not simply public relations exercises. Executives in large private companies also spend a great deal of their time in this way. A former secretary of state said that visits 'call attention to departmental bottle-necks, oversights and failures in communication'. An Energy Department junior minister who visited 28 coal mines in two years claimed that his meetings with people working in the industry were an enormous opportunity to gather information from sources outside the department. An army minister said, 'The purpose of the visits was to see what was on the ground, what the chaps were doing, how they were – to get a feel of the state of morale, hear their grumbles about comforts (mail, leave, food), and to report back on all that to those responsible for that sort of thing.' This minister felt that he could speak with greater authority inside the department because of his knowledge of what was happening in the ranks. Inasmuch as they were not concerned with policy, procurement and overall strategy, but rather personnel cases, service morale and detailed administration, the pattern of visits undertaken by service ministers was sensible. A permanent secretary said, 'for a minister, any minister, to pass through, shake hands and so on, makes a big difference to morale.' In large and dispersed departments (for instance the social security operation of the Department of Health and Social Security or regional offices of the Department of the Environment) this activity has value as a means of increasing the coherence of the organization in addition to alerting ministers of problems and difficulties.

There is an international dimension to this work. Foreign Office ministers naturally spend much of their time abroad, negotiating agreements, consulting on policy, on 'good will' missions and so on. A recent study of the Foreign Office pointed to the advantages of this: 'ministers gain access to their opposite numbers more easily and their presence raises the stakes in negotiations.' But the drawback is that 'it inevitably means that decisions are often prepared in their absence, and at best all they can do is to race home to orchestrate presentation. Many ministers can thus become no more than tactical advisers to the foreign policy machine, taking its tablets of stone and applying a rough political cosmetic to make them more acceptable.'[20] Trade ministers also spend a great deal of time on crucial but unspectacular international trade negotiations. The Treasury, too, has interests in international financial questions which involve ministers (particularly the economic secretary among the junior ministers, though the present minister of state deals with European Economic Community business) in negotiations and conferences overseas. Denis Healey, Chancellor of the Exchequer 1974–9, has been criticized for tending to send civil servants rather than his junior ministers when he could not attend important meetings. For instance, in 1976 the permanent secretary substituted for Healey at the International Monetary Fund conference in Manila. (On the home front, Healey apparently preferred to send the second permanent secretary in charge of industrial policy, rather than a junior minister, to those sessions of the National Economic Development Council he was unable to attend.)

Then there are international organizations. In 1964 the UK's permanent representative at the United Nations, Sir Hugh Foot, was raised to the peerage as Lord Caradon, appointed a Foreign Office minister of state, and continued to be based in New York. After 1970 a Foreign Office minister of state continued to have a departmental responsibility for the UN, and to visit it regularly for meetings, but not to be based there. The European Community has embroiled 'domestic' ministers, not just Foreign Office ones, in the ceaseless round of meetings in Brussels. At the monthly meeting of the EEC's Foreign Ministers' Council, the UK is generally represented by the Foreign Office minister of state with responsibility for European affairs; other departments send ministerial representatives when their subjects are up for discussion. Ministers also attend other, specialized, councils and may even have a six-month stint as President in charge of the meetings. There are meetings with EEC commissioners and with ministers from other states, bilateral and multilateral. Of 205 trips abroad made by ministers in the year ending 30 September 1977, 117 were connected with EEC business, or nearly six out of every ten. Four departments – the Foreign Office, the Ministry of Agriculture, the Scottish Office, and the Department of Energy – accounted for four-fifths of those EEC visits. Those four departments were much more likely than others to send their secretary of state to meetings, alone or leading a delegation including one or two junior ministers, as well as officials. Other departments, to which the EEC might be considered more marginal, sent only parliamentary secretaries on their few visits (Employment, Prices, Industry, Health and Social Security, and Trade, though this department is conventionally described as having extensive EEC contacts).[21] In interview, a Cabinet minister explained why he sent his parliamentary secretary on EEC trips, despite the protests of his officials who wanted a higher ranking minister to go: 'Work in Brussels is slow and frustrating – it's hard to get and see fast results. You spend a hell of a lot of time there doing precious little, so why spend the time there?'

In the post-war period these diverse 'ambassadorial' duties have become more burdensome. As government does more and increasingly impinges on society, and the multitude of private interests and groups within it, contacts between these groups and departments have intensified. The growth of the public sector has been accompanied by the proliferation of governmental organizations outside Whitehall and complicated relations between central government and local government. Hence, for ministers, there are more deputations to receive, more visits to make and more social functions to attend, to say nothing of the more difficult decisions to take! Satisfactory measurements of the increase in 'ambassadorial' work are difficult to find. However, it is possible to measure the load of international work that ministers and junior ministers undertake because of published lists of ministerial visits abroad. Table 6.4 indicates the number of government ministers of different ranks travelling abroad at different times since 1946. It can readily be seen that, whereas in 1946 full ministers went abroad on two-thirds of the visits made by members of the government, in 1964–5 they made only half the trips, and in 1976–7 only one-third, and that the share of visits made by junior ministers changed proportionately in the opposite direction. In general, there were more visits to be made, and Cabinet ministers themselves made more visits, but junior ministers took a much greater share. It is also clear that ministers of state have undertaken more foreign trips than parliamentary under-secretaries. As noted above, some 'domestic' departments involve their ministers in a fair amount of overseas travel, not least since entry to the EEC. But it is important to remember that those departments making few or no international trips have heavy loads of home-based 'ambassadorial' work: the Department of the Environment, the Department of Health and Social Security, the Department of Education, the Department of Employment, the Department of Industry and, of course, the Welsh and Northern Ireland Offices. Foreign Office ministers accounted for nine of the trips in 1946, 32 in 1964–5, 86 in 1976–7, and eight in 1978–9. Between a quarter and two-fifths of all overseas trips made by ministers are made by Foreign Office ministers. This proportion is not surprising: the Foreign Office is the lead department for United Nations work, a central department for EEC policy and its ministers are constantly travelling abroad for negotiations and discussions. The burden of international travel on ministers has increased because of the greater number of states and international forums, the intensity of contacts between them and the ease of international air travel since 1945. Making

TABLE 6.4 Ministerial visits abroad

Year	Time	Total trips	By Cabinet minister or departmental head	By minister of state	By parliamentary under-secretary
1946	3–4 months	31	20	2	9
1964–5	8 months	133	65	42	26
1976–7	12 months	205	76	67	62
1978–9	1 month	23	7	12	4

Figures refer to numbers of ministers travelling abroad rather than to numbers of separate visits (one visit by two ministers together thus counts as two ministerial visits).
Sources: HC (1945–6) 427 c. 218–24 (w); HC (1964–5) 713 c. 55–62 (w); HC Library (1976–7) 7337; HC (1978–9) 961 c. 88–90 (w).

due allowance for differences in the home scene, the general trend of a growing workload and greater delegation of work of this type to junior ministers seems clear.

A cynical view would be that Cabinet ministers and civil servants are only too happy to employ junior ministers in all these varied 'ambassadorial' activities, particularly if – perhaps for different reasons – they do not want them involved in departmental administration and decision-taking. An alternative view would be that, in parliament and as departmental ambassadors, junior ministers perform essential ministerial roles which only secretaries of state could otherwise do, but for them to do so would be a gross misuse of their time. But junior ministers can only take some, not all, the pressure off Cabinet ministers.

To some extent, the office of minister of state was created to provide more authoritative representation for departments in which ministers had to carry out a large number of visits. It is no coincidence that the first minister of state as a junior minister (leaving aside the wartime ministers resident overseas and Lord Beaverbrook's Cabinet appointment in 1941) was in the Foreign Office, and that others soon followed in the Colonial Office, Commonwealth Relations Office, Board of Trade and Scottish Office. In interview, a minister (who had been a parliamentary secretary, minister of state and a secretary of state) said, 'There's a fair amount of visiting and waving the flag. A minister of state did that – it was a question of status, a "senior junior minister" was needed for the job. The outside world often wants that – organizations want a minister of state not a parliamentary under-secretary. If they get the latter, it can seem that they're being fobbed off with a nobody.' In contrast, a Foreign Office parliamentary under-secretary said:

Foreign diplomats want to go to the top man if they possibly can, but often they cannot, and are happy to see the junior minister. In a matter of first rate importance they will want to see the secretary of state, but on a lot of things they are perfectly happy to deal with a junior minister. On visits, most foreigners don't know the difference between a minister of state and a parliamentary under-secretary. They are happy to get a visit from a 'Foreign Office minister' or a 'junior minister'.

However, it does seem likely that the large increase in the number of ministers of state in the post-war period, and their spreading to almost all departments, does owe *something* to feelings of 'rank consciousness'. As seen in table 6.4, ministers of state make more overseas visits than their more junior colleagues, and it is significant that four out of five Foreign Office junior ministers are in fact ministers of state.

The final responsibility and authority of the secretary of state mean that organizations will want to see him on what they consider to be major issues. On the appointment of a Scottish Office minister of state in 1951, William Ross, a Labour MP and future Secretary of State for Scotland, said that deputations would not be satisfied with seeing the minister of state and would appeal to the Scottish Secretary. The minister of state would become 'a very expensive office boy in Scotland'. In less emotive language, Edward Heath admitted that this disadvantage applied to the 'giant' departments he created in 1970. He acknowledged that the second-tier ministers may not be able to make their own 'political and public position' as pressure groups and the media bypass the delegated responsibilities of the junior ministers and want to go to the secretary of state. And looking back on his time as Scottish Secretary, William Ross noted that outside groups had a 'determination . . . to see the man at the top. Seeing the Minister of State became, too often, an intermediate step in the pressure-group process. A meeting with the Secretary of State is merely delayed. Yet it gives the Secretary of State time – a commodity which with him is always in short supply.'[22]

7

Junior Ministers in the Limelight

Ask the next man in the street the names of the current Ministers of
State at the Home Office, or the Parliamentary Secretaries in the
Department of the Environment, and you'll get some blank looks.
Norman Shrapnel[1]

Until recently, most junior ministers have belonged in the broom
cupboards of Whitehall. A few individual junior ministers have achieved
public recognition, but for the most part their colleagues have been
unremarked upon. That position has been changing since 1964. The
trend towards clearly designated departmental responsibilities has meant
that, increasingly, junior ministers are known to and within relevant
'policy communities', those networks of press commentators, academics,
interest-group leaders and local authority councillors and administrators
existing around particular fields of government policy. Speaking at
conferences, making visits, receiving deputations, answering parliamentary questions and letters on individual cases, it is natural that junior
ministers will come to be identified with a particular policy or decision,
which is often rightly regarded as theirs and not that of their secretary of
state. It is clearly beneficial if 'in the public mind identifiable people . . .
replace the impossible morass of "the government".'[2] Some junior
ministers have moved even more decisively into the political limelight,
possessing distinct ministerial titles and responsibilities which have
brought them a political and public identity much better defined than
that of their peers. This chapter examines the role of three junior
ministers who have been thus favoured: the Ministers for the Arts, for
Sport and for the Disabled. These ministers are the best examples of this
phenomenon and have been the longest lasting offices of this type (the
first two dating from 1964, the third from 1974). In due course we will
note other junior ministers with similarly prominent positions.

The Minister for the Arts

Before 1964 the government's stance towards the arts was one of aloof benevolence. The Arts Council, established in 1946 under a Royal Charter, was appointed by the Chancellor and received moneys from the Treasury, but determined its own policies. The philosophy of 'arm's length government' meant that the Council was more than a conduit for the direction of public money into the arts – it, not ministers, decided priorities and allocated funds. It was a buffer between government and the arts. It was feared that a Minister for the Arts would presage a government policy and undermine the independence of the Arts Council. There was no pressure from the arts world for the creation of a ministry or minister. The idea of appointing an Arts Minister in 1964 was Harold Wilson's – it was meant as a radical gesture, a symbol of a new prime minister and a new governing style. Jennie Lee (now Baroness Lee of Asheridge), widow of Aneurin Bevan and a close friend of Wilson's, was the obvious choice for the post: she had extensive contacts in the arts world and had long been associated with Labour's arts policy. She was at first a parliamentary secretary in the Ministry of Public Building and Works, but in February 1965 moved across to the Department of Education and Science, being promoted to minister of state in 1967. Jennie Lee defined her job as to 'improve priority for the arts, to get more interest in the House [of Commons] and in the country and to get more money for the arts'. She was able to treble the grant to the Arts Council over her period of office, from £3.2 million in 1964–5 to £9.3 million in 1970–71. Her impact on expenditure was directly related to her public and political role, a result of her being in the limelight. When the Treasury was responsible for links with the Arts Council, its ministers 'were not in a position to press vigorously for larger monetary allocations or to whip up greater public support by means of speeches and personal television appearances'.[3] Jennie Lee *could* effectively evangelize. She championed the Arts Council's cause in Whitehall's annual expenditure round, approaching the prime minister directly if she felt the need; knowledge of her privileged access strengthened her position. She provided the authority and charisma to put the arts on the national political agenda.

The formal status and position of the Arts Minister has not been stable. Arts Ministers were parliamentary under-secretaries in the Department of Education 1965–7 and 1974–6, and ministers of state there 1967–70, 1973–4, 1976–9 and 1981–3. Viscount Eccles held the office in conjunction with that of Paymaster-General (non-Cabinet)

1970–3. Norman St John Stevas (1979–81) was in the Cabinet as Chancellor of the Duchy of Lancaster and was also Leader of the House of Commons. The Earl of Gowrie (1983–5) was successively Minister of State in the Privy Council Office and then in the Cabinet as Chancellor of the Duchy of Lancaster, combining the Arts portfolio with oversight of the Management and Personnel Office. And from September 1985 Richard Luce (also supervising the MPO) was Minister of State at the Privy Council Office. During the tenure of Eccles, the DES Arts and Libraries branch moved to a building in Belgrave Square, London, away from the main DES site in York House. In 1977 Arts was moved back to York House, the relocation preventing potential 'empire building' by Arts Ministers and representing a tightening of control by DES officials. Under St John Stevas the Office of Arts and Libraries had been separate from the DES, but following his departure was abolished and its staff reintegrated into the DES hierarchy, only to re-emerge as a distinct organization under Gowrie, housed in a separate building and with its own parliamentary vote.

Whatever their rank, all Arts Ministers have had to work with, through and – if necessary – around the Arts Council. Norman St John Stevas defined the minister's role in Bagehotian terms as 'the right to be consulted, the right to encourage, and the right to warn'. While accepting that it was not for him to make artistic judgements, Hugh Jenkins (Minister 1974–6) thought that the arm's length principle reduced the Arts Minister to an 'understudy Pontius Pilate'. The power to appoint and dismiss members of the Arts Council affords opportunities only for general and indirect influence. The education secretary (when the minister was based in the DES) and even the prime minister are involved in major appointments (Chairman and Vice-Chairman). In 1982 the Arts Minister, Paul Channon, opposed the sacking of Arts Council Vice-Chairman Richard Hoggart, and it was not his officials who reviewed candidates and recommended a replacement, but the education secretary's. Arts Council Chairmen are usually powerful and well-connected individuals in their own right, with access to higher-ranking ministers, including the prime minister. Sir William Rees-Mogg, Chairman since 1982, is known to enjoy the particular confidence of Mrs Thatcher, who is thought to have ensured that the Arts Council has emerged 'relatively unscathed' from public expenditure cuts.[4] In addition, the Chairmen and Secretaries-General of the Council tend to hold office far longer than individual ministers.

There are, of course, close and informal contacts between the Arts Council and the minister and his officials. The minister does not attend meetings of the Council; his officials go as non-voting observers.

Raymond Williams thought that the Arts Council was 'in the pocket' of ministers, but the position is not so simple. In March 1986 Richard Luce said that without the Arts Council to act as an intermediary between the minister and the arts, ministers would come 'under enormous pressure to reduce the funding of a theatre company that produces a controversial play'. But at times the arm's length relationship has been strained. In 1980 the minister let it be known that he was angry at not being consulted over an Arts Council decision to stop the grants to 41 of its clients. Sidestepping the Council, the minister also ordered an inquiry into the financial efficiency of the Royal Opera House and the Royal Shakespeare Company. And on a number of occasions, the government has given the Arts Council money which has been earmarked for specific projects.[5]

The Arts Minister's scope for direct action is also limited by the fact that two-thirds of public expenditure on the arts and libraries is spent by local authorities. The minister must come to terms with these bodies interposed between him and the arts world. If not, he will dissipate his energies in pointless and unsuccessful arguments. His arm's length relationship with institutions with their own powers of decision explains much of the way in which the Arts Minister operates: the tours, speeches, visits to artistic events and performances which take up so much of his time. (Hugh Jenkins made 38 visits outside London in two years.) The minister's visibility demonstrates the government's concern, can fuel demands for more money and may help influence the decisions of local authorities and the Arts Council.

Several Whitehall departments impinge on the arts. Broadcasting and the BBC are a Home Office responsibility, the film industry is dealt with by the Department of Trade and Industry, ancient monuments and historic buildings are the concern of the Department of the Environment. The writ of the Arts Minister does not run to these territories. In 1974 the minister was given a 'general co-ordinating role in relation to artistic and cultural matters' and 'an effective interest both in the work of the film industry and in ancient monuments and historic buildings'. Broadcasting was excluded, but in the other areas the minister recalled, 'I was given neither means nor authority to make my co-ordination and interest effective in any real sense of the word.' In contrast to the Minister for the Disabled, the Arts Minister did not operate through a coordinating Cabinet committee. In fact, contacts with other ministers concerned with related topics (films, sport) were only intermittent. The minister was relatively detached from the rest of the government. At the few committees he attended, Jenkins reports that most other ministers were apathetic and regarded the Arts Minister's schemes as unimportant.

When Fred Mulley became Education Secretary in 1975 he would allow Jenkins to attend committees only if he was unable to go; Jenkins had normally to prepare briefs for Mulley on arts business.[6]

When the Arts Minister was an Education Department junior minister, the education secretary was not much concerned with day-to-day arts business. He or she played a role in key Arts Council appointments and in expenditure negotiations with the Treasury. The arts do not generally raise controversial policy questions, but when they have done so, secretaries of state have had a very significant power to thwart what their Arts Minister has been doing, if they have inclined to intervene or have been roused to step in. Their role has been negative rather than positive. Jennie Lee's personal position and political connections afforded her more power than her formal rank suggested. Paul Channon, Arts Minister 1981–3, apparently had a letter from the Prime Minister guaranteeing his independence and direct access to No. 10, but was over-ruled on some important matters (such as the sacking of Richard Hoggart). Hugh Jenkins tried to run Arts as 'an autonomous republic within the Education and Science kingdom', but his controversial policies (for instance on the 'democratization' of the Arts Council) were opposed by the leaders of the Arts Council and scotched by his political superiors. His civil servants, recognizing that he was not supported by his secretary of state or the Cabinet, took important decisions direct to the education secretary and used the Whitehall grapevine to put pressure on their minister. Relations between Jenkins and Fred Mulley deteriorated to the point where they took their respective private secretaries along to meetings with each other, and disputed accounts of what had passed at them![7]

Various proposals have been made to widen the jurisdiction and enhance the status of the Arts Minister. Some reformers would place the Arts Minister in the Cabinet by adding 'and Arts' to the title of the Secretary of State for Education and Science, or by appointing a Cabinet minister responsible for the Arts and related functions (Communications and Entertainments, or Heritage and Tourism). Others would leave the existing distribution of functions between departments largely intact, and appoint a non-departmental Cabinet minister to supervise and coordinate policy for the arts, sport and leisure (or perhaps the arts and film). Such a minister would have a small staff of his own, supporting junior ministers, and would negotiate with the Treasury for funds. These proposals have many drawbacks. An Arts Minister in the Cabinet, it is feared, may not respect the integrity of independent bodies funded by his department, threatening the always fragile arm's length principle. A coordinating minister would face political and administrative obstacles to his authority. And, as Lord Redcliffe-Maud put it, it may be difficult to find 'a senior Cabinet Minister who would be happy to confine his energy and influence to such a post'.[8] Whenever the Arts Minister has been in the Cabinet the job has been 'part-time' in the sense that it has been coupled with another responsibility: Leadership of the House of Commons or supervision of the Management and Personnel Office. Cabinet appointments have also been short-lived, suggesting a lack of political will to increase the authority of the Arts Minister. The narrow focus of the Arts Minister inside Whitehall, and the existence of the Arts Council and local authorities as policy-making bodies, both inhibit the upgrading of the office to Cabinet rank and full departmental status. The arts are neither controversial enough nor the subject of such expenditure to warrant the continuous and undivided attention of a Cabinet minister and a permanent secretary. At the same time, governments have found it useful to have an Arts Minister for the sake of creating an impression of concern, radicalism and imagination, and the arts world and the Arts Council have been able to tolerate a minister who has provided a point of contact with Whitehall, fought for money and further legitimized their public position, without impinging too much on their autonomy and decisions.

The Minister for Sport

In the late 1950s pressure put on the government to give more support to sport took the form of proposals for a Sports Council, analogous to the Arts Council, to distribute increased funds, an idea endorsed at the 1959 election by both main parties. However, the Macmillan government did nothing until December 1962 when Lord Hailsham, Lord President of the Council, was named as minister with special responsibility for coordinating the sports policies of government departments, though the Ministry of Education, Ministry of Housing and Scottish Office retained executive responsibility. In 1964 Hailsham, then Hogg, became the first Secretary of State for Education, and the DES – which accounted for about two-thirds of government sports expenditure – became the focal point for sport inside Whitehall. Although Labour had promised a Sports Council and not a Sports Minister, Harold Wilson appointed Denis Howell a DES parliamentary under-secretary with responsibility for sport and schools. Like the simultaneous appointment of an Arts Minister, the post was the result of the new prime minister's desire to make imaginative gestures in policy and government structure, giving priority to subjects which had been neglected in the past. Again like Arts, there was the availability of a suitable politician, Denis Howell, an ex-First Division football referee, with a background in local government. Unlike the Arts Minister, the Minister for Sport has always been a junior minister: a DES parliamentary under-secretary 1964–9, a minister of state at the Ministry of Housing and Local Government 1969–70 (the transfer from DES reflecting the substantial local authority role in sport), an Environment Department parliamentary under-secretary 1970–4 and since 1979, and a DOE minister of state 1974–9. If the rank of the Sports Minister is taken as a measure of government commitment, Conservative governments seem to give sport a lower priority than the arts, and a lower one than Labour governments do.

It seems that in 1964 Labour had planned an executive Sports Council, but as that would have required legislation (for which no time could be found) it instead established an advisory Sports Council, appointed by the education secretary and chaired by the Sports Minister. The Sports Council had neither the independence nor the authority of the Arts Council; it had no responsibility for the distribution of money (controlled by the DES and Scottish Office). The Sports Minister was more than a point of access to the government. As one close observer put it, Denis Howell 'found it convenient, congenial, and politically advantageous to be in the chair, to be "The Boss", making sure that he got what he wanted, providing the money and determining the priorities.' In Opposition before 1970, the Conservatives pledged to make the Sports Council, not the minister, responsible for determining policy and allocating funds. Whitehall officials also wanted an arm's length relationship, with an independent Sports Council and the minister disengaged from the detailed running of sport. A Royal Charter, granted in 1972, ensured the independence of the Sports Council and prevented the minister from playing the executive role Howell had favoured in the 1960s. As Howell himself said in 1975, 'As soon as the Tories got in they changed the whole thing . . . and I haven't had the same control since.' One of Howell's successors, (Sir) Hector Monro, Sports Minister 1979–81, gave his view of the job: 'The Sports Council should be given the cash and allowed to get on with the job. Obviously it will be for me to maintain close links with the Council and act as the channel through to Cabinet.'[9] The minister apparently has regular meetings with the Sports Council's Chairman. He goes to some, but not all, meetings of the Sports Council, depending on whether they can be fitted into his diary; his position in this respect is quite different from that of the Arts Minister and the Arts Council. He receives the papers and minutes of the Sports Council's meetings, and his officials always attend and report back.

In addition to the Sports Council, local authorities interpose between the minister and sports programmes; they account for about 80 per cent of relevant public spending. This institutional context explains why the Sports Minister has a pronounced 'ambassadorial' role. Howell admitted, 'I am a preacher . . . I rush around the country giving sermons.'[10] Visits to sports facilities, conferences and events (in Britain and abroad) help the minister to influence those bodies with decision-taking powers, in addition to demonstrating the government's commitment to sport. Like the Arts Minister, the Sports Minister is a long way from the grass roots, and must enlist the cooperation of institutions beyond Whitehall to achieve his goals.

Inside Whitehall, other departments' responsibilities relate to sport, chiefly the Department of Education, the Scottish and Welsh Offices (these have their own Sports Councils and Arts Councils) and the Department of Employment (tourism, formerly a Trade responsibility). In 1974 the Department of the Environment was given 'a leading responsibility' for the coordination of active recreation policies, to be exercised by the minister 'for Sport and Recreation'.[11] However, the distribution of functions between departments was not altered, and while the minister would liaise with other ministers, there was no coordinating Cabinet committee for sport and recreation. Any contacts the Sports Minister had with other ministers were issue-specific and intermittent, rather than through a continuing process of policy coordination. Sport in general is peripheral to the interests and preoccupations of senior Cabinet ministers. As long as it is run smoothly and without political repercussions under the junior minister, more senior figures will not be impelled to intervene. They do so only in major crises (e.g. the South African cricket tour 1970, the Olympic boycott 1980) or on issues which have aroused acute public controversy (football hooliganism), and where the question has wider political implications beyond the sports world.

The Sports Minister has always been a 'part-time' minister. At Education in the 1960s Howell devoted about half his time to sports business and the rest to his educational responsibilities. Eldon Griffiths, Sports Minister 1970–4, apparently had responsibilities within the DOE for the environment, pollution and aspects of transport, planning and housing. He told a House of Lords Select Committee that 99.7 per cent of his time was devoted to his DOE work, the rest to sport.[12] In the 1974–9 government, Howell dealt with countryside matters, ancient monuments, pollution and the environment, and water resources in addition to sport. After 1979, Conservative Sports Ministers spent less than half their time on sport, also dealing with a range of other DOE business. In 1986, for instance, Richard Tracey is responsible for sport and recreation and designated as assisting Lord Elton (Minister of State) on planning and regional affairs, new towns, the implementation of the 1985 Local Government Act, historic buildings, ancient monuments, royal parks and palaces, and gypsies.

Apart from budgetary allocations and top-level Sports Council appointments, secretaries of state at either the DES or DOE have not been persistently or intimately involved in sports questions. It seems that Sports Ministers would occasionally deal direct with the Treasury over funds for specific projects, but the overall sports budget was a matter for agreement within the DOE (or DES earlier) after the secretary of state had negotiated with the Treasury in the annual public expenditure round. A former Conservative Sports Minister said in interview, 'Sport cropped up with the secretary of state when I raised it or not at all.' On day-to-day sports matters, Sports Ministers have been given a free hand. The Environment Department's Sports and Recreation division is headed by an under-secretary. Relations with officials have been coloured by the political and personal relationship between the minister and his secretary of state. The minister just quoted said on this point, 'They saw that I would have my own way; that I had made arrangements with my superiors on how we would do it.' Denis Howell was Minister for Sport for 11 years, building up experience and political contacts which greatly strengthened him in relation to officials. But Howell's career suffered as a result. An ambitious politician, knowing his way round the Labour Movement, he was, in a sense, trapped in a political ghetto. One of his ministerial colleagues said of him in 1978, 'He was an obvious choice for the job thirteen years ago . . . But there was a time when he should have said to Wilson "I won't do the job any more." He's almost a person you can't take seriously in a higher dimension after all those years with Sport, but he could be a very useful member of the Cabinet.'[13]

Proposals for a Cabinet-ranking Minister for Sport raises problems analogous to those for the Arts. The idea of the 1972–3 House of Lords Select Committee for a non-departmental coordinating minister runs up against the difficulties of a minister with limited administrative backing coordinating departments and ministers which have kept day-to-day control of budgets and programmes.[14] Denis Howell's well-known desire for a Department of Leisure Resources, controlling sport, arts and tourism, faces strong countervailing forces in the sports world, among local authorities and inside Whitehall. The junior ministerial status and limited executive power of the Sports Minister can be justified by the roles played by the Sports Council and local authorities, and are unlikely to be modified in the foreseeable future.

The Minister for the Disabled

It was not until the mid-1960s that the disabled were identified as a community of clients of government programmes. Until then they had been marginal to the public debate about welfare policies and, apart from wartime and industrial injuries pensions, neglected by government. In the 1960s groups were formed to campaign on their behalf, and the disabled became more self-conscious and demanding of government. Community concern and pressures fuelled political initiatives which culminated in the enactment of the Chronically Sick and Disabled Persons Act of 1970 (CSDPA). This private member's measure codified and strengthened legislation affecting the disabled, but also demonstrated the weakness of government organization in this area of policy. The basic problem was how to articulate programmes for the disabled as a client group within a government machine organized along functional lines. Departmental responsibilities for the disabled were diffuse: the CSDPA impinged on 11 Whitehall departments. This fragmentation had inhibited policy initiatives. During the debates on the CSDPA, one MP, taking the Minister for Sport as a precedent, called for a Minister for the Disabled, and in the Lords there were proposals for a coordinating division inside the Department of Health and Social Security. But the government argued that no special ministerial appointment or organizational reconstruction was necessary to ensure that the needs and interests of the disabled were not overlooked or given the special attention they were now acknowledged to require.[15]

In Opposition 1970–4, the Labour Health and Social Security team included Alf Morris, the CSDPA's sponsor, as a junior Shadow spokesman for the disabled. In 1971 Morris called for the appointment of a senior non-departmental minister to coordinate departmental responsibilities for the disabled. The Conservative government's Secretary of State for Health, Sir Keith Joseph, opposed the appointment of a Minister for the Disabled, and other ministers and officials objected to dividing responsibilities on the basis of client groups for fear of blurring and confusing departmental responsibilities, and arousing expectations which could not be fulfilled. At the February 1974 election all parties promised increased help for the disabled. Forming his government in March 1974, Harold Wilson appointed Alf Morris Minister for the Disabled, with the rank of a parliamentary under-secretary in the Department of Health and Social Security. Wilson's personal commitment to policy initiatives for the disabled, and his penchant for appointing junior ministers with special titles and responsibilities, were vital factors in the emergence of the new minister. Wilson thought that his appointment of an Arts Minister and a Sports Minister 'had contributed greatly to the quality of life in Britain'. Between 1963–4 and 1970–71 public spending on the arts had almost trebled and on sports it had doubled.[16] Within the constraints of government expenditure, Alf Morris's appointment was clearly intended to have similar consequences.

The Minister for the Disabled, through the administration of cash benefits, was more directly connected to programme implementation than the Ministers for the Arts and for Sport. The arm's length principle affected him in the administration of services for the disabled, chiefly provided by local authorities. In general, local authority service provision, both before and after the 1970 CSDPA and the appointment of a Minister for the Disabled in 1974, has been geographically uneven and patchy. Alf Morris said, on his appointment, that he wanted to reduce disparities in the levels of service provision, subject to resource availability, but had only limited success in this respect. The minister could try to encourage, persuade and influence local authorities by receiving deputations, making speeches and visits, holding conferences, and seeking to have the disabled included on local authority circulars. The minister's educative role was very important. He could publicize the plight of the disabled and signal government concern: changing public attitudes was as important as changing public policies. The minister had several meetings each week with disabled people and their organized lobbies. Information and opinion could be exchanged and publicity generated. In 1975 and 1976 weekend conferences at Sunningdale brought together a wide variety of government departments and organized interests to discuss problems of disablement policy. Special campaigns and committees were established, for instance the Jubilee Year Committee (1977) on disabled mobility and activities, the Snowden Committee on access to buildings and the integration of the disabled into society, and – after Morris had left office – the 1981 International Year of the Disabled. These galvanized action and could be guaranteed to call for more spending by government. The minister was a 'gatekeeper', affording a route of access to government for the disabled and their lobbies. One close observer commented, 'Alf Morris was marvellous at that sort of thing: letting people know how to deal with government, where to go, when, who to see, and so on – showing them the way in.'

From the outset the minister was intended to have a trans-departmental role. Within the DHSS the relevant aspects of policy were dealt with by different branches of a large and heterogeneous department. Across government the principal departments participating in the formulation and implementation of disablement policy were the Treasury (cash benefits and other expenditure), Department of the Environment (housing, access to public buildings), Education (education of disabled children), Transport (special vehicles), Employment (training and work), and the Scottish, Welsh and Home Offices. Morris was, officially, 'available for consultation' by other departments and 'concerned with all matters affecting disablement . . . even though they are the direct responsibilities of other Ministers'. The main instrument of coordination was a Cabinet committee, the Disablement Committee, chaired by Morris and including ministers and officials from interested departments. As one commentator wrote, this committee was 'an indication of the importance attached by the Prime Minister to the problems of disabled people . . . the appointment of a Minister can always be regarded as a public relations gesture. But a Cabinet committee . . . is an instrument for getting things done . . .'[17] As a policy subject, disablement gave rise to more transdepartmental problems than either the arts or sport, so the minister had, of necessity, a more significant coordinating role in Whitehall than his counterparts.

The Cabinet committee was effective in stimulating and facilitating measures for the disabled. Other ministers and departments were made aware of the implications of their policies for the disabled and could make adjustments, and the committee offered a forum for the minister to introduce his ideas and concerns. To the extent that initiatives in disablement policy came from the Education Department, Department of the Environment, Department of Employment and Home Office, as well as from the DHSS base of the minister, the role played by the committee was valuable. However, coordination need not breed integration. The minister could agitate and secure action from other departments, but policies and programmes remained fragmented and partial, not integrated and comprehensive. There were policies for the disabled, not a disablement policy. The minister was successful in increasing expenditure on the disabled: DHSS spending (cash benefits and central services) rising from £482.6 million in 1973–4 to £1,622 million in 1978–9.[18] The minister dealt with the Treasury mostly through his secretary of state at the DHSS, who he would often accompany at meetings with Treasury ministers. Within the DHSS, the secretary of state settled expenditure priorities.

During the 1974–9 Labour government, the Minister for the Disabled was a DHSS parliamentary under-secretary. The 1979 Conservative government upgraded the post, but linked it to a wider responsibility, appointing a DHSS Minister of State for Social Security and Disablement. The Disablement Committee of the Cabinet was discontinued. The 'Minister for the Disabled' then became very much a 'part-time' minister, spending no more than one-third of his time on disablement questions. He corresponded with other ministers and departments and met informally with other junior ministers on particular issues; his coordinating role was thus diluted. However, in interview both Labour and Conservative former DHSS ministers said that this change was not very significant as the minister's workload before 1979 had not justified a full-time appointment. In the view of some, Alf Morris's distinctive contribution was more to do with his 'ambassadorial' and publicity skills than the working out of policy schemes with officials or dealing with day-to-day administrative problems. But it can be argued that in the 1970s the disabled needed such a gifted publicist. It is clear that Morris may have been the figurehead of the disablement policy field, but he was not its prime mover. He was defeated on a number of key issues. For instance, in 1974 he favoured providing special cars for the immobile disabled, but DHSS officials and Professor Brian Abel-Smith, Barbara Castle's special adviser, preferred cash benefits, and won the day.[19] After 1979 a hostile economic climate acted as a fundamental and restrictive influence on policy developments.

Alf Morris's isolated call for a senior non-departmental minister to coordinate disablement policy has not been repeated. In contrast to the arts and sport, there has been no proposal for a Cabinet minister and department to run all programmes connected with the disabled. Such a department would be too small to command the services of a politically senior minister and would not carry much weight in Whitehall. The Minister for the Disabled as a junior minister has performed a useful role evangelizing for the disabled, and supplying an angle of vision to supplement rather than replace the primary functional organization of government.

Other Ministers in the Limelight

Junior ministers have moved into the limelight for a number of reasons. Appointing junior ministers with distinct ministerial titles and clear areas of responsibility allows the government to signal that it regards a particular policy subject as important, whilst avoiding major upheavals in the machinery of government (which impose heavy administrative costs). This can happen not only immediately after a general election – the 'new broom' effect as seen with the appointment of the Arts and Sports Ministers in 1964 and the Minister for the Disabled in 1974 – but also at other points on the political/election cycle (the Minister for Information Technology was appointed in January 1981, for instance).[20]

These sort of appointments are often a response to lobbying from interested groups, with the minister then subsequently acting as a 'door-keeper', channelling access to Whitehall. A former Cabinet minister said bluntly in interview, 'It is important that groups outside have identifiable ministers.' And a senior civil servant commented on the appointment of Alf Morris as Disablement Minister: 'It was his label. All the lobbies and organizations had their man in as a spokesman.' Additionally, these ministers have been concerned with subjects generating too little work to command the time and attention of a Cabinet minister, and too narrow in focus for any senior and ambitious politician to want to be confined there for long. Neither have they been sufficiently complex or weighty to command the full-time attention of a permanent secretary. Usually assistant and under-secretaries, and occasionally deputy secretaries, have been the most senior officials working with the relevant ministers. Top ministers and officials have taken up only isolated issues which have broken through to their level because of the implications for wider policy or because of their politically charged nature. It is wrong to dismiss these ministers are mere public relations gimmicks. A former Cabinet minister said in interview, 'Ministers like those were a Wilson fad for ministers for everything who had no clear job or real function. A minister needs a ministry. These ministers are rather meaningless figures. They just sit there, encouraging something without really achieving anything.' In their defence, though, one can point to the increased expenditure secured through their championing of their clients; their liaison work with organizations at arm's length from Whitehall, local authorities and interest groups, helping keep the government in touch with problems and views outside; and the consolidation of responsibilities within Whitehall achieved under them, even though only the Disablement Minister had a significant inter-departmental role. Moreover, from time to time other junior ministers have come to play a similar role in the political limelight.

The Minister for Overseas Development, now a minister of state in the Foreign Office, can be considered a minister of this type. This post has in fact a chequered history. Before 1964 Whitehall's organization for purposes of overseas aid was 'dispersed, if not muddled'. Financial assistance was provided by six different departments. Technical assistance was brought under the Department of Technical Cooperation in 1961. The Secretary for Technical Cooperation was, like the earlier Ministers for Mines and Overseas Trade (see chapter 1), in day-to-day charge of his small department, but beholden to superior ministers for policy directions. The Secretaries of State for Foreign Affairs, Colonies and Commonwealth Relations were responsible for matters of general policy, but the Secretary (who was paid and classed as a minister of state) had his own statutory powers to coordinate, promote and carry out technical assistance programmes. At this time, the objectives of aid policies were still unclear, and the aid lobby only embryonic – hence the government's haphazard arrangements. Additionally, representing the first tentative step towards the eventual merger of the Foreign, Colonial and Commonwealth Offices, there was much to be said for piecemeal adaptations. At the same time, not being directly under these major departments would help defuse potential opposition to 'neo-colonialism'. Before the 1964 election, the Secretary for Technical Cooperation was suggesting that his department's scope be widened to encompass all forms of aid, but still to be concerned with the management rather than the formulation of aid policy, which would be left to the relevant Cabinet ministers.[21]

The 1964 Labour government included a Minister for Overseas Development in the Cabinet. This was a major achievement for the aid lobby in the party and outside in the voluntary organizations. The aid lobby rejected any subordination of aid policy to Foreign Office diplomatic policies, and so the status of the department and its ministerial head became important indicators of the priority given to aid. Under Barbara Castle (1964–5) the political commitment was high, but after 1967 the minister was no longer in the Cabinet and the aid programme experienced cut-backs. In 1970 overseas aid became the ultimate responsibility of the foreign secretary, with a Foreign Office minister of state designated as having charge of the aid wing, called the Overseas Development Administration, which was housed separately from the rest of the Foreign Office and retained its own representation on some ministerial and official committees. During the 1974–9 Labour government, Overseas Development again became a separate Ministry (the minister sitting in the Cabinet 1975–6), but in 1979 it was reintegrated into the Foreign Office. One observer of foreign policy-making in Britain considered that these changes in the department's and minister's formal status affected the pattern of aid policy-making 'relatively little'. The failure of Overseas Development to maintain a fully independent and Cabinet position is due to a lack of sustained political support and to the opposition of other departments, reflecting the fact that development has not been able to override other foreign policy objectives.[22] Designating a Foreign Office junior minister as responsible for aid thus seems the most sensible and defensible arrangement.

Consumer affairs is another policy area downgraded from Cabinet to junior ministerial level. A Cabinet minister and a department had been responsible for Prices and Consumer Protection 1974–9. In 1979 the Conservative government abolished the department, but appointed a Minister of State for Consumer Affairs in the Department of Trade.

When the incumbent, Mrs Sally Oppenheim resigned in February 1982 she was not immediately replaced. The failure of the government to retain the post was criticized by consumer groups, which were active behind the scenes lobbying for a new ministerial appointment. They argued that it could be an electoral handicap not to have a Consumers' Minister, and that 'it is better to have a focus for consumer anxieties, even if the Minister has a narrow brief and low status within the government, than to have no focus at all.'[23] Dr Gerard Vaughan was moved across from the Department of Health to become Minister of State for Consumer Affairs in March 1982. For consumers' groups the minister's importance was as a route of entry to Whitehall and to symbolize the government's attention to consumer problems. Following the 1983 election, the post of Minister for Corporate and Consumer Affairs was downgraded still further to that of a parliamentary under-secretary; the minister's responsibilities and rank had changed, but the government remained anxious to retain his title.

The post of Minister for Information Technology (IT) was created in January 1981 as a result of the chivvying of one MP, Kenneth Baker, who in 1980 had proposed to the then Industry Secretary, Sir Keith Joseph, a ten-point programme to promote IT. His scheme accorded with the government's desire to make a public signal of commitment to what it regarded as this increasingly important area of industrial policy. Baker, formally a minister of state in the Department of Industry, thus became the world's first IT Minister. One of his aims was to coordinate policies in the department and he held weekly 'prayer meetings' (the IT Action Group) of senior civil servants from divisions dealing with aspects of IT policy. Baker also tried to raise public awareness of IT, using familiar techniques of speeches and conferences to promote the Information Technology Year, 1982. Meetings with ministers from other departments were essential, for IT posed complex inter-departmental problems. Fourteen Whitehall departments have an interest in IT, prominent among them being the Ministry of Defence, the Department of Employment, the Department of Education, the Department of Health and Social Security and the Home Office. In his three years in office Baker quadrupled the funding for IT research and development, helped by pressure from outside groups and a climate of opinion (which he helped to focus) holding that IT was a key to the future economic health of the country. However, although the minister's frenetic activity helped to raise the prominence of IT policy, the most recent study of this policy field suggests that he had a less dramatic impact on policy content. The domestic IT industry remains small and has a falling share of the market. While individual programmes have some merits, there has been no overall coordinated government IT strategy, chiefly because of the constraints of Whitehall's fragmented organization and the nature of the administrative culture and policy style (co-opting private companies and research bodies already in the field) prevalent at the centre of government. Under Baker's successor, Geoffrey Pattie, government subsidies for the IT industry were actually reduced, showing that Britain may have an IT Minister but lacks a coherent IT policy.[24]

While IT policy may be in a rut, the original IT Minister has prospered, showing the way in which able and ambitious ministers can use posts of this type to further their careers. Baker had been Heath's PPS and campaign manager in the 1975 Conservative Leadership battle, and was denied a post in 1979. After being, at least in ministerial terms, a success in the IT job, he was transferred sideways to support the beleagured Environment Secretary, Patrick Jenkin, in 1984, steering through the Commons the Bill to abolish the Greater London Council and the Metropolitan councils. In 1985 he entered the Cabinet as Environment Secretary after Jenkin was sacked, and in 1986 succeeded Sir Keith Joseph in the Education Department hot seat. In just five years he had moved from the backbenches to one of the most crucial Cabinet posts and has been talked of as a possible future party Leader.

The periodic designation of Denis Howell, Minister of Sport 1974–9, as unofficial 'Minister for the Weather' is an example of coordinating and 'ambassadorial' roles coming together. During the drought of August to September 1976 and the wintry blizzards of February 1978 and January 1979, Howell was named as emergency coordinating minister, as a focus for information and decision where responsibility was divided between departments and between central and local government. His flair for press relations, experience with water issues as a Birmingham councillor in the 1950s and his departmental responsibilities for water resources suggested him in 1976. Once established, the practice of appointing him to head working parties of officials from responsible departments, tour affected areas (by helicopter when roads were blocked by snow) and report to the prime minister and Cabinet became the routine response to meteorological calamities, and worked well. The 'Minister for Flaps' was the subject of a 'poetical portrait' in 1978,[25] the flavour of which is well represented in the verse:

> The Minister for Drought
> Began to go about
> Extolling every means of saving water.
> To husband what we had
> A garden hose was bad,
> Or flushing lavvies when we didn't oughter.

'Let every flower die!'
Became his battle cry.
'Thrice use your washing water and your suds.'
He kept this up for weeks
Although a lot of Sikhs
Prayed once for rain, precipitating floods.

As this indicates, Howell's assignments caught the popular imagination, though the Conservative government after 1979 apparently had an ideological aversion to reacting to very bad weather in this fashion.

There are periodic calls for further ministerial appointments or assignments of this type, using existing ministers as precedents. In 1977 the Labour government, concerned that the Conservatives might seize the issue and use it against them, apparently considered the appointment of a Minister for the Family, to play a role similar to that of the Minister for the Disabled, but senior ministers were unenthusiastic, fearing that it would be an empty publicity gimmick or that the minister would interfere in their departmental business. In 1983 an all-party group of MPs urged the appointment of a Family Minister but the government did not respond.[26] Ministers for the Aged, for Children and for Women have also been mooted. They would have publicity value, liaise with pressure groups and outside organizations, including local authorities, and perhaps seek to coordinate within Whitehall. Whether problems or policy areas receive their own minister chiefly depends on political factors: the prime-minister's attitude, senior ministers' views on subjects straddling departments and the pressures of interested groups. The achievements of such ministers would doubtless be modest, but valuable all the same. Appointing junior ministers with special titles and responsibilities is a welcome development. It continues the trend, established over the past 20 or so years, of giving clear departmental responsibilities to junior ministers and allowing them a greater role in policy-making. It thus provides further opportunities for politicians to exercise authority before they reach the Cabinet, a necessary part of a minister's apprenticeship. And it helps to keep government sensitive to the views of different groups and sections of the public, as well as recognizing that policy problems do not always fit neatly into the overall organization of Whitehall.

8

Junior Ministers in Perspective

A considerable part of this book has been devoted to putting in perspective the role and careers of contemporary junior ministers by reviewing the history and development of the offices they hold. Historical analyses are a particularly fruitful way in which to approach the study of British government because of the manner in which traditional and modern elements are blended in British institutions. However, there is always the danger of academic isolationism. Students of British government can in fact learn a great deal about British institutions through comparative studies. By focusing exclusively on the peculiar governmental arrangements of a specific country, one can fail to appreciate that which may be the general experience of a number of countries. Of course, great care must be taken to allow for differences in historical and constitutional development, and social and political environments. There can be no straightforward comparisons of like with like. Nevertheless, even such brief comparisons between British junior ministers and their counterparts in other states as can be drawn here will show that the problematic position of subordinate political office-holders in Britain, and their difficulties in establishing a clear role, are not unique to this country. Comparisons also illuminate the different pathways to office that politicians typically follow in other states. The parliamentary route to ministerial office is not the only or even the main channel of executive recruitment in many states outside Britain, a point often seized upon by reformers eager to improve the performance of British institutions by changing the skills and experience of ministers and those who aspire to be ministers. Yet this laudable aim remains difficult to act on, showing that administrative and political practices cannot simply be transplanted from one system of government to another.

International Comparisons

In 1976 there were about 200 junior ministers around the world. According to Jean Blondel, they were appointed in only a minority of states: 37 countries, about one-third of the countries outside the Communist world. These posts were found in several liberal democracies: Britain, France, West Germany, Canada, Holland, Belgium, Ireland, Italy, Japan. They appeared also in India, Pakistan and almost half of the black African states (16 out of 38). In most of these states there were only a few junior ministers. In eight countries there was only one junior minister; in another six only two; others had only a handful. Only in a few countries were junior ministers found in numbers similar to those of full ministers and in most government departments. Elsewhere, the position was exceptional and found in only some departments, particular appointments reflecting special political needs or circumstances. In these cases, junior ministers did not really constitute a fully developed layer of the ministerial hierarchy, either in the sense of the distribution of authority or in terms of the organization of political careers. As Blondel puts it, 'the device of "junior ministers" . . . does not correspond to a clear-cut theory of what government should be and how it should connect with the civil service.' Even where junior ministers were appointed to assist ministers they were sometimes drawn from civil service rather than political circles, blurring the boundaries between government and the bureaucracy.[1] Britain, accounting for one-quarter of the world's junior ministers, and with more than twice as many junior as Cabinet ministers, usually with teams of three or more in each department, is thus a unique case.

Comparisons across governments are not always helped by problems of nomenclature. Ministerial titles, let alone functions and powers, vary in confusing ways. Thus in France and Belgium junior ministers are called secretaries of state, in Germany parliamentary state secretaries and in Japan parliamentary vice-ministers. Canadian junior ministers are known as parliamentary secretaries and ministers of state, but the most senior *officials* are called deputy ministers. It is also worth pointing out that in some continental countries ministers have *cabinets* of personal assistants and advisers: these are not to be confused with the Cabinet, the collective political executive, often known as the Council of Ministers.

In Canada, the office of parliamentary assistant was introduced in 1943 to relieve some of the burdens on departmental ministers. In 1959 legislation regularized this arrangement and changed the title of the position to parliamentary secretary.[2] The seven parliamentary assistants of 1943 had become 15 or 16 parliamentary secretaries by the early 1960s. Parliamentary secretaries were to be members of the House of Commons and were appointed for a term of one year, which was renewable. From 1971 their number was to correspond with the number of full ministers – now 28 – and their term of office was to be two years, which was renewable. The role of these parliamentary secretraies is not well defined; indeed, they are apparently not officially regarded as junior ministers but instead as non-ministerial assistants to ministers. The doctrine of collective ministerial responsibility is held not to bind them in the same way as it does Cabinet ministers, leaving them free to express their own views. Some have put down questions on the Order Paper and made statements in parliament as private members, but the realities of party politics and prime ministerial patronage ensure that they adhere to the government's line. Their role depends chiefly on the minister in charge of the department. A parliamentary secretary may appear in parliament to answer questions or at a committee, guiding a Bill through the House of Commons. They may stand in for the minister at public speaking engagements. They may sometimes substitute for the minister at meetings of Cabinet committees. Their departmental role is usually extremely limited. While it is common for them to receive copies of most departmental memoranda and to attend some of the meetings between the minister and officials, few are given responsibility for specific aspects of the department's business on a day-to-day basis or even for particular assignments.

As in Britain, ministers in charge of departments carry full individual responsibility to parliament, which tends to centralize decision-taking. On controversial matters, the Opposition will want to confront the minister in person, not his or her parliamentary secretary. Then, as Kathryn Randle observes, 'Ministers don't choose their own parliamentary secretaries, often have little in common with them, sense that they are actual or potential rivals for cabinet positions, and are reluctant to share their authority and the credit that goes with it.' One of the senior officials she interviewed told her that parliamentary secretaries are underemployed because 'Ministers are often paranoid about other people getting the credit for something.' And whether the minister ignores the parliamentary secretary or brings him into policy discussions and delegates authority conditions how senior officials react to him. Ministers may prefer to rely on their personal staff – executive and special assistants – who are their own appointees and whose numbers have grown rapidly. The effectiveness of parliamentary secretaries is further limited by their short average tenure, which Matheson indicates is only 1.8 years in individual departments.

Parliamentary secretaryships have been used to reward veteran party stalwarts but also to try out future Cabinet talent. Between 1943 and 1975 35.8 per cent of all parliamentary secretaries eventually reached the Cabinet. More than half of the parliamentary secretaries to the prime minister and to the Department of External Affairs and four-fifths of those in the Department of Finance reached the Cabinet, suggesting that they had more scope than their colleagues in other departments to play a real role, demonstrate their abilities and impress party leaders. As in Cabinet appointments, the representation principle has applied to the selection of parliamentary secretaries. Every Cabinet must mirror the various strands in Canadian life: the different provinces, religious/ethnic groups and economic interests must be given representation. Fear that the creation of junior ministerial positions might mean the relegation from the Cabinet of certain provinces or groups lay behind the tardy development of subordinate political offices in Canada and also the reluctance to define parliamentary secretaries as ministers at all. Thus, in practice, no province is represented by a parliamentary secretary instead of a minister at Cabinet level. Indeed, the representative principle often means that appointments are balanced within departments by selecting, for instance, an Ontario, English-speaking, Protestant parliamentary secretary to serve under a Quebec, French-speaking, Catholic minister and vice versa.

Overall, it seems that Canadian parliamentary secretaries carry much less weight than even British parliamentary under-secretaries. Many have relatively little to do. One told Matheson, 'my priorities are my constituency responsibilities, my House work and my position as parliamentary secretary, in that order.' In terms of responsibility for decision-taking, they are 40 or more years behind their British namesakes.

In 1970 the Canadian government introduced a new type of minister, the minister of state.[3] Some ministers of state have been in charge of Ministries of State – such as Science and Technology, Urban Affairs, Federal-Provincial Relations – and have played a policy-planning and coordinating role, albeit without much success. The most common kind has been the 'minister of state to assist', who have been quite definitely junior ministers. These have been assigned to assist a departmental minister with regard to a specified segment of his portfolio (although in the Department of Finance and in Transport ministers of state have been general assistants rather than designated as overseeing a particular sphere of policy). Thus ministers of state have been appointed to assist the Minister of Industry, Trade and Commerce with regard to small business, to work on the problems of multiculturalism under the

Secretary of State, to support the Minister of National Health and Welfare on matters of fitness and amateur sport, to assist the Minister of the Environment with regard to fisheries, and so on. Two junior ministers have assisted the Minister for External Relations, with the status though not the title of ministers of state. Ministers of state sit in the Cabinet which, because of the pressure to be representative, is large: Trudeau's Cabinet of 1980 had 33 members; Mulroney's in 1984 had 40, the largest number in Canadian history. Only 12–15 senior ministers sit on the key Priorities and Planning Committee, a kind of 'inner Cabinet'.

The number of ministers of state has increased. In 1980 Trudeau appointed six, in 1984 Mulroney appointed 11. A number of influences lay behind the creation and expansion of the office of minister of state to assist. First, the development of larger departments, grouping a wider range of functions and interests, has meant that there is a danger of departmental ministers being overloaded and unable to exert effective political control over officials. Ministers of state were seen as a way of redressing the departmental balance of influence in favour of political rather than bureaucratic objectives and values. Secondly, the appointment of a minister of state has often been a response to pressure from particular groups, signalling that their interests are to receive special political attention. It may be, though, that a minister of state can only demonstrate sympathy and concern rather than 'deliver' on greater expenditure and policy initiatives; the Minister of State for Youth was a good example of this type of gesture politics. Then there are the prime minister's patronage calculations, including the need to accommodate demands for office and to train promising individuals for major posts. Half of Mulroney's ministers of state were from Quebec, with little or no previous political experience, who were thus placed in these junior Cabinet slots as an apprenticeship.

According to Chenier, ministers of state are 'constrained by the bureaucracy, often mistrusted and ignored by the senior minister, unsure of a mandate and lacking in resources'. Legally, it is clear that they exercise the minister's authority, not their own; political and personal relationships are thus of crucial importance. Mulroney apparently encouraged his ministers to discuss with their ministers of state the role the junior minister should play and put agreements in writing for the prime minister's approval. Ministers of state work closely with officials dealing with their subjects in the department and with the deputy minister. Civil servants have in practice a dual responsibility: often the minister of state's sphere is not self-contained and the same officials also work to the top minister on certain issues. The deputy minister's prime loyalty must be to the minister in charge of the department rather than to the minister of state. Where relatively autonomous functions can be identified (for instance, Fitness and Amateur Sport, the Wheat Board) the minister of state can play an effective role, but where his responsibilities are broad and diffuse, he experiences structural as much as political constraints.

In Canada ministers must be parliamentarians but there is less emphasis on a lengthy backbench apprenticeship than in Britain. Half of all Liberal Cabinet ministers 1921–70 had less than five years parliamentary experience and a third less than one year. Junior non-Cabinet posts are only one of several routes into the Cabinet: of the 28 ministers in Trudeau's 1974 Cabinet, only 16 had been parliamentary secretaries. Liberal prime ministers often appoint 'extra-parliamentary notables' such as provincial premiers, civil servants and businessmen, who are then found seats. Canada's political elite is thus more open than Britain's to a wide range of experiences and skills.[4]

In the Federal Republic of Germany junior ministers date only from 1967, with the creation of the office of parliamentary state secretary (*parliamentarischer Staatssekretär*).[5] This partly reflected the fact that the demand for ministerial office exceeded its supply when the 'Grand Coalition' between the SPD and the CDU/CSU was formed in 1966. After 1969, when one of the two main parties has been in government along with the smaller FDP, coalition bargaining has sometimes meant that a department's minister and parliamentary state secretary are drawn from different parties. Partly, too, the establishment of these posts was intended to furnish a ministerial apprenticeship for younger politicians angling for Cabinet appointments. And finally it was hoped that these junior ministers would support their departmental chiefs in their political roles.

As is the case with their British equivalents, the role of West German junior ministers in practice depends significantly on their relations with their minister and the department to which they are appointed. Nevil Johnson describes them as operating in 'a twilight zone', constrained because their role is not well defined in a system which strongly emphasizes legal definition of relationships and powers. In the *Bundestag* parliamentary state secretaries make frequent appearances to answer for their department at question time and to speak in plenary debates; they also attend sessions of the specialized parliamentary committees which scrutinize legislative proposals and general departmental policies. Ministers have traditionally been assisted by their state secretaries – equivalent to the British permanent secretaries – in the conduct of parliamentary business, senior officials thus playing a more openly 'political' role than could be conceivable in Britain, but the parliamentary state secretaries have taken over more of this work from them. Junior ministers have also assisted their ministers by helping to maintain contact with the different party groups supporting the government, and by substituting for them at meetings of the Cabinet and its committees, at which official state secretaries may also appear. Inside the department, the official rather than the parliamentary state secretary functions as the minister's deputy. The top political officials (*politische Beamte*) are appointed directly by ministers and must be in a relation of trust to them, being liable to displacement on political grounds. This system provides for ministers a combination of administrative expertise, substantive knowledge of policy fields and a degree of political commitment to their basic objectives. Parliamentary state secretaries may supervise particular divisions or sections of the department's work, but ministers inevitably rely much more on their senior bureaucratic aides in the process of policy-making. Junior ministers have no definite position in the administrative chain-of-command.

In West Germany, although ministers are professional party and parliamentary politicians, they are more likely to have a background of specialist knowledge or relevant executive experience than in Britain. It is often noted that about 40 per cent of German MPs are public servants, but a large proportion of these are teachers or university professors and perhaps only one-third come from the higher civil service. However, it would be more accurate to describe them as former officials, for by the time they become MPs or enter ministerial office they have spent many years in full-time political activity, usually starting with elected office at local authority level or in a provincial (*Land*) government. But political executives are not moulded by the generalist tradition still dominant in Britain. Page noted, for instance, a tendency to recruit parliamentarians with specialist knowledge for junior minister posts related to that specialism, but Johnson is right to point out that the 'specialist minister' is now almost invariably a 'parliamentary specialist'. Aspiring ministers' subject specialism *is* developed in a parliamentary context, but in a parliament that gives priority to expert investigation in specialized committees rather than to general debate on the floor of the chamber. Arguably, this means that West German politicians are better prepared for ministerial office by their parliamentary apprenticeship than are their British counterparts.

In the Fifth French Republic junior ministers go by the title of secretaries of state (*secrétaires d'état*), though they were known as under-secretaries in the Third Republic and both designations were used in the Fourth Republic.[6] The number of junior ministers in de Gaulle's first government was between four and ten, but more were appointed by his successors. In 1978, for instance, the government, under the prime minister, was composed of 19 full ministers and 18 secretaries of state. Two of those junior ministers headed independent Secretariats (minor departments) for Posts and for War Veterans; the others took on specific aspects of the work of their ministries on behalf of the minister rather than being general assistants with miscellaneous duties. All full ministers attend the Council of Ministers, which is chaired by the president, secretaries of state attending only if invited for particular items on the agenda concerning their responsibilities. When de Gaulle was President junior ministers apparently attended meetings of the Council of Ministers on a regular basis, and Pompidou adopted this practice for some periods of his presidency. After 1974, to compensate for their absence from the Council of Ministers, Giscard d'Estaing arranged for his junior ministers to be briefed regularly on its discussions by a senior minister.

According to the constitution, ministers are proposed by the prime minister to the president, who formally appoints them. In practice, before 1986, the president had a decisive say in the selection of ministers and the allocation of posts. Appointments reflected the president's priorities: thus in 1974 Giscard d'Estaing appointed junior ministers for penal reform, feminine affairs and immigrant affairs, areas of policy where he planned reforms. In 1976 he appointed a junior minister for industrial affairs without consulting the prime minister at all. However, in 1986 when – for the first time in the history of the Fifth Republic – the prime minister came from the opposing party to the president, as a result of the electoral defeat of the Socialist government, ministerial appointments were decided by the prime minister, with the president reputedly vetoing one nominee for the post of foreign minister but being obliged to acquiesce in some other selections he disliked. The chief constraint on the prime minister's freedom of choice then became the need to bargain with his coalition partners.

As is well known, a crucial role in the French political-administrative system is played by ministerial *cabinets*. These number between ten and 20 staff in the *cabinets* of full ministers, and five to ten for junior ministers; their membership is drawn predominantly from the elite of the higher civil service. Their role is to act as ministerial advisers, as extra eyes, ears, arms and legs in the ministry, and to link with other ministers and the prime minister's and president's staffs. The existence of *cabinets* affects the role of junior ministers. For instance, ministers do attend, though are not members of, the National Assembly to participate in debates on legislation and to answer questions, but junior ministers do not seem to have such a significant parliamentary role as in Britain partly because the National Assembly has a more limited role than the House of Commons, and has shorter sessions, but also because the top minister's *cabinet* handles important aspects of legislative business, such as contacts and negotiations with deputies. The relations between junior ministers and the minister's *cabinet* are potentially fraught with tension. Some junior ministers have apparently complained of a lack of contact with their minister who is shielded by his *cabinet*. Vincent Wright has given examples of several well-publicized disputes between junior ministers and their chiefs, including one at the Ministry of Agriculture in 1974–5 when the minister and the secretary of state were reduced to conducting their relations by exchanging notes. Inevitably, much depends – as elsewhere – on personalities and political circumstances.

The main route to ministerial office in the Third and Fourth Republics was through parliament and especially its committees. Under the Fifth Republic, however, the road to ministerial rank has pre-eminently been through the civil service, what Dogan has called 'the mandarin ascent'. Up to 40 per cent of deputies have been civil servants (the majority being teachers) and between 41 and 65 per cent of ministers have had a civil service background. Before 1974 it was common for officials to acquire some parliamentary experience before receiving ministerial posts (when they then had to give up their seats or put them into cold storage), but Giscard d'Estaing often chose ministers with no experience in the National Assembly. Under Mitterrand the basic pattern of ministerial recruitment appeared to change little, though many more teachers were appointed at secretary of state level, reflecting their numbers among the Socialist party in parliament. As Dogan points out, the contrast in 'the recruitment, socialisation, and cast of mind' between French ministers appointed in this fashion and British ministers, formed in the House of Commons, is quite striking.

If in West Germany and France the career paths and even the division of roles between officials and ministers are blurred at the edges compared to the British position, the picture is much more confused in the United States. The institutionalized separation of powers and the appointment of a large number of political executives, penetrating deep into the administrative structures of the federal government, mean that there is no simple equivalent of the British junior minister.[7] At the top levels of the government machine are 550 or so presidential appointees in the Executive Schedules, ranging from the Cabinet secretaries heading departments, to agency directors, and the ranks of deputy secretaries, under-secretaries, deputy under-secretaries and assistant secretaries, occupying sub-Cabinet posts and often heading major divisions in departments. Beneath them are 8,000 posts in the Senior Executive

Service, of which 10 per cent can be filled by political appointments. As James Fesler has put it, 'When an administration changes, each department is more than beheaded.' This point can be easily illustrated. In the British Ministry of Defence, for instance, five ministers (the secretary of state, two ministers of state and two parliamentary under-secretaries), together with two PPSs, work with about 120 senior civil servants. In the US Defense Department, there are around 30 presidentially appointed senior staff and another 90 non-career executives, a total of about 120 political appointees, working with almost 1,300 senior bureaucrats. Thus in Washington, political appointees take on roles which in Whitehall would be performed by career civil servants, not ministers or junior ministers.

American political executives are on the whole not trained for office in the legislature. Only 6 per cent of the executives in Stanley, Mann and Doig's study of the Roosevelt to Johnson administrations had experience in Congress. Ambitious Senators and Representatives hope to secure committee chairmanships, not sub-Cabinet or Cabinet appointments. The majority of the presidential appointees studied by Stanley et al. had some previous experience in government. Twenty-nine per cent had earlier held high political positions in the same agency, 11 per cent in other agencies; 24 per cent had served at a more junior level (such as special assistant, personal aide and so on) in the same agency and 37 per cent in other agencies. In total, two-thirds had some prior administrative service before taking up their Executive Schedule appointments. According to Hugh Heclo, 'public careerists' – individuals who move around the loosely-structured career lines of Washington, combining stints in government with service on congressional staffs and in law firms, 'think tanks', with lobby groups and so on – are becoming a major source of senior political appointments. Half of President Reagan's top appointments in the winter of 1980–1 had held subordinate posts in previous administrations. To some extent, then, there is some sort of career ladder in the American system, but it is not so orderly as the British ministerial hierarchy or the transition from Opposition frontbench team to government. The popular image of 'in-and-outers' does not stand up to close examination, though. From 1933 to 1965, nine out of every ten senior political executives held no more than two government posts, four-fifths served only one president, and nine out of ten served in only one agency. Heclo has shown how the combination of short average tenures (half hold their jobs for less than two years) and fragile teams means that political executives constitute 'a government of strangers'. According to one US Senator, some have all the impact of a snowflake on the bosom of the Potomac. The overall result is tremendous administrative disruption following the election of a new president, and problems in ensuring political responsiveness within the bureaucracy.

The Prospects for Reform

It is easy to disparage junior ministers. Maurice Kogan thought that their position 'underlines the cruelty of the system – get to the very top or be nothing'. According to William Rodgers: 'The fact is that a junior Minister is a political eunuch. He has lost the power to speak out boldly and to influence events, to be creative in the broad political arena.'[8] In interview, a former permanent secretary referred – apparently in all seriousness – to parliamentary secretaries as 'one of the lower forms of political life'. But, the useful and, indeed, essential work that junior ministers do should not be overlooked. Steering Bills through Standing Committee, replying at adjournment debates, dealing with MPs' letters, receiving deputations, making visits, appearing at Cabinet committees, supervising blocks of departmental business are all intrinsically important ministerial activities. The workload on Cabinet ministers is already too heavy; without the support of junior ministers it would be simply impossible. If junior ministers did not deal with much unglamorous, not to say tedious, business, Cabinet ministers would probably have to spend even more time than they presently do speaking *for* rather than *to* their departments. Junior ministers free Cabinet ministers to concentrate on their primary roles of policy formulation, decision-taking, Cabinet discussions and major political and parliamentary controversies. At the same time, the role of junior ministers in the 1970s and 1980s is much more significant than in the 20 years after 1945: real responsibility for overseeing areas of departmental work has been delegated, and as a result the balance between politicians and bureaucrats has been maintained despite the greater burdens of government.

The problems of junior ministers are partly constitutional and partly political. As we have seen, the constitutional convention of ministerial responsibility is a major limitation on the scope and authority of junior ministers, but it is unlikely to be relaxed or abandoned. Regulating the relations between parliament, ministers and civil servants, and celebrated as a cornerstone of the British constitution since the nineteenth century, the convention of ministerial responsibility has ramifications far wider than its deleterious effects on the position of junior ministers and for that reason is likely to be enduring. Political realities further constrain junior ministers. To the extent that their influence depends largely on their relationship with their secretary of state, the vagaries of ministerial appointments and careers and the pressures of a Cabinet and parliamentary system combine to make their role a sometimes limited one.

Many observers believe that there are too many junior ministers and, as a result, some of these do not have a real job to do. To adapt Dunning's famous motion on the influence of the Crown (1780): 'The number of junior ministers has increased, is increasing and ought to be diminished.' This seems to be the view of a number of permanent secretaries and even Cabinet ministers. One permanent secretary recalled:

> Each of my secretaries of state in the 1970s felt that there were too many junior ministers. The secretary of state can be a little perplexed about what to give the junior ministers to do. You simply do not need, say, six ministers with six private offices and so on. Even though the work has increased, it is not conducive to the efficient conduct of business. It is desirable to cut down the numbers, both from the view of top politicians and that of bureaucratic orderliness.

The growth in the number of junior ministers, and the elaboration of the ministerial hierarchy with the proliferation of ministers of state, has owed something to the heavier burdens on ministers. Given (a) the nature of the relations between the executive and legislature in Britain, (b) the enlargement of the government's sphere of responsibility, (c) the intensification of contacts between government and outside groups, and (d) the disappearance of the non-Cabinet minister heading a small department, there has clearly been a need both for more junior ministers and for those appointed to have a better-defined role. At the same time, impressionistic evidence and examination of ministers' engagement diaries does suggest that some junior ministers are busy but under-employed, spending relatively little of their time on problems of administration and policy-making. But cutting the number of junior ministers – if it was intended to mean that those left would have a bigger say in decision-taking over a wider area of departmental affairs – would have to involve a rethinking of government's relations with parliament and with outside groups and organizations. It is not easy to see ministers being able to disengage from their time-consuming 'ambassadorial' duties without fundamental changes in the organization of government and the conduct of political life.

A further obstacle to reducing the number of junior ministers is that prime ministers and whips need ministerial posts to distribute among backbenchers anxious for office. Fewer posts may simply mean the frustration of MPs' expectations of advancement and create problems of party management. Mrs Thatcher's greatly increased parliamentary majority after 1983 led to the creation of a small number of extra junior posts (see table 2.1). Patronage calculations mean that a drastic slimming of the ranks of the government is unlikely so long as MPs have an 'executive mentality'. If an alternative career ladder were to develop around Commons Select Committees, and ambitious and able back-benchers were to covet Committee assignments and ultimately Chair-manships as much as they appear to aspire to (even lowly) ministerial office, then there may be scope for adjustments in the size of governments. At the moment this is not happening. Governments resist increases in the power of Select Committees and steps which might lead to the development of another career ladder, such as extra remuneration for Chairmen, and MPs themselves have been willing to accept junior minister posts rather than remain members of Select Committees.

One reason why governments in Germany and France are smaller than in Britain (a total of 35–40 ministers and junior ministers instead of 80) is that in those states top civil servants are politicized. That is to say, not only are senior and sensitive appointments subject to political confirm-ation (state secretaries, divisional directors, the staffs of *cabinets*), but those officials play political roles in a way unknown in Britain: appearing alongside ministers at inter-departmental committees, and liaising with parliament, even participating in the work of parliamentary committees. At a time when the politicization of the British civil service is being openly discussed ('made in Britain' versions of *cabinets*, greater ministerial influence over top-level appointments) the consequences for junior ministers should be considered. For instance, there could be clashes between junior ministers and *cabinets*, just as there are between special advisers and junior ministers. And in the context of this discussion of the expectations and behaviour of backbenchers, the 'knock-on' effects of establishing a layer of political officials, if this seemed to imply a reduced need for so many junior ministers, may be serious indeed.[9]

Can anything be done to give junior ministers a stronger role in government? Such diverse figures as Tony Benn, Cecil Parkinson and a Fabian Society Study Group identify junior ministers as a potential resource for increasing political control of the Whitehall machine.[10] The case for reform is first to prepare politicians better for high office by changing the way in which ministers are selected and appointed, and second to reinforce the influence of the accountable ministerial element in government by allowing junior ministers more influence over government policy and in relation to civil servants.

From the mid-1960s onwards, would-be civil service reformers have emphasized the need for officials to have more specialist knowledge of the subjects they deal with, to have improved management skills and for Whitehall to be open to regular infusions of 'new blood' – outsiders with different skills and experiences to those fostered by the career bureaucracy. Critics of the way in which British politicians prepare for ministerial office make similar proposals. As chapter 2 made clear, ministerial careers in Britain follow a Victorian pattern. MPs are recruited on the basis of their parliamentary ability and for political reasons, not for demonstrating specialist subject expertise or possessing executive or managerial skills. Once on the career ladder, they find that there is no planned career system designed to equip them with specialist knowledge of a field of policy or with an understanding of the workings of large, complex organizations. They become generalists, moving from department to department if they are successful. As Sir John Hoskyns has put it, 'Being a *professional* politician turns out to mean being an *amateur* Minister.' Reformers argue that instead of trying to train Cabinet 'all-rounders', the real question is how to develop in politicians the competence to run particular departments. This aim would require a career system with the following characteristics:

1 A greater stress on the specialist subject skills of potential ministers, perhaps developed on Select Committees.
2 A better match between Opposition and government portfolios to build up expertise.
3 Allowing Cabinet ministers more of a say in the choice of their own juniors, to encourage delegation and closer working relations and give junior ministers more experience of decision-taking and policy formulation.
4 Select as Cabinet ministers those junior ministers who have moved up the ministerial hierarchy in a single department, or at least closely related ones in a particular policy field.
5 Introduce more outside talent; break down the closed and introspective system of career politics centred on Westminster. According to Hoskyns, 'For the purposes of government, a country of 55 million people is forced to depend on a talent pool which could not sustain a single multinational company.'[11]

To list these changes is to realize just how difficult they are to secure. The nature of competitive party politics in parliament precludes any major development of subject specialisms at the expense of broad political capabilities and perspectives. Prime ministers would be reluctant to loosen their grip on power, which a diminution of their patronage would imply; they want the freedom of manoeuvre to switch Opposition spokesmen and ministers from post to post for political reasons.

Ambitious ministers would prefer being promoted to an unfamiliar department, if it meant that they got their feet under the Cabinet table, to staying at minister of state level working on one particular field of policy over a number of years. The emphasis on parliamentary performance, and the sheer amount of time ministers have to spend on parliamentary business, puts outsiders brought in to government office at a 'disadvantage. It is rare for them to enter the House of Commons in middle age and be a success, and it is difficult to fill senior departmental positions with newly created peers except in a small number of cases (for instance, Lord Young at Employment in 1985). The prognosis in this respect must, therefore, be gloomy. Improvements in the supply of specialized, executive-type ministers are contingent on far-reaching changes in British political life, including the workings of the party system and the organization of parliament. In the absence of such change the ministerial generalist will continue to prevail.

Even within the present career system junior ministers could be better prepared for Cabinet office. They could and should be put more into the picture and allowed to see, as a matter of routine, policy papers outside their departmental responsibilities, so that they would be able to explain and defend government policy in parliament and to the public as more credible and acceptable spokesmen than they have been to date and, in addition, play a greater part in decision-taking. The problem here is that information is power. Top ministers and senior civil servants may want to restrict access to information rather than share it. 'Collective government' can look like a power game based on limited knowledge and limited discussion. Instituting regular ministers' meetings each morning in all departments would help both the secretary of state in managing his team and the junior ministers, who could thus keep in touch with wider policy issues. Secretaries of state employ their own special advisers for understandable reasons, but should also be encouraged to aim for a more collegial atmosphere in departments. As a former parliamentary secretary said, 'If you're a secretary of state your ministerial colleagues should be your first political advisers – you should discuss major problems of policy in the department with them. It's a scandal and a failure that not enough real political discussion takes place between ministerial colleagues.' Much depends on the top minister's personal style and temperament, and the extent of his confidence in his subordinates (over whose appointment he will have had perhaps little influence); there will probably always be 'loners' among ministers. Coordination is a way of life at the top of the civil service, departmentally and inter-departmentally. It is up to ministers to do more to ensure that as a political team in each department they are better coordinated.

Whitehall is honeycombed by civil service departmental and inter-departmental committees and working groups, which ministers do not attend or even know about often. Former ministers have argued that there is a danger that 'agreed' civil service positions can be evolved on these committees by officials secluded from direct ministerial concerns and committed to the enduring interests of their departments, which are then merely registered by ministers who lack the time to consider the issues properly. In the Fulton Committee Report on the Civil Service, Lord Crowther-Hunt inserted a personal note that junior ministers should be members of 'the more important of these committees' to 'strengthen the political direction of departments',[12] but there is also a case for including them on *inter*-departmental groups to ensure that options are not pre-empted or ministerial policy initiatives not watered down. Shirley Williams has candidly written that 'mixed committees have the great advantage of demonstrating to Ministers that there are differences of view between officials and between departments.'[13] In interview several junior ministers supported these steps:

> You're at the apex of this huge pyramid and you don't see much of it. I'd like to see how things were built up from the bottom; ministers never get to see that. So I'd have junior ministers chair committees of civil servants. Junior ministers could be usefully used that way. Of course, everyone argues, they [the civil servants] would go over things, hold them back, have their own separate meetings first. But everyone does that in politics anyway.

Another minister said, 'ministers should use their junior ministers as their eyes and ears on civil service committees, to give officials a political push. Instead, you get a grave misuse of junior ministers' time.'

Mixed committees of this type do occasionally appear in Whitehall, but there is much to be said for greatly extending their use. One problem is that there are not enough junior ministers, nor do they have the time, to sit on *all* committees. They would have to be selective, attending only those dealing with major policy initiatives or sensitive subjects. Another drawback is that to work properly the idea would need strong backing from the prime minister and secretaries of state. Only then could probable civil service scepticism be overcome and junior ministers carry conviction with the officials they were supervising. This raises the familiar problem of facilitating trust and mutual confidence in ministerial teams. Given the political will, this is a way in which junior ministers could come to play a much more positive role in government.

Notes

The following abbreviations are used in these notes:

Hans. Hansard
HC   House of Commons
HL   House of Lords
PP   Parliamentary Papers
PRO   Public Record Office

Preface

1 Simon Hoggart, 'Tomorrow's men: a guide to form', *Guardian*, 9 October 1979.
2 Robert Stewart, *The Penguin Dictionary of Political Quotations* (Harmondsworth, 1986), p. 104.

Chapter 1 Historical Background

1 *First Report of the Commissioners appointed to inquire into Fees received at Public Offices*, PP 1806, vii (309).
2 Henry Parris, *Constitutional Bureaucracy: the Development of British Central Administration since the Eighteenth Century* (London, 1969), p. 42.
3 D. M. Young, *The Colonial Office in the Early Nineteenth Century* (London, 1961), p. 84.
4 H. J. Hanham (ed.), *The Nineteenth Century Constitution: Documents and Commentary* (London, 1969), pp. 100–1.
5 E. Jones-Parry, 'Under Secretaries of State for Foreign Affairs, 1782–1855', *English Historical Review*, 49 (1934), p. 311.
6 Dorothy Marshall, *The Rise of George Canning* (London, 1938), p. 109.
7 D. J. Heasman, 'The emergence and evolution of the office of Parliamentary Secretary', *Parliamentary Affairs*, 23 (1970), pp. 351–2.

8 Parris, *Constitutional Bureaucracy*, p. 123.
9 *Select Committee on the Reduction of Salaries*, PP 1830–1, iii (322), p. 6; Treasury Minute of 15 April 1831, PP 1830–1, vii (1), p. 494.
10 Philip Guedella, *The Queen and Mr Gladstone* (London, 1933), vol. 2, pp. 130–1; *Select Committee on Official Salaries*, PP 1850, xv (611), q. 300.
11 J. P. Cornford, 'The parliamentary foundations of the Hotel Cecil', in *Ideas and Institutions of Victorian Britain: Essays in Honour of George Kitson Clark*, ed. R. Robson (London, 1967), pp. 290–1.
12 Vt Gladstone, 'The Chief Whip in the British Parliament', *American Political Science Review*, 21 (1927), p. 520.
13 Sir Sidney Low, *The Governance of England* (London, 1925), pp. 114–15; *Select Committee on Miscellaneous Expenditure*, PP 1847–8, xviii–1 (543), q. 4771–2.
14 Hanham, *The Nineteenth Century Constitution*, p. 151.
15 Cornford, 'Parliamentary foundations of the Hotel Cecil'; W. L. Guttsman, *The British Political Elite* (London, 1965); Harold Laski, *The British Cabinet: a Study of its Personnel 1801–1928*, Fabian Tract 223 (1928).
16 Randolph S. Churchill, *Winston S. Churchill, Companion Vol. II, part 2, 1907–11* (London, 1969), p. 862; Vt Grey of Fallodon, *Twenty Five Years* (London, 1925), pp. 1–2.
17 A. Lawrence Lowell, *The Government of England* (New York, 1909), vol. 1, p. 58; John P. Mackintosh, *The British Cabinet*, 3rd edn (London, 1977), p. 304; Guedella, *The Queen and Mr Gladstone*, p. 4.
18 Mackintosh, *The British Cabinet*, p. 108, n. 99.
19 K. B. Smellie, *A Hundred Years of English Government*, 2nd edn (London, 1950). p. 55.
20 *Select Committee on the Board of Admiralty*, PP 1861, v (438), q. 937; 3 Hans. D. (194) 1868–9, c. 859; Grey, *Twenty Five Years*, pp. 2, 25; Churchill, *Winston S. Churchill*, p. 862.
21 F. M. G. Willson, 'The routes of entry of new members of the British Cabinet 1868–1958', *Political Studies*, 7 (1959), pp. 227–8.
22 *Select Committee on Official Salaries*, q. 82.
23 *Select Committee on Miscellaneous Expenditure*, q. 4754.
24 3 Hans. D. (201) 1870, c. 968, 1054–61; 3 Hans. D. (219) 1874, c. 1613.
25 3 Hans. D. (172) 1863, c. 364; Parris, *Constitutional Bureaucracy*, p. 124.
26 Sir Robert Biddulph, *Lord Cardwell at the War Office* (London, 1904), p. 102.
27 R. B. McDowell, *The Irish Administration 1801–1914* (London, 1964).
28 Lucy Masterman, *C. F. G. Masterman, a Biography* (London, 1968), p. 230.
29 *Select Committee on Education*, PP 1865, vi (403), q. 760; R. R. James, *Rosebery* (London, 1963), pp. 122, 125.
30 L. Creighton, *Dorothy Grey* (1907), quoted in K. Robbins, *Sir Edward Grey: a Biography of Lord Grey of Fallodon* (London, 1971), p. 38; *Select Committee on the Admiralty*, PP 1861, v (438), q. 1070.
31 *Select Committee on Official Salaries*, q. 1941; Lushington to Childers, 8 March 1886, PRO, H045/9611/A7070B/2e.

32 A. C. Benson and Vt Esher, *Letters of Queen Victoria, 1st series 1837–1861, vol. 3: 1854–1861* (London, 1907), pp. 568–9.

33 Kenneth Rose, *Superior Person: a Portrait of Curzon and his Circle in Late Victorian England* (London, 1969), pp. 306–8; F. Gosses, *The Management of British Foreign Policy before the First World War* (Leiden, 1948), p. 149; Low, *The Governance of England*, p. 300.

34 *Royal Commission on Civil Establishments*, C. 5226, PP 1887, xix, q. 10,410.

35 *Select Committee on Miscellaneous Expenditure*, q. 4801–3; *Royal Commission on Civil Establishments*, C. 6172, PP 1890, xxvii, q. 27,931.

36 Palmerston to Queen Victoria, 25 February 1838, in Benson and Esher, *Letters of Queen Victoria, 1st series*, vol. 1, pp. 136–7; Parris, *Constitutional Bureaucracy*, pp. 107–11; *Select Committee on the Reduction of Salaries*, p. 38.

37 *3 Hans. D.* (319) 1887, c. 1110; L. Wolf, *Life of the First Marquess of Ripon* (London, 1921), vol. 2, p. 323.

38 *Select Committee on the Admiralty*, PP 1871, vii (180), q. 228, 770–3.

39 *Select Committee on Trade with Foreign Nations*, PP 1864, vii (493), q. 3437; Walter Bagehot, *The English Constitution* (London, 1963), p. 211; Henry Parris, *Government and the Railways in Nineteenth Century Britain* (London, 1965).

40 *Select Committee on Miscellaneous Expenditure*, q. 4747; Maurice Wright, *Treasury Control of the Civil Service 1854–1874* (London, 1969), pp. 44–5.

41 *Select Committee on Official Salaries*, q. 4410–1; *Select Committee on Miscellaneous Expenditure*, q. 47.

42 Wright, *Treasury Control of the Civil Service*, pp. 44–7, 252–4.

43 Ibid., pp. 50–2; *3 Hans. D.* (194) 1868–9, c. 842–63; *Treasury Minute on Duties of the Third Lord of the Treasury*, PP 1868–9, xxxiv, pp. 621–2.

44 *Royal Commission on Civil Establishments*, 1887, q. 1840, 5546, 5551, 5560–1, 5591.

45 *Select Committee on Public Offices*, PP 1854, xxvii (1715), pp. 47–8; *Select Committee on Official Salaries*, q. 1548.

46 Gillian Sutherland (ed.), *Studies in the Growth of Nineteenth Century Government* (London, 1973), p. 142; H. L. Hall, *The Colonial Office, a History* (London, 1937), p. 51.

47 G. Tayar (ed.), *Personalities and Power: Studies in Political Advancement* (London, 1971), p. 79; Henry Pelling, *Winston Churchill* (London, 1977), pp. 98–9.

48 *Select Committee on the Diplomatic and Consular Services*, PP 1871, vii (238), q. 1146, 1156.

49 *Select Committee on the Diplomatic and Consular Services*, PP 1870, vii–2 (382), q. 729, 3881; Mary A. Anderson, *Edmund Hammond: Permanent Under Secretary of State for Foreign Affairs, 1854–1873* (University of London, unpublished PhD thesis, 1956), p. 250.

50 *Select Committee on the Diplomatic and Consular Services*, 1871, q. 1155, 1203; *Royal Commission on Civil Establishments, 1890*, q. 27, 929.

51 *Select Committee on the Diplomatic and Consular Services*, 1871, q. 1146; *Royal Commission on Civil Establishments*, 1890, q. 27, 930–1.

52 David Marquand, *Ramsay MacDonald* (London, 1977), p. 304; Hugh Dalton, *Call Back Yesterday, Memoirs 1887–1931* (London, 1953), p. 249.

53 The data here include the 1945–51 Labour government. P. W. Buck, *Amateurs and Professionals in British Politics 1918–59* (Chicago, 1963), pp. 48–51, table 22, p. 115.

54 H. E. Dale, *The Higher Civil Service of Great Britain* (Oxford, 1941), p. 119.

55 Duff Cooper, *Old Men Forget* (London, 1953), pp. 161–2.

56 M. A. Hamilton, *Arthur Henderson*, quoted in Ben Pimlott, *Hugh Dalton* (London, 1985), p. 190; Lord Butler, *The Art of the Possible* (London, 1971), p. 61; Kenneth and Jane Morgan, *Portrait of a Progressive: the Political Career of Christopher, Viscount Addison* (Oxford, 1980), pp. 173–4, 177.

57 Sir Geoffrey Shakespeare, *Let Candles Be Brought In* (London, 1949).

58 Richard Crossman, *The Charm of Politics* (London, 1958), pp. 78–9.

59 PRO, PREM 5/130, *Representation of the Ministry of Agriculture in the House of Lords*.

60 R. K. Mosely, *The Story of the Cabinet Office* (London, 1969), p. 13; PRO, CAB 21/1331, *Access of Junior Ministers to War Cabinet Minutes and Secret Documents*, Cabinet Procedure, Note by the Prime Minister, 25 November 1937; Cooper, *Old Men Forget*, p. 162.

61 PRO, CAB 21/459, *Issue of Foreign Office Telegrams to Junior Ministers*.

62 PRO, CAB 87/71, *Machinery of Government Committee – Official Committee*, 52nd meeting, 2 May 1944, Geoffrey Vickers, para 3.

63 D. N. Chester and F. M. G. Willson, *The Organisation of British Central Government 1914–1964* (London, 1968), pp. 79–81.

64 Ibid., pp. 89–90; Emanuel Shinwell, *Conflict Without Malice* (London, 1955), p. 107.

65 PRO, CAB 87/71, *Machinery of Government Committee – Official Committee*, 50th and 52nd meetings; PRO, CAB 87/72, *Machinery of Government Committee – Official Committee Memoranda*, MGO 53 Official Committee Report on External Economic Relations; PRO, CAB 87/73, *War Cabinet Committee on the Machinery of Government*, MG (44) 18th meeting, 5 September 1944.

66 PRO, CAB 87/71, *Machinery of Government Committee – Official Committee*, 51st and 52nd meetings; PRO, CAB 87/72, *Machinery of Government Committee – Official Committee Memoranda*, MGO 21 and MGO 37; PRO, CAB 27/57, *Committee to Examine the Machinery for Trade and Commerce*, (1919), pp. 91 and 106.

Chapter 2 Appointment and Careers of Junior Ministers

1 Anthony Seldon, *Churchill's Indian Summer: the Conservative Government 1951–55* (London, 1981), p. 79; Anthony King, 'Margaret Thatcher: the

style of a Prime Minister', in *The British Prime Minister*, 2nd edn, ed. Anthony King, (London, 1985), p. 103.

2 Harold Wilson, *The Governance of Britain* (London, 1976), p. 30.

3 Francis Williams, *A Prime Minister Remembers: The War and Postwar Memoirs of the Rt Hon Earl Attlee* (London, 1961), p. 84.

4 Wilson, *Governance of Britain*, p. 33.

5 Reginald Maudling, *Memoirs* (London, 1978), p. 52.

6 Gerald Kaufman, *How to be a Minister* (London, 1980), p. 13; Seldon, *Churchill's Indian Summer*, p. 261; R. K. Alderman, 'The Prime Minister and the appointment of Ministers: an exercise in political bargaining', *Parliamentary Affairs*, 29, 2 (1976), p. 129, n. 76; *Guardian* 14 February 1986; G. M. F. Drower, *Neil Kinnock: the Path to Leadership* (London, 1984), p.40.

7 Richard Rose, 'The making of Cabinet Ministers', in *Cabinet Studies: a Reader*, ed. Valentine Herman and James E. Alt (London, 1975), pp. 12–14; Wilson, *Governance of Britain*, p. 34.

8 Richard Crossman, *The Diaries of a Cabinet Minister, vol. 1, Minister of Housing 1964–66* (London, 1975), pp. 494–5; Harold Wilson, *The Labour Government 1964–70: a Personal Record* (London, 1971), p. 714; Richard Crossman, *The Diaries of a Cabinet Minister, vol. 2, Lord President of the Council and Leader of the House of Commons 1966–68* (London, 1976), p. 761.

9 Bruce Headey, *British Cabinet Ministers: the Roles of Politicians in Executive Office* (London, 1974), p. 89; Gavin Drewry (ed.), *The New Select Committees: A Study of the 1979 Reforms* (Oxford, 1985).

10 Anthony King, *British Members of Parliament: a Self-portrait* (London, 1974), p. 70; Headey, *British Cabinet Ministers*, pp. 62, 107; Maurice Kogan, *The Politics of Education* (Harmondsworth 1971), p. 86; David Judge, *Backbench Specialisation in the House of Commons* (London, 1981), pp. 93–4, 97, 100.

11 Philip Norton, *Dissension in the House of Commons 1945–74* (London, 1975); *Conservative Dissidents: Dissent within the Parliamentary Conservative Party 1970–74* (London, 1978); *Dissension in the House of Commons 1974–79* (Oxford, 1981).

12 Kenneth Harris, *Attlee* (London, 1982), p. 325; Williams, *A Prime Minister Remembers*, p. 84.

13 Richard Rose, *Understanding the United Kingdom: the Territorial Dimension in Government* (London, 1982), p. 93; J. G. Kellas, *The Scottish Political System*, 2nd edn (London, 1975), pp. 41–3; M. J. Keating, 'A test of political integration: the Scottish Members of Parliament', *Studies in Public Policy* (6), University of Strathclyde (1977), pp. 24–5.

14 R. J. Jackson, *Rebels and Whips: an Analysis of Dissension, Discipline and Cohesion in British Political Parties* (London, 1968); Harold Macmillan, *Riding the Storm 1956–59* (London, 1971), pp. 191–2; Anthony King and Anne Sloman, *Westminster and Beyond* (London, 1977), p. 108; Norton, *Conservative Dissidents*, p. 233; Uwe Kitzinger, *Diplomacy and Persuasion*

(London, 1973), p. 154; Robert McKenzie, 'The pursuit of power – John Biffen', *The Listener*, 2 July 1981.

15 R. M. Punnett, *Front-Bench Opposition: the Role of the Leader of the Opposition, the Shadow Cabinet and Shadow Government in British Politics* (London, 1973), pp. 360, 380–3.

16 *Guardian*, 9 October 1979.

17 *Observer Magazine*, 6 April 1986.

18 Crossman, *The Charm of Politics*, p. 78.

19 William Rodgers, *The Politics of Change* (London, 1982), p. 162.

20 Headey, *British Cabinet Ministers*, p. 104.

21 Ibid., p. 90; Philip Norton, *The Commons in Perspective* (Oxford, 1981), p. 76; George Thomas, *Mr Speaker: The Memoirs of Viscount Tonypandy* (London, 1985), p. 91.

22 Gerald Kaufman *How to be a Minister*, p. 75.

23 Richard Rose, *The Problem of Party Government* (Harmondsworth, 1976), p. 451; Philip Williams, *Hugh Gaitskell: a Political Biography* (London, 1979), p. 113.

24 D. J. Heasman, 'Ministers' apprentices', *New Society*, 16 July 1964.

25 Headey, *British Cabinet Ministers*, p. 104; Rose, 'The making of Cabinet Ministers', p. 16.

Chapter 3 The Constitutional Position

1 Lord Morrison of Lambeth, *Government and Parliament: a Survey from the Inside*, 3rd edn (London, 1964), p. 73.

2 Harold Wilson, *Final Term: The Labour Government 1974–1976* (London, 1979), pp. 60–1; *Guardian*, 14 April 1984, 10 May 1986.

3 Robert Pyper, 'The F.O. resignations: individual ministerial responsibility revisited?', in *Updating British Politics*, ed. Lynton Roberts (London, 1984), p. 51.

4 Ibid., pp. 52–5.

5 PRO, CAB 21/778, *Cabinet Procedure*; PRO, CAB 21/1624, *Cabinet Procedure: Consolidated Version of the Prime Minister's Directives*; Tony Benn, *The Case for a Constitutional Premiership* (Nottingham, 1979), p. 13.

6 See *Report of a Tribunal appointed to inquire into allegations reflecting on the official conduct of Ministers of the Crown and other public servants* and *Proceedings of the Tribunal*, Cmd 7616 (1949); Stanley Wade Baron, *The Contact Man: the Story of Sidney Stanley and the Lynskey Tribunal* (London, 1966); John Gross, 'The Lynskey Tribunal', in *Age of Austerity 1945–51*, ed. M. Sissons and P. French (Harmondsworth, 1964); R. S. Milne, 'The junior minister', *The Journal of Politics*, 12, 3 (1950), pp. 437–49.

7 HC Deb. 460 (1948–9), c. 1854, 1951.

8 CP (49) 31, in PRO, CAB 21/1642 *Duties of Parliamentary Secretaries and Junior Ministers*.

9 HC Deb. 672 (1962–3), c. 1078–9; HC Deb. 673 (1962–3), c. 640–1.

10 *Guardian*, 5 September 1985; *New Statesman*, 14, 21, 28 February 1986; letter to the author from Rt Hon Tony Benn, MP.

Chapter 4 The Departmental Role of Junior Ministers

1 Headey, *British Cabinet Ministers*, pp. 33–7.
2 Philip Williams (ed.), *The Diary of Hugh Gaitskell 1945–1956* (London, 1983), p. 38.
3 The following paragraphs are based on: PRO, PREM 8/1485, *Duties of Parliamentary Secretaries and Junior Ministers* (1951), and Seldon, *Churchill's Indian Summer*, pp. 121, 128, 134–6, 153, 157–60, 208, 273, 383–5.
4 C. M. Woodhouse, *Something Ventured* (London, 1982), pp. 157–8.
5 PRO, FO 366/3046, *Work of the Minister of State and the Parliamentary Under Secretaries* (1953).
6 *HC Deb.* 494 (1950–1), c. 381, 521–4.
7 Morrison, *Government and Parliament*, pp. 80–3.
8 *HC Deb.* 577 (1957–8), c. 27–8; *The Economist*, 16 November 1957.
9 Kogan, *Politics of Education*, p. 86.
10 Headey, *British Cabinet Ministers*, pp. 104–5; William Rodgers, 'Westminster and Whitehall: adapting to change', in *Policy and Practice: the Experience of Government*, Royal Institute of Public Administration (London, 1980), p. 11; Jeremy Bray, *Decision in Government* (London, 1970), p. 64; Wilson, *The Labour Government 1964–70*, p. 10; 'Harold Wilson: post experience', interviewed by Norman Hunt, in *The British Prime Minister*, ed. Anthony King, (London, 1969), p. 110.
11 Bray, *Decision in Government*, p. 64; Hugo Young, 'But who is responsible for burials?', *Sunday Times*, 17 April 1977.
12 Susan Crosland, *Tony Crosland* (London, 1982), p. 177; Kogan, *Politics of Education*, p. 157.
13 Lord Strang, *Home and Abroad* (London, 1956), p. 300; Peter Kellner and Lord Crowther-Hunt, *The Civil Servants: an Inquiry into Britain's Ruling Class* (London, 1980), p. 226; Kogan, *Politics of Education*, p. 157.
14 Jo Grimond, Enoch Powell, Harold Wilson, Norman Hunt, *Whitehall and Beyond* (London, 1964), pp. 46–7.
15 Martin J. Painter, 'Policy co-ordination in the Department of the Environment 1970–1976', *Public Administration*, 58 (Summer 1980), p. 139.
16 Sir Patrick Nairne, 'Managing the DHSS Elephant: reflections on a giant department', *The Political Quarterly*, 54, 3 (1983), p. 253; *HC Deb.* 805 (1970–1), c. 939.
17 Richard Crossman, *The Diaries of a Cabinet Minister, vol. 3, Secretary of State for Social Services 1968–70* (London, 1977), p. 682.
18 R. K. Alderman and J. A. Cross, 'The Parliamentary Private Secretary', *The Parliamentarian*, 48, 2 (April 1967), p. 75; *HC Deb.* 386 (1942–3), c. 354–6; PRO, PREM 11/253, *Cabinet Procedure: Parliamentary Private Secretaries, Note by the Prime Minister* (1952).

19 Rudolf Klein and Janet Lewis, 'Advice and dissent in British Government: the case of the Special Advisers', *Policy and Politics*, 6 (1977), pp. 19–20; David Owen, *Face the Future* (Oxford, 1981), p. 146.

20 Klein and Lewis, 'Advice and dissent', p. 20.

21 Maurice Peston, 'A professional on a political tightrope', *Times Higher Education Supplement*, 11 July 1980.

22 Crossman, *Diaries*, vol. 1, p. 48; Kogan, *Politics of Education*, p. 185; Crosland, *Tony Crosland*, p. 177.

23 Painter, 'Policy co-ordination in the Department of the Environment', p. 138; Joel Barnett, *Inside the Treasury* (London, 1982), p. 84; Hugo Young and Anne Sloman, *But Chancellor: an Inquiry into the Treasury* (London, 1984), p. 37.

24 Malcolm Rifkind, 'Reflections of a Scottish Office Minister', in *The Scottish Government Yearbook 1982*, ed. H. M. and N. L. Drucker (Edinburgh, 1981), p. 61; Kellner and Crowther Hunt, *The Civil Servants*, p. 227.

25 Crossman, *Diaries*, vol. 1, pp. 21, 385.

26 Kaufman, *How to be a Minister*, p. 37; Kellner and Crowther-Hunt, *The Civil Servants*, pp. 226–7.

27 Morrison, *Government and Parliament*, p. 81; Crossman, *Diaries*, vol, 1, p. 614.

28 Kellner and Crowther-Hunt, *The Civil Servants*, pp.227–8; Charles Medawar, *Parliamentary Questions and Answers* (London, 1980), pp. 22–6; Painter, 'Policy co-ordination in the Department of the Environment', pp. 140, 151.

29 Kogan, *Politics of Education*, p. 179; *The Civil Service, Eleventh Report of the Expenditure Committee Minutes of Evidence*, HC 353–II (1976–7), q. 1,898; Rodgers, 'Westminster and Whitehall', p. 15.

30 Christopher Hood and Andrew Dunsire, *Bureaumetrics* (London, 1981), pp. 121–3; A. Clark, 'Ministerial supervision and the size of the DOE', *Public Administration*, 55 (Summer 1977), pp. 197–204; HC Deb. 805 (1970–1), c. 938.

Chapter 5 Junior Ministers and the Problems of Collective Government

1 Tessa Blackstone, 'Helping Ministers do a better job', *New Society*, 19 July 1979; PRO, CAB 21/1331, *Access of Junior Ministers to War Cabinet Minutes and Secret Documents*, note by Sir Edward Bridges, 25 May 1944; PRO, CAB 21/1624, *Cabinet Procedure: Consolidated Version of the Prime Minister's Directives, Questions of Procedure for Ministers*, CP (49) 95, para. 24; *New Statesman*, 21 February 1986, p. 14.

2 Crossman, *Diaries*, vol. 2, p. 236.

3 Wilson, *Governance of Britain*, p. 44; Michael Cockerell, Peter Hennessy and David Walker, *Sources Close to the Prime Minister* (London, 1984), pp. 15–16.

4 *The Times*, 11 December 1961; Peter G. Richards, *The Backbenchers* (London, 1972), p. 93; *The Times*, 25 May 1976; *Guardian*, 23 February 1983.
5 *Guardian*, 19 October 1983.
6 Painter, 'Policy co-ordination in the Department of the Environment', p. 139; Crosland, *Tony Crosland*, p. 354; Bruce Reed and Geoffrey Williams, *Denis Healey and the Politics of Power* (London, 1971), pp. 196–7, 210–11.
7 Rodgers, 'Westminster and Whitehall', pp. 9–10; Kaufman, *How to Be a Minister*, p. 44.
8 Bruce Page, 'The secret constitution', *New Statesman*, 21 July 1979.
9 Mackintosh, *The British Cabinet*, p. 523; Kellner and Crowther-Hunt, *The Civil Servants*, p. 232.
10 Headey, *British Cabinet Ministers*, p. 36.
11 Kaufman, *How to Be a Minister*, p. 75.
12 Crossman, *Diaries*, vol. 2, pp. 109, 168, 199, 470.
13 Edmund Dell, 'Collective responsibility: fact, fiction or facade?', in *Policy and Practice: the Experience of Government*, Royal Institute of Public Administration (London, 1980), p. 42; Patrick Gordon Walker, *The Cabinet* (London, 1972), p. 44; Barbara Castle, *The Castle Diaries 1974–76* (London, 1980), p. 280.
14 Williams, *The Diary of Hugh Gaitskell*, pp. 38–9.
15 Shirley Williams, 'The decision makers', in *Policy and Practice: the Experience of Government*, Royal Institute of Public Administration (London, 1980), p. 88; Kaufman, *How to Be a Minister*, pp. 42, 49; *The Times*, 16 May 1983.
16 'Harold Wilson: post experience', p. 110.

Chapter 6 Junior Ministers in Parliament and as Departmental Ambassadors

1 Headey, *British Cabinet Ministers*, pp. 36, 167–71; Philip Norton, ' "Dear Minister, . . ." The importance of MP-to-Minister correspondence', *Parliamentary Affairs*, 25, 1 (1982), p. 63; Simon Jenkins and Anne Sloman, *With Respect, Ambassador: an Inquiry into the Foreign Office* (London, 1985), pp. 112–13.
2 Headey, *British Cabinet Ministers*, pp. 105–6.
3 *HC Deb.* 13 December 1985, c. 1205–10; *HC Deb.* 6 March 1986, c. 218 (w); *Guardian*, 7 January 1986.
4 Williams, *Hugh Gaitskell: a Political Biography*, p. 134.
5 Lord Avon/Sir Anthony Eden, *Full Circle* (London, 1960), p. 273. See also D. N. Chester, 'Double-banking and deputy ministers', *New Society*, 11 June 1964.
6 S. A. Walkland, 'Committees in the British House of Commons', in *Committees in Legislatures: a Comparative Analysis*, ed. John D. Lees and Malcolm Shaw (Oxford, 1979), p. 258.

7 Crossman, *Diaries*, vol. 1, p. 629; Martin Kettle, 'Point of law and order', *New Society*, 25 February 1982; *HC Deb.* 1974: Standing Committees, vol. V, Scottish Grand Committee, c. 168, 9 July 1974.

8 Walkland, 'Committees in the British House of Commons', p. 259; J. A. G. Griffith, *Parliamentary Scrutiny of Government Bills* (London, 1974), pp. 39–40; J. A. G. Griffith, 'Standing Committes in the House of Commons', in *The Commons Today*, ed. S. A. Walkland and Michael Ryle (Glasgow, 1981), pp. 130–1; Crossman, *Diaries*, vol. 3, p. 903.

9 *Standing Committees: Return for Session 1983–84*, HC 107 (1984–5).

10 Crossman, *Diaries*, vol. 3, pp. 826, 902–3.

11 Norton, ' "Dear Minister, . . ." ', pp. 60–3; *Guardian*, 17 September 1976 and 27 March 1986; *The Times*, 24 March 1982; *Sunday Times Magazine*, 24 April 1980; King and Sloman, *Westminster and Beyond*, p. 18.

12 PRO, CAB 21/2009, *Appointment of a Tribunal to Conduct a Judicial Inquiry into Alleged Irregularities in Government Departments*, 'Letters to Ministers from MPs', note of 8 January 1949.

13 *Guardian*, 17 September 1976; Lord Crowther-Hunt, 'Whitehall – just passing through', *The Listener*, 16 December 1976; *The Times*, 20 and 21 June 1978.

14 S. A. Walkland (ed.), *The House of Commons in the Twentieth Century* (Oxford, 1979), pp. 480, 490–1; Kaufman, *How to Be a Minister*, p. 93.

15 Headey, *British Cabinet Ministers*, p. 33; Crossman, *Diaries*, vol. 3, p. 635; vol. 1, p. 546; Geoffrey Moorhouse, *The Diplomats: the Foreign Office Today* (London, 1977), p. 150.

16 Lord Brabazon of Tara, *The Brabazon Story* (London, 1956), p. 122; *HC Deb.* 6 March 1986, c. 275 (w).

17 Wyn Grant and David Marsh, *The Confederation of British Industry* (London, 1977), pp. 123–4.

18 William Wallace, *The Foreign Policy Process in Britain* (London, 1976), p. 92.

19 Owen, *Face the Future*, p. 137.

20 Jenkins and Sloman, *With Respect, Ambassador*, p. 112.

21 House of Commons Library 7337 (1976–7), 9 November 1977, *Overseas Visits by Junior Ministers and Ministers during the Year ending 30 September 1977*.

22 *HC Deb.* 494 (1950–1), c. 492; *The Civil Service, Report from the Expenditure Committee*, q. 1,888; William Ross, 'Approaching the arch-angelic', in *The Scottish Government Yearbook 1978*, ed. H. M. Drucker (Edinburgh, 1978), p. 8.

Chapter 7 Junior Ministers in the Limelight

1 Norman Shrapnel, *Bluff your Way in Politics* (London, 1975), pp. 33–4.

2 *Sunday Times*, 17 April 1977.

3 *HC Deb.* 711 (1964–5), c. 178; John S. Harris, *Government Patronage of the Arts in Great Britain* (London, 1970), p. 62.

4 Robert Hutchinson, *The Politics of the Arts Council* (London, 1982), p. 17; Hugh Jenkins, *The Culture Gap* (London, 1979), pp. 25, 189; Peter Smith, 'Dr Hoggart's Farewell', *Marxism Today*, March 1982, pp. 31–2; *Guardian*, 22 May 1986.

5 Raymond Williams, 'The Arts Council', *The Political Quarterly*, 50, 2 (April–June 1979), p. 159; *Guardian*, 12 March 1986, 22 May 1986; Muriel Nissel, 'Financing the Arts in Great Britain', in *Funding the Arts in Europe*, ed. John Myerscough (London, 1984), p. 71.

6 *HC Deb.* 870 (1974), c. 4 (w); Jenkins, *The Culture Gap*, pp. 124, 177, 180.

7 Smith, 'Dr Hoggart's Farewell', p. 32; Jenkins, *The Culture Gap*, pp. 76, 96, 203, 205.

8 *The Arts: the Way Forward*, Conservative Party (1978), p. 15; *The Arts and the People*, Labour Party (1977), p. 14; *Public and Private Funding of the Arts*, Eighth Report from the Select Committee on Education, Science and the Arts, 1981–2; Lord Redcliffe-Maud, *Support for the Arts* (London, 1976), pp. 30–1; *Guardian*, 27, 29 and 30 November 1976.

9 Vincent Hanna, 'Hot gospeller for sport', *Sunday Times*, 16 November 1975; *Sunday Telegraph*, 13 May 1979.

10 Hanna, 'Hot gospeller for sport'.

11 *HC Deb.* 877 (1974), c. 102 (w).

12 *House of Lords Select Committee on Sports and Leisure*, 2nd report (1972–3), HL 193–I, *Evidence*, q. 1242.

13 *Sunday Times*, 8 January 1978.

14 *Lords Select Committee on Sports and Leisure*, Report para. 114–18.

15 *HC Deb.* 798 (1969–70), c. 862; *HC Deb.* 795 (1969–70), c. 111–12 (w); *HL Deb.* 303 (1969–70), c. 255–6, 848–9.

16 *Harding Award Speech, Royal Society of Medicine* (London, 1971), p. 12; Lord Windlesham, *Politics in Practice* (London, 1975), p. 62; Wilson, *Final Term*, p. 18.

17 *HC Deb.* 870 (1974), c. 1323–4; Geoffrey Smith, 'A new deal for the disabled, but so far not enough', *The Times*, 11 April 1975.

18 *HC Deb*, 982 (1979–80), c. 405 (w).

19 Castle, *The Castle Diaries*, pp. 151–2.

20 Christopher Pollitt, *Manipulating the Machine: Changing the Pattern of Ministerial Departments, 1960–83* (London, 1984).

21 Wallace, *Foreign Policy Process in Britain*, p. 194; D. J. Morgan, *Official History of Colonial Development* (London, 1980), vol. 3: *Reassessment of British Aid Policy*, pp. 256, 261; vol. 4: *Changes in British Aid Policy 1951–70*, p. 17.

22 Wallace, *Foreign Policy Process in Britain*, pp. 204, 197.

23 Rosemary Collins, 'One of our ministers is missing', *Guardian*, 23 February 1982.

24 J. Moon, J. Richardson and P. Smart, 'Government policy for the development and acquisition of information technology: the role of the

Department of Trade and Industry', in *Policy Change in Government: Three Case studies*, ed. Nicholas Deakin (London, 1986), pp. 63–91; *Guardian*, 26 March 1986; *New Statesman*, 1 February 1985.
25 *Sunday Times Magazine*, 7 May 1978.
26 *Guardian*, 23 September 1983.

Chapter 8 Junior Ministers in Perspective

1 Jean Blondel, *The Organization of Governments; a Comparative Analysis of Government Structures* (London, 1982), pp. 211–15.
2 On Canadian parliamentary secretaries see: Kathryn J. Randle, 'Fifth wheel or firm ally? Parliamentary secretaries and the public service', *Parliamentary Government*, 4, 3 (October 1983), pp. 12–15; W. A. Matheson, *The Prime Minister and the Cabinet* (Toronto, 1976), pp. 68–74; Alan Alexander, 'Canada's parliamentary secretaries: their political and constitutional position', *Parliamentary Affairs*, 20 (1966–7), pp. 248–57; J. R. Mallory, *The Structure of Canadian Government* (Toronto, 1971), pp. 94–5.
3 On ministers of state in Canada see: John A. Chenier, 'Ministers of State to assist: weighing the costs and the benefits', *Canadian Public Administration*, 28, 3 (Fall 1985), pp. 397–412; G. Bruce Doern and Peter Aucoin (eds), *Public Policy in Canada: Organisation, Process and Management* (Toronto, 1979), pp. 228–36; Colin Campbell, 'Cabinet committees in Canada: pressures and dysfunctions stemming from the representational imperative', in *Unlocking the Cabinet*, eds. T. Mackie and B. Hogwood (London, 1985), pp. 73–7, 82.
4 Matheson, *The Prime Minister and Cabinet*, p. 73; R. M. Punnett, *The Prime Minister in Canadian Government and Politics* (Toronto, 1977), pp. 59–61; Patrick Weller, *First Among Equals: Prime Ministers in Westminster Systems* (Sydney, 1985), pp. 82–3.
5 On German parliamentary state secretaries see: Nevil Johnson, *State and Government in the Federal Republic of Germany : the Executive At Work* (Oxford, 1983), pp. 77–8, 99; Renate Mayntz, 'German Federal Bureaucrats: a functional elite between politics and administration', in *Bureaucrats and Policymaking: a Comparative Overview*, ed. Ezra Suleiman (New York, 1984), pp. 195–7; Edward Page, *Political Authority and Bureaucratic Power: A Comparative Analysis* (Brighton, 1985), pp. 88–9; David Southern, 'Germany', in *Government and Administration in Western Europe*, ed. F. F. Ridley (Oxford, 1979), pp. 127–8.
6 On junior ministers in France see: F. Ridley and J. Blondel, *Public Administration in France*, 2nd edn (London, 1969), pp. 13–15; Vincent Wright, *The Government and Politics of France*, 2nd edn (London, 1983), pp. 85, 95; Mattei Dogan, 'How to become a Cabinet Minister in France', *Comparative Politics*, 12, 1 (October 1979), pp. 1–25; Pierre Birnbaum, 'The Socialist Elite, "les Gros" and the State', in *Socialism, the State and Public*

Policy in France, eds. Philip G. Cerny and Martin A. Schain (London, 1985), pp. 129–42.

7 See Hugh Heclo, *A Government of Strangers: Executive Politics in Washington* (Washington, DC, 1977); D. T. Stanley, D. E. Mann, and J. W. Doig, *Men Who Govern* (Washington, DC, 1967); Hugh Heclo, 'In search of a role: America's higher civil service', in *Bureaucrats and Policymaking: a Comparative Overview*, ed. Ezra Suleiman (New York, 1984), p. 18; James W. Fesler, 'The higher civil service in Europe and the United States', in *The Higher Civil Service in Europe and Canada: Lessons for the United States*, ed. Bruce L. R. Smith (Washington, DC, 1984), pp. 88–9; Michael D. Hobkirk, *The Politics of Defence Budgeting* (London, 1984), pp. 71–2.

8 Kogan, *Politics of Education*, p. 55; Rodgers, 'Westminster and Whitehall', p. 11.

9 Kevin Theakston, 'Politicising the higher civil service', *Teaching Public Administration*, 6, 1 (Spring 1986), pp. 25–6.

10 *FDA News*, February 1983, April 1983; David Lipsey (ed.), *Making Government Work*, Fabian Tract 480 (1982).

11 Sir John Hoskyns, 'Conservatism is not enough', *The Political Quarterly*, 55, 1 (January–March 1984), pp. 13–14.

12 *The Civil Service, Report of the Committee 1966–68* (Fulton), Cmnd 3638, p. 94.

13 Williams, 'The decision makers', p. 88.

Index